Coding
For Kids

FOR

DUMMIES®

A Wiley Brand

by Dr. Camille McCue, PhD

FOR
DUMMIES®
A Wiley Brand

Coding For Kids For Dummies®

Published by: **John Wiley & Sons, Inc.,** 111 River Street, Hoboken, NJ 07030-5774, www.wiley.com

Copyright © 2015 by John Wiley & Sons, Inc., Hoboken, New Jersey

Published simultaneously in Canada

For general information on our other products and services, please contact our Customer Care Department within the U.S. at 877-762-2974, outside the U.S. at 317-572-3993, or fax 317-572-4002. For technical support, please visit www.wiley.com/techsupport.

Wiley publishes in a variety of print and electronic formats and by print-on-demand. Some material included with standard print versions of this book may not be included in e-books or in print-on-demand. If this book refers to media such as a CD or DVD that is not included in the version you purchased, you may download this material at http://booksupport.wiley.com. For more information about Wiley products, visit www.wiley.com.

Library of Congress Control Number: 2014943276

ISBN 978-1-118-94032-7 (pbk); ISBN 978-1-118-94033-4 (ebk); ISBN 978-1-118-94034-1 (ebk)

Manufactured in the United States of America

10 9 8 7 6 5 4 3 2

Contents at a Glance

Table of Contents

Week 4: Multiturtles, Keyboard Control, Shooters 211

Introduction

So you want to learn to *code* — awesome! You are embarking on an adventure that will transform you from a user of technology into a maker of technology. And it's a lot easier than you might guess! *Coding* — writing computer programs — has something for everyone: creativity, logic, art, math, storytelling, design, and problem solving. From games and toys to animations and simulations, this book coaches you step by step through coding *real* programs you can share with family and friends.

About This Book

Although coding is emerging as a critical skill, it is not usually taught until high school — if at all. There are some super camps and great websites where you can get started with coding, but most affordable resources either stop with the very basics or club you over the head with too much, too soon. What you'll find in this book is a complete introductory to intermediate treatment of coding in a single programming language — one that has stood the test of time with generations of students, and is conceptually transferrable to every other programming language. And this treatment isn't boring or theoretical: Like content in all of the *For Dummies* series, this book is fun, clear, and organized in an easy-access format.

Coding For Kids For Dummies is assembled as a series of projects with steps for constructing each project from start to finish. As you work through each project, keep in mind the following writing conventions:

✔ Programming code and web addresses appear in monofont. If you're reading a digital version of this book on a device connected to the Internet, note that you can click the web address to visit that website, like this: `www.dummies.com`.

✔ Command sequences use the command arrow. Here's an example: From the menu bar, choose File⇨New Project Size⇨ MicroWorlds Small to set the size of a new project to the MicroWorlds small size.

Foolish Assumptions

In this book, I make a few assumptions about you in regard to getting started:

✔ You have a reasonable comfort level in typing on a computer and using a mouse. Your experience can be either on a Windows or Mac system — either one will do! Instructions for coding each project are written for both platforms, and figures are shown for MicroWorlds EX operating on a Mac.

✔ You're capable of installing software, because you will be installing the MicroWorlds EX program on your computer.

Further, I've made some assumptions with regard to your entering into the world of coding:

✔ You've played with a few games on a computer, so you have some idea regarding how people interact with computer games (as opposed to video games on a gaming console).

✔ You're comfortable with basic math, math operations such as adding whole numbers, and logical operations such as comparing two whole numbers. I introduce algebraic variables in this book, but you don't need to have any prior knowledge of variables.

Lastly, if you struggle with spelling, you may need to spend extra time troubleshooting your code for misspellings. A programming language doesn't understand spelling errors, but can give you clues about which commands it doesn't understand.

Icons Used in This Book

The Tip icon marks tips and shortcuts that you can use to make coding easier. Some tips are repeated multiple times throughout the book — especially when you might run into the very issue addressed by the tip.

The Coding Connection icon describes how a coding concept you're working on connects to other programming languages and to the big picture of coding in any language.

The Math Connection icon shows ways in which math (including school math!) is used in coding. Finally, from computation and algebra to geometry and logic, you learn how that stuff really is used!

The Warning icon tells you to watch out! It marks important information that may save you headaches.

Beyond the Book

I have made available a lot of extra content that you won't find in this book. Go online to find the following:

- ✔ **An online Cheat Sheet for the programming language and interface is available at** www.dummies.com/cheatsheet/codingforkids. Key commands are condensed into a Cheat Sheet that shows their syntax and placement within a coding project. This sheet may also be ideal for teachers who want to provide a quick "how-to" guide to students in the classroom.

- ✔ **Online articles covering additional topics are available at** www.dummies.com/extras/codingforkids. Additionally, you'll find a bonus project called Silly Story as well as Action Plans for the projects in the book.

- ✔ **Updates to this book, if there are any, can be found at** www.dummies.com/extras/codingforkids.

Where to Go from Here

MicroWorlds EX was developed as a *constructionist* tool — a tool you can use to construct ideas from your head in the real world. It was never really intended to be a Step 1, Step 2–style programming language, but rather a creative programming playground. However, because you and I are not physically together in a classroom with your peers, we're going to work in a method that has worked well for hundreds of *For Dummies* books: This book uses printed instructions and example screenshots to guide you through a series of fun projects!

Early projects in this book are fairly simple. Later projects increase in difficulty as you gain experience. Each project includes new *primitives* — coding commands built into MicroWorlds EX — and may introduce new *procedures* — coding commands you invent to do new things in your program. The projects are intended to be completed sequentially, but you are always welcome to "jump around" and work on projects in any order you choose. Most projects are sufficiently self-contained that you will be able to complete them simply from the pages within that chapter. As such, you may notice that there is some repetition of concepts and steps from one project to the next — this is deliberate so that you don't feel lost if you do choose to code projects out of order.

After you gain a little experience coding, there are a bazillion new directions you can go, from learning more advanced concepts in MicroWorlds EX to tackling more challenging programming languages. I congratulate you on taking the first step!

Week 1
Basic Drawing, Motion, and Text Handling

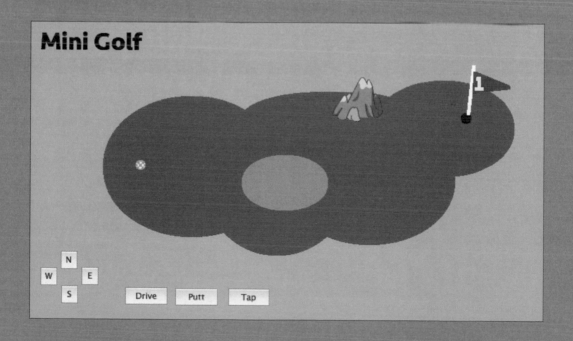

This week you'll build . . .

Getting Started with Coding

Until the last few decades, education focused on skills called the three Rs — reading, writing, and arithmetic. (I know what you're thinking . . . adults who believe all these words begin with the letter *R* need to return to kindergarten!) If you mastered the three Rs, you were considered an educated person. But now, technology has changed everything. In your personal life, in school, and in your parents' jobs, technology is in constant use. And communicating with technology requires a new skill called *coding,* or *computer programming.*

In this chapter, I explain what coding is and describe the types of projects you can create. Then, I introduce you to MicroWorlds EX, which is the software that you will use to create the projects in this book, as well as connect you with additional resources for extending your learning.

Understanding What Coding Is

Coding means writing instructions that a piece of technology — usually a computer — understands so that the technology will perform a task. A computer programming language provides the *vocabulary* (words) and *syntax* (rules and punctuation) for communicating with a computer.

The instructions that you write and that the computer reads are a program. A *computer program* comprises code and communicates instructions about what is supposed to show on a computer screen and when it is supposed to happen. As you learn a computer programming language, you will be able to read and understand programs already written. Most importantly, you will be able to *code* — that is, design and write your own original programs.

Learning to understand and create code in a computer programming language allows you to communicate with technology. Just like there are tons of human languages, there are tons of computer programming languages. If you're wondering which programming language you should learn, the answer is . . . any one of them! After you learn one programming language, there will be many similarities between that language and any other programming language you may need. Still, there are some programming languages that are much easier to start with and much more fun to learn if you're a kid. And you *are* a kid, right?

Learning to Code with MicroWorlds EX

In general, to get started coding, you need only a computer, the programming language software, and an up-to-date version of a consumer-grade operating system (Windows or Mac OS). Some languages, such as Scratch, operate in a web browser, so you must also have a browser such as Firefox to work with those options.

The programming language software that you will use with this book is MicroWorlds EX (MWEX), which is my favorite computer programming language of all time.

Examining why MWEX is a good language to start with

MWEX is a perfect first language for many reasons:

- ✔ **It uses natural language for *commands* — instructions the computer follows.** Vocabulary such as IF, FORWARD, SETSHAPE, and STOP are written in standard English, and you know what they mean. Abbreviations such as FD (for FORWARD) and RT (for right turn) make sense. And MWEX isn't picky about capitalization; for example, FD and fd are equivalent.

- ✔ **It doesn't go overboard with punctuation.** Most of the punctuation makes good sense — some commas, quotation marks, parentheses, and square brackets. For example, if you want to command a UFO to fly, you type ufo, fly in your program. In more advanced programming languages, you need to master periods (.) and curly braces ({ }), but MWEX keeps punctuation fairly simple.

- ✔ **It has drag-and-drop palettes and also areas for writing new code.** Some programming languages have only drag-and-drops. Although this makes program creation easy, it limits your ability to create entirely new code. On the other hand, programming languages that expect you to create all the code yourself are a bit scary — too much empty canvas and not enough paint-by-number. MWEX has a nice, balanced, interface: plenty of palettes and panes to access tools easily and develop program components quickly, and plenty of empty canvas to be inventive.

- ✔ **It has built-in paint tools and a Shape Editor for painting original backgrounds and characters.** Also, there's a big collection of pre-made backgrounds and characters (including shapes that can be used for animation) in the MWEX library. You can even import graphics from the web and from graphics editing programs.

✔ **It can import music and sound effects, as well as record audio.** Best of all, there is a built-in music editor that allows you to create simple music in a variety of instruments. There's even a say command that invokes synthesized speech.

✔ **It has built-in error-checking and helpful troubleshooting assistance.** Many programming languages have error-checking tools to catch errors or *bugs* in your code. MWEX has an *interpreter* that checks your code as it runs or *executes*: If there's an error, MWEX displays a message indicating the problem and where it occurred. Then, you can revise your code accordingly.

MicroWorlds EX programming paradigm

For the tech ninjas who want to know the programming paradigm of MicroWorlds EX, it is a hybrid: MWEX blends sequential programming with event-driven programming with a few other paradigms (including object-oriented programming):

✔ *Sequential programming* means following step by step through a series of instructions.

✔ *Event-driven programming* means that what happens in a program is determined by events such as user inputs (mouse or button clicks) received through the graphical user interface, or messages from within the program.

Additionally, there are elements of object-oriented programming in MWEX: digital objects, called *turtles,* that possess attributes (data) and have methods of interacting (procedures).

Taking a look at what projects you can make

By working in MicroWorlds EX, you'll sample important yet easy-to-understand programming paradigms that allow you to make cool projects *now* — and set the stage for more advanced coding in the future.

What kinds of things can you make? Everything! Up until now, you've probably been a user or consumer of technology. You play games, run a simulation or model for a science class, word-process a story, conduct web research, communicate with friends via social media, and order goods online. But by learning to code, you are now a *maker* of software, a producer in the world of technology!

In this book, you will make four different types of projects:

- ✔ **Toys** are things you play with that have no specific goal or scoring: for example, a spirograph drawing toy or *Mad Libs*.

- ✔ **Games** have a goal (and sometimes scoring) such as a search-and-find game that challenges you to find an object, or Frogger, where the goal is to get the frog across the road and to the pond without being struck by a number of objects. Games present challenges that can be won or lost.

- ✔ **Animated scenes** are little movies such as a winter snow scene with blinking holiday lights.

- ✔ **Simulations (sims)** are programs that are meant to mimic or *model* the real world — for example, a viral epidemic, or births of babies in a hospital.

Ultimately, the coding skills you learn in this book are just the beginning. I hope you create all sorts of exciting new programs that are wilder and wackier than anything contained in these pages. And I hope you level up and tackle learning new programming languages as you increase your skill level in the coming years.

Getting Started with MicroWorlds EX

Your purchase of this book comes with a 35-day, 90 saves-allowed trial of MicroWorlds EX, so you can work through all the projects at the rate of approximately one part each week! At any time, you can purchase MicroWorlds EX at a deep discount so you can continue developing your coding skills creating new projects to share with friends and family.

Downloading and installing the software

To download and install the trial version of MicroWorlds EX, navigate to www.dummies.com/go/microworlds. Then follow the onscreen download and installation instructions.

For PCs, MicroWorlds EX is supported on Windows 7, Windows 8, and Windows 8.1. For Macs, MicroWorlds EX is supported on OS X Version 10.7 and later.

Starting a project

After you've installed it, follow these steps to start MicroWorlds EX:

1. Click on the yellow backpack icon (shown in the margin).

   The backpack serves as the icon for MWEX because objects in this programming language are called *turtles,* and every turtle totes a backpack carrying important information just like your backpack.

   As MicroWorlds EX starts, you see the splash screen shown in Figure 0-1.

2. Click on the splash screen to dismiss it.

   A yellow Welcome to MicroWorlds EX screen opens and presents several options to you, as shown in Figure 0-2.

Figure 0-1

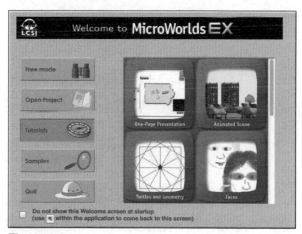

Figure 0-2

3. Choose Free Mode to start a new project, or Open Project to open a saved project. (For additional guidance and other project examples in MWEX, choose Tutorials or Samples on the left, and then choose a specific project on the right.)

Upon choosing any option, you are presented with the MWEX interface. Free Mode presents a somewhat empty interface, as shown in Figure 0-3, because you haven't created any code or graphics yet.

Getting to know the interface

Note the following key areas of the MicroWorlds EX interface, shown in Figure 0-3:

Toolbar

Menu bar   Workspace   Pane

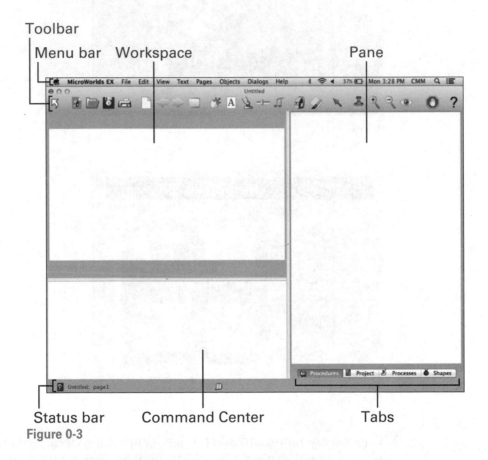

Status bar   Command Center   Tabs

Figure 0-3

- ✔ **Menu bar:** Contains menus for opening and saving files, editing (copying and pasting), changing the view of the interface, formatting text, creating and naming new pages, creating new objects and dialogs, and help.

- ✔ **Toolbar:** Contains button versions of File items on the menu bar, as shown in Figure 0-4. A few buttons merit special mention:

  - *Regular Pointer:* As you program, your mouse pointer will sometimes appear as a cursor (in places where you can type), sometimes as a pointer (for dragging a turtle, button, or other element), and sometimes as a hand for placing shapes in the workspace. If the mouse pointer is a hand, you can change it back to a pointer by clicking the Regular Pointer button. Another way to revert to a pointer is simply to click in the Command Center (discussed later in this list).

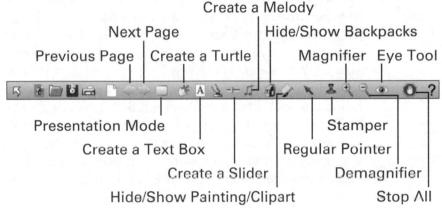

Figure 0-4

- *Eye Tool:* The Eye Tool button can open a turtle backpack, or a dialog box for a button, text box, slider, or sound. Just click it! This button is also useful for locating hidden objects (turtles) — just click the Eye Tool to reveal their locations.

- *Stop All:* This button is useful for stopping program execution. When characters are flying around the screen or the OnTimer function keeps ticking away, click Stop All to halt everything and take a breath.

- *Presentation Mode:* Use this button to view your project as an end user would see it. Clicking this button limits the view to the workspace only. Because this mode hides the other areas of the MWEX interface, it allows end users to experience a more polished presentation of your project. Press the Escape key (Esc) to return to the regular MWEX view. This is also how your project will be viewed by people seeing your project posted on the web.

➤ **Project title and page number:** The project title appears at
the top of the MWEX interface and also in the lower-left corner. This second location, called the *status bar,* also shows the
page number of the current page within the project. If the page
is named, this name appears instead of the default, for example, `page1`.

➤ **Workspace:** This is where you create the physical appearance
of your project. Here, you can add a background and then create turtles, buttons, and other elements of your project. At the
start of a new project, you can change the size of the workspace by choosing File⇨New Project Size, and then selecting
one of these options: MicroWorlds Small, MicroWorlds
Standard, Web Player, Full Screen 640 x 480, or Full Screen
800 x 600. Or you can create a project size of your own dimensions by typing `newprojectsize [width height]` in the
Command Center (discussed next). Note that a project size
can be changed only at the start of a project.

➤ **Command Center:** This region is used for several different
purposes:

- You can try out a command or snippet of code and instantly
see the results.

- You can issue a command that doesn't need to be reused
(so there's no purpose in typing it more permanently into a
procedure). For example, if you've created 50 fish and you
want all of them to swim in the same direction, you can
command everyone to head in a specific direction and be
done with it.

- You can see any error messages. If MicroWorlds EX encounters a problem with your code, it will tell you in the Command
Center. There are other uses for the Command Center that
you will discover as you gain experience working in MWEX.

✔ **Panes:** The right side of the MWEX interface features four panes stacked on top of each other. Only one pane shows at a time, and you can move among panes by clicking these tabs at the bottom-right side of the interface:

- *Procedures:* For writing new commands

- *Project:* For viewing all pages and elements in a project

- *Processes:* For viewing program processes in detail as they execute and for adjusting the execution speed of your project

- *Shapes:* For creating shapes for objects and performing additional image editing functions

Detailed use of each pane will be discussed further in the projects.

 The divider bars separating the workspace, Command Center, and panes can be moved to increase or decrease your view of each area as needed.

Coming Up with Your Ideas, Your Projects

As you get started with the projects in this book, keep in mind that you can customize every project with your own personal creativity. Many video games have the same underlying structure, as do many toys. The coding of the gameplay is often the same for multiple games. Think about how many different forms a shooter game can take, all with the same code: a squid shooting ink at an approaching shark; a pig dropping water balloons on cows; a pea shooter aiming at targets in a carnival game; or a bomber dropping bombs on enemy battleships. If you remove the graphics and sound effects, you simply have an object shooting at another object, with target objects moving and some sort of lives and scoring system. Many simulations also involve the scattering or distribution of lots of objects in a region — the underlying code is the same whether these objects are walruses lounging on an ice floe, trees in a forest, or people walking around a mall.

I encourage you to invent new characters and new actions and make every project your own. Now get coding!

Exploring help resources

The number of MWEX primitives vocabulary covered in this book is tiny compared with the entire library of vocabulary available. The Help menu, which you can access from the MWEX menu bar, contains an option for viewing the language vocabulary, sorted alphabetically. Each MWEX command is explained and accompanied by an example. I am constantly using this resource to locate new primitives and learn how to use them in my code. I hope you find it as valuable a resource as I do! The Help menu also provides assistance in fundamentals, programming, and more techniques — all are excellent resources.

Another great help resource for learning how to use primitives is available as you code: With your cursor in the Command Center or project Procedures pane, hover over any MicroWorlds EX primitive — a tooltip appears with information telling you how to format the primitive.

Additionally, the startup screen of MicroWorlds EX offers access to tutorials and samples you may find helpful. Every example you can view and play with is a learning opportunity. I also encourage you to modify the code of each example, and then extend the code to hone your coding skills.

Lastly, the MWEX website located at `www.microworlds.com` is a great source of links to examples from kid coders around the world — take a look for inspiration and motivation.

Art Toy

Coding the Art Toy introduces you to MicroWorlds EX *primitives,* which are built-in commands including setting background and *turtle* (object) colors; putting the turtle pen up and pen down; setting the pen size; moving the turtle forward and backward; and turning the turtle left and right. It also introduces the `home` and `clean` primitives.

In this project, you'll code your first *procedures* — new commands you create by putting together primitives in new ways, many using the `repeat` command. As you build Art Toy, you'll craft a user interface by making a text box title and buttons, as well as tinker with setting your buttons to execute once versus forever. The fun is in creating your own toy, and then playing with it. Now you're coding!

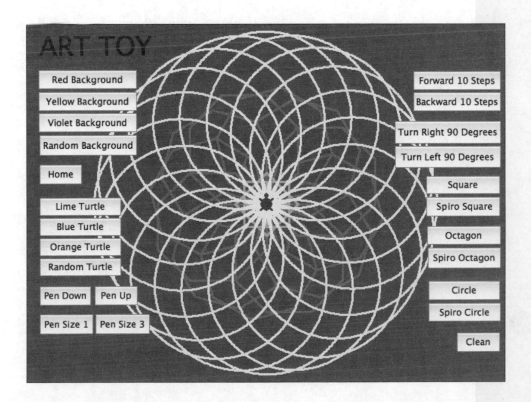

Brainstorm

All projects can be adapted to appear in new ways to the user or player. Many times, by using different graphics with the same computer code, you can create projects or games that look very different.

You can create a few different looks for Art Toy, but mostly, this project gives the *end user,* the person who will be playing with your art toy, a chance to make things look differently because that person uses your buttons to make their own art.

In future projects, you will have many chances to brainstorm cool new ways to change the look of your user interface. For now, get coding by following these simple steps.

Start a New Project

Begin creating your Art Toy by starting a new project as follows:

1. Start MicroWorlds EX.

2. On the yellow MicroWorlds EX startup screen, select Free Mode.

   A new project opens.

3. From the menu bar, choose File⇨New Project Size⇨Full Screen 640 x 480.

   This is the next-to-the-largest project size available and provides plenty of space for creating your Art Toy. Other project size options consist of MicroWorlds Small, MicroWorlds Standard, Web Player, and Full Screen 800 x 600.

   You must set the project size at the outset of a new project. You cannot resize projects later.

Add a Title to the Toy

The region in which your toy appears is the *workspace*. Add a title to the workspace as follows:

1. On the toolbar, click the Create a Text Box button (shown in the margin). Move into the workspace.

   The cursor becomes a white pen.

2. Drag the mouse anywhere on the workspace to draw a medium-sized rectangle, creating the text box.

   A text box called text1 appears in the workspace.

3. Click inside the text box. Type a title — Art Toy — in the white area of the text box, as shown in Figure 1-1.

4. Use the mouse to select (highlight) the text inside the text box, as shown in Figure 1-1.

   The text can now be formatted. Note that the Windows menu options for formatting text may vary slightly from Mac menu options described here.

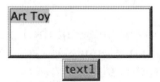

Figure 1-1

5. From the menu bar, choose Text⇨Font and choose a font from the pop-up menu of fonts.

6. Choose Text⇨Size to choose a text size for your title.

7. Choose Text⇨Style to choose a text style for your title from the pop-up menu.

   Options consist of Plain, Bold, Italic, and Underline.

8. Choose Text➪Color.

   A Colors dialog box appears, as shown in Figure 1-2.

Figure 1-2

9. Move the slider, which is on the right, and click a color on the color wheel to choose a text color for your title. Click OK to apply the color to your text title.

10. If needed, resize your text box to better fit the text you type inside it. Ctrl-click (Windows) or Command-click (Mac) outside the text box and drag over a side of the text box. Sizing dots appear — click and drag any of them to resize the text box.

11. Right-click (Windows) or Ctrl-click (Mac) inside the title text box and select Transparent from the pop-up menu.

   Making the text box transparent makes the text inside the box visible and the box itself invisible.

12. Click your title text and drag it into a position in the workspace where you would like to place the title.

You can edit text only when the text box is opaque (not transparent). To change a text box from transparent to opaque, right-click (Windows) or Ctrl-click (Mac) the text and select Opaque from the pop-up menu.

Add a Turtle

All programming languages have ways to create objects. Objects are usually the physical things that move around the computer screen — cars, birds, paintballs, and so on. Programming languages have different name for objects. In another programming language you may have heard of, GameSalad, an object is called an *actor*. In MicroWorlds EX, an object is called a *turtle*.

In certain programming languages, such as object-oriented programming languages (OOPs), objects can be physical things but can also be informational things — abstract entities that possess data and behave in certain ways in a program.

In your Art Toy, your turtle will do the drawing! He is an object that can move around the workspace in many ways. Also, the turtle carries a *pen* that is capable of drawing in a variety of colors and pen sizes.

Create a turtle for your Art Toy as follows:

1. On the toolbar, click the Create a Turtle button.

2. Move into the workspace and click.

   A turtle hatches in your workspace.

You can drag the turtle and move it anywhere in the workspace. You can also click its snout and turn the turtle around in a circular motion to point in any direction.

Test Primitives in the Command Center

There are two types of commands in MicroWorlds EX:

- ✔ **Primitives:** These are built-in commands that already exist in the MicroWorlds EX vocabulary.

- ✔ **Procedures:** These are new commands you create by putting together primitives and other procedures you have already coded.

You can type any command, primitive, or procedure, at any time into the Command Center for the purpose of testing out the command. The Command Center is located just below the workspace, at the bottom of the MicroWorlds EX window (see Figure 1-3).

Turtle

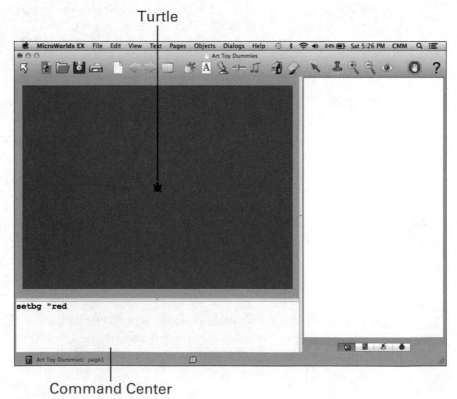

Command Center

Figure 1-3

Try out a few of these primitives at the Command Center:

✔ **setbg:** This command sets the background color. In the
Command Center, type setbg "red and then press Enter
(Windows) or Return (Mac). This command sets the back-
ground color to red, as shown in Figure 1-3.

Now try setbg 15. The background is still red! That's because
MicroWorlds uses both names and numbers to represent colors.
The color name red is the same as the color number 15.

Try a few more color names such as yellow, green, and
violet. Also test a few more color numbers using any number from 0 to 139. You can type a new line of code each time,
or replace the color you typed previously and then press
Enter/Return.

Computer programming languages have their own *syntax,* which are
the rules for how the language is communicated. The syntax includes
grammar (where the words go, and in what order) as well as punctuation (where parentheses, brackets, commas, and quotes must be
placed). In MicroWorlds EX, opening quotation marks are often used
with names, but closing quotation marks are never used. Quotation
marks are not used with numbers, except in special cases.

Most computer programming languages have a *compiler,* a separate
program that checks your code for syntax errors before you can try
executing your code. Compilers give you error messages to help you
fix, or *debug,* your code. MicroWorlds EX has something similar, a
built-in interpreter, that checks for errors as you code. Error messages
appear in the Command Center — read them to see what changes
you need to make to correct your code.

✔ **setbg random:** This command sets a random color for the
background. In the Command Center, type setbg random
140 and then press Enter (Windows) or Return (Mac). This
command sets the background color to a color number
selected randomly from 0 to 139. Execute the command a few
times to see many new colors appear.

Random number generation is often used in computer code. Randomness allows you to make actions in your computer code behave like actions in the real world: dogs run in crazy zig-zag motions, dice rolls result in different combinations, and some people get sick during flu season while others don't. In MicroWorlds EX, random whole numbers are made from 0 up to one less than the number you provide. For example, the code `random 6` results in one of these numbers: 0, 1, 2, 3, 4, or 5. The code `random 140` results in one of these numbers: 0, 1, 2, 3 . . . all the way up to 139. Each number in the group is as likely to appear as any other number in the group.

- **home:** This command moves the turtle to the home position, which is the exact center of the workspace. To try out this command, drag the turtle to any location in the workspace. In the Command Center, type `home` and then press Enter (Windows) or Return (Mac). The turtle moves to the home position and points toward the top of the workspace.

Some commands, such as `home`, are standalone, while others require additional inputs, such as `setbg 15` or `setbg "red`. The command `setbg` cannot be executed without providing an input indicating a color code or color.

In geometry, coordinates are used to describe the position of a point on a graph. MicroWorlds EX also uses coordinates. The west-east position of a turtle is its *x-coordinate,* or XCOR. The north-south position of a turtle is its *y-coordinate,* or YCOR. The exact center of the workspace is located where XCOR = 0 and YCOR = 0. Another way to write this in math is (0,0). This special position is called the *origin.*

- **setc:** This command sets the color of the turtle. In the Command Center, type `setc "yellow` and then press Enter (Windows) or Return (Mac). This command stands for *set the turtle color to yellow.* Try a few more colors such as pink, lime, cyan, and brown. The color of the turtle is the same as the color of its drawing pen.

- **setc random:** This command sets the turtle color to a random color. In the Command Center, type `setc random 140` and then press Enter (Windows) or Return (Mac). This command stands for *set the turtle color to a color number selected randomly from 0 to 139*. Execute the command a few times to see the turtle turn many different colors. The color of the turtle is the same as the color of its drawing pen.

✔ **fd or bk:** These commands move the turtle forward or backward. In the Command Center, type fd 10 and then press Enter (Windows) or Return (Mac). This translates to *move forward 10 steps*. Now type fd 100 and note the difference. Then type fd 1000 and see what happens when it moves off one side of the workspace! The maximum value for forward and backward is 9999.

The opposite of moving forward is moving backward. Type bk 10 and then press Enter (Windows) or Return (Mac). This command translates to *move backward 10 steps*. Type some other distances and observe the change in the turtle's position.

The MicroWorlds EX workspace is similar to a flat map of Earth. If a turtle walks off of one side of the workspace, it reappears on the opposite side of the workspace.

✔ **pd or pu:** These commands set the turtle's pen down or up. In the Command Center, type pd and then press Enter (Windows) or Return (Mac). This translates to *pen down*. It looks as if nothing happens! That's because the turtle pen is below the center of the turtle — when he's not moving, you can't see whether his pen is up or down.

Try the forward and backward commands to see the turtle draw as it moves. The command pu stands for pen up, but don't give the pen up command now; just leave the pen down.

✔ **setpensize:** This command sets the pen size. The pen size indicates the line width when the turtle moves with the pen down. The starting (or default) value is 1. Larger sizes make wider pen widths. In the Command Center, type setpensize 3 and then press Enter (Windows) or Return (Mac). This sets the pen size to the value 3. Try several values to create pen sizes of different widths. You can see the effect of changing the pen size only when the pen is down and the turtle is moving.

✔ **rt or lt:** These commands turn the turtle right or left. In the Command Center, type `rt 90` and then press Enter (Windows) or Return (Mac). This translates to *turn right 90 degrees*. Now type `lt 90` and press Enter/Return. This translates to *turn left 90 degrees*. Try other degree angles such as `45`, `180`, `270`, and `360`.

Circle measurements are made in units called *degrees*. There are 360 degrees in a circle. To make a turtle face the opposite direction from where it is currently facing, give the command `rt 180` or `lt 180`.

Turtle turns are always made from the viewpoint of the turtle. If the turtle is facing north and you give the command `rt 90`, the turtle faces east. If you give the command `rt 90` again, the turtle faces south. Give the command `rt 90` a third time and the turtle now faces west.

✔ **clean:** This command clears any graphics from the workspace. In the Command Center, type `clean` and then press Enter (Windows) or Return (Mac). Notice that the background color remains. The turtle also remains and does not change its position.

To delete a turtle, right-click (Windows) or Ctrl-click (Mac) the turtle and select Delete from the pop-up menu.

To try out combination commands, type a short sequence of commands in the Command Center to explore the simple art you can create in the workspace. An example with six commands is shown in Figure 1-4.

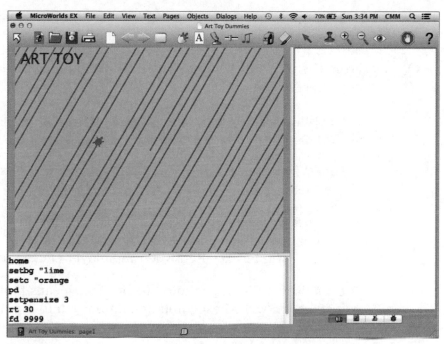

Figure 1-4

Create Buttons to Execute Primitives

The Command Center is a good place to test out commands as you develop a program. But users of your program don't want to type in commands! Users want a simple way to operate your program.

You operate your television, phone, and computer through a *graphical user interface* (also called a *GUI*), which has buttons, pictures, menus, and other tools for communicating with each device. MicroWorlds EX provides ways for you to build your own GUI to make it easy for people to use your computer program.

Instead of asking a user to type in a command such as `setbg "red` to change the workspace of the Art Toy to the color red, you can make a button to do the work instead. To create a button, you provide two pieces of information: a label for the user, and an instruction for the computer.

Make a button to change the background color of the workspace as follows:

1. From the toolbar, click the Create a Button button. Then click anywhere in the workspace.

2. In the Button dialog box, fill in the following information (as shown in Figure 1-5):

   - *Label:* Type Red Background in the Label text box. These are the words the user will see on the button.

   - *Instruction:* Type setbg "red into the Instruction field. The command that you enter in the Instruction field — setbg "red — will be executed when the player clicks the button.

   - *Do It:* Select the Once radio button. This means that the instruction will be executed one time when the button is clicked.

   - *Visible:* Select this check box to leave the button visible on the screen.

button		
Name:	button1	
Label:	Red Background	
Instruction:	setbg "red	
Do It:	⦿ Once	☑ Visible
	◯ Forever	Cancel OK

Figure 1-5

3. Click OK to close the Button dialog box.

The completed Red Background button (shown on the left in Figure 1-6) is added to the workspace.

Original button

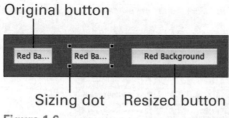

Sizing dot   Resized button

Figure 1-6

4. The button doesn't show all the words, so resize the button to show the entire label. Ctrl-click (Windows) or Command-click (Mac) the button. Sizing dots appear (Figure 1-6, center) — click and drag any of them to resize the text box (Figure 1-6, right).

5. Position the completed button by dragging it to any location in the workspace.

6. To make sure that people playing with your Art Toy don't accidentally move your buttons or text boxes, right-click (Windows) or Ctrl-click (Mac) any button or text box and select Freeze from the pop-up menu to freeze it in place.

7. Repeat Steps 1–6 to create buttons for all the primitives you have learned so far (as discussed in the preceding section).

   Be creative by using any colors, distances, and turn angles you want! On some of the buttons, try setting the Do It radio button to Forever so that the button command executes over and over (until you click the button again to halt the execution, or click the Stop All button on the toolbar). Executing the button instructions forever will produce interesting effects for forward, backward, turn, and random instructions.

8. Play with your toy to create a unique digital work of art.

   Your Art Toy now looks something like Figure 1-7.

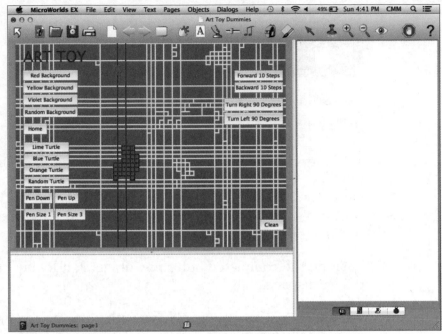

Figure 1-7

Write New Procedures in the Procedures Pane and Add Associated Buttons

A *procedure* is a new command you create from primitives and other procedures. Procedures are used as shortcuts to describe a long list of steps. For example, if you want the turtle to draw a square that is 30 steps on a side (with the pen already down), you could type the following into the Command Center; press Enter/Return after each line:

```
fd 30 rt 90
fd 30 rt 90
fd 30 rt 90
fd 30 rt 90
```

But if you want to draw many squares, it would be faster to give this collection of steps a new name: square.

In the following sections, you write a square procedure and then use that procedure to write a procedure called spirosquare. You will also create two buttons.

Write the square procedure and create a button

Write a procedure to create the new command as follows:

 1. Click the project Procedures tab (located in the lower-right corner of the MicroWorlds EX window) to open the project Procedures pane.

2. Type the following code, as shown in Figure 1-8:

```
to square
fd 30 rt 90
fd 30 rt 90
fd 30 rt 90
fd 30 rt 90
end
```

```
to square
fd 30 rt 90
fd 30 rt 90
fd 30 rt 90
fd 30 rt 90
end
```

Figure 1-8

A new procedure starts with to followed by the name of the procedure, in this case, square. Do not use spaces in the name of the procedure. Always end the code for your new procedure with end. The end command must be on its own line, so be sure to press Return/Enter after typing it.

Procedure names may not have spaces. If you want to separate words in a procedure name, use the underscore symbol: wiggle_around. You can also use the dash symbol, but this is not recommended because the dash can be confused with a minus sign.

3. Test your new procedure by typing square in the Command Center to check whether it works as expected.

A common mistake among new programmers is leaving off the word to at the start of your procedure definition. If this occurs, the Command Center issues an error message like the one shown in Figure 1-9. If you see an error message, simply edit your procedure and test it again until it executes as expected.

```
square
I don't know how to square
```

Figure 1-9

4. A key principle of writing computer code is keeping your code *efficient,* meaning as simple as possible. Because the square procedure is executing the same command (fd 30 rt 90) four times, a more efficient way to write the code is to use the repeat command. In the Procedure pane, edit your square procedure to appear as follows (see Figure 1-10):

```
to square
repeat 4 [fd 30 rt 90]
end
```

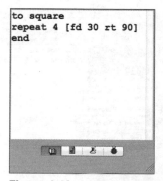

```
to square
repeat 4 [fd 30 rt 90]
end
```

Figure 1-10

Notice that the primitive repeat is followed by a number showing how many repetitions to perform, and then the repeated phrase is placed inside square brackets: [fd 30 rt 90].

5. Test your revised procedure by typing square in the Command Center to check that it works as expected. It may be helpful to drag the turtle to a new location first so that the new square isn't drawn on top of the previously drawn square.

6. Follow Steps 1–3 in the earlier section "Create Buttons to Execute Primitives" to create a button with the label *Square* and the instruction square.

7. Drag the Square button to a position in the workspace where it doesn't block the artwork the user will be making.

8. Test the button a few times, moving the turtle to different locations as you draw squares (see Figure 1-11).

Use the clean command (or button, if you made one!) to erase drawings from the workspace if it becomes too crowded.

A square can be constructed using four right turns *or* four left turns, so the square procedure could just as easily have used an lt instead of an rt command!

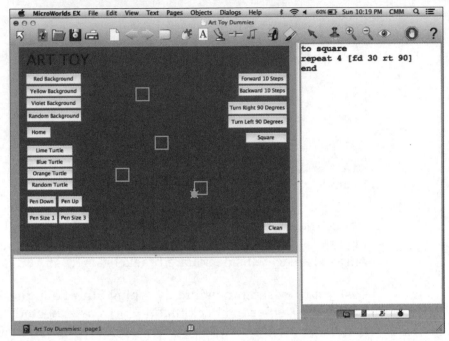

Figure 1-11

Write the spirosquare procedure and create a button

Now that you have written a procedure to create a square command, you can use it anywhere in the current project — you can even use it in another procedure! When one procedure is used inside another procedure, we say it is *nested*. Try writing the following spirosquare procedure:

1. In the Procedures pane, enter the following code (see Figure 1-12):

```
to spirosquare
repeat 8 [square rt 45]
end
```

```
to square
repeat 4 [fd 30 rt 90]
end

to spirosquare
repeat 8 [square rt 45]
end
```

Figure 1-12

2. Test your new procedure by typing `spirosquare` in the Command Center.

Figure 1-13 shows a time-lapse picture of `spirosquare` as it executes. Note that a new background color and turtle color are used for this drawing.

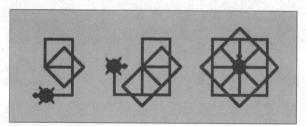

Figure 1-13

Here's how the `spirosquare` procedure works: The `to spirosquare` command names the new procedure. Next, the turtle repeats the instructions inside the brackets a total of eight times (`repeat 8`). The instructions inside the brackets draw a `square` and then turn right 45 degrees (`rt 45`). The `end` primitive indicates the end of the procedure.

Drawing spiro shapes

You can make spiro shapes in many different ways. The general rule is to draw a polygon and then turn a little, and then repeat that process until the turtle returns to its starting point. Similar to the way a turtle draws a single polygon, the turtle must make an *overall path* of a complete circle when drawing a spiro shape. Like a *Dancing with the Stars* competitor, the turtle may perform many small spins along the way, but the overall path around the room is one complete circle. This can be done in different ways. For example, the spiro octagon can be made using any of these commands:

```
repeat 6 [octagon rt 60]
```

or

```
repeat 12 [octagon rt 30]
```

or

```
repeat 20 [octagon rt 18]
```

or

```
repeat 30 [octagon rt 12]
```

Here the octagon is a group of small spins. But it's the `repeat` number and the turn angle that result in one complete circle in the creation of the entire spiro octagon. As with drawing the polygon itself, the repeat number times the turn angle equals 360; for example, 6 x 60 = 360 and 12 x 30 = 360.

3. Follow Steps 1–3 in the earlier section "Create Buttons to Execute Primitives" to create a button with the label *Spiro Square* and the instruction `spirosquare`.

Note that it is okay to use a space in the label of a button, just not in the instruction.

4. Drag the Spiro Square button to a position near its companion button, Square. Test the button a few times to ensure it functions properly, moving the turtle to a new location after each test.

5. When testing more complex procedures such as `spirosquare`, it is helpful to slow down the execution of the procedure to see more clearly how it operates. Control the speed of execution by clicking the project Processes tab (located in the lower-right corner of the MicroWorlds EX window).

The Processes pane appears, as shown in Figure 1-14. The top of the Processes pane shows three execution speeds: green (full speed), yellow (slow speed), and orange (very slow speed).

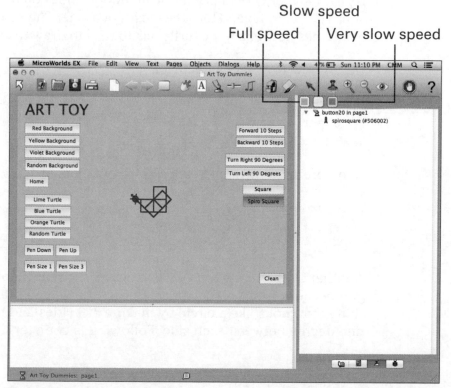

Figure 1-14

6. Click the yellow or orange speed and then click the Spiro Square button to see the procedure executed in slow motion.

   The Processes pane reports the execution of all parts of MicroWorlds EX as they happen.

7. Try creating procedures to draw other *polygons* (closed shapes that don't cross over themselves), such as an octagon and a circle. Write the code for each procedure in the project Procedures pane.

   You use this basic code to write the procedures:

   ```
   to procedure
   repeat numbersides [fd sidelength rt turnangle]
   end
   ```

   Replace *procedure* with the name of the new procedure. The repeat number should match the number of sides on the polygon. The fd command tells the length of a side. The rt command tells how much the turtle has to turn to draw the next side.

   Here's how to create an octagon:

   ```
   to octagon
   repeat 8 [fd 60 rt 45]
   end
   ```

   And here's one way to create a spiro octagon:

   ```
   to spirooctagon
   repeat 12 [octagon rt 30]
   end
   ```

   Another shape to try drawing is a circle. A circle is not a polygon because it has no flat sides. But the turtle can draw something that looks like a circle by making 360 sides and turning one degree between each side. Following is code for a circle:

   ```
   to circle
   repeat 360 [fd 2 rt 1]
   end
   ```

And here's one way to create a spiro circle:

```
to spirocircle
repeat 20 [circle rt 18]
end
```

8. Test each procedure in the Command Center and then make a button for each procedure.

9. Arrange the new buttons in the workspace to complete your Art Toy, as shown in Figure 1-15.

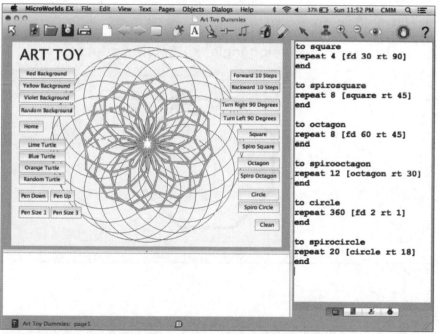

Figure 1-15

When arranging your buttons in any project, think carefully about the GUI. The user or player will expect buttons and other parts of the interface to be organized in an easy-to-understand layout. For the Art Toy, you may want to position all the buttons for setting colors and pen sizes on the left side of the workspace, and all of the buttons for drawing on the right side.

Polygon angles and turtle turns

Turtle turn angles in polygons are called *exterior* angles. Polygons also have *interior* angles, the angles inside the polygon. See the following figure. Adding up all the exterior angle turns of a polygon always equals 360 degrees; this is because the turtle makes one complete circle as it draws any polygon. That's why the repeat number times the turn angle always equals 360. However, adding up all the interior angles of a polygon results in different numbers for different polygons. A triangle has an interior angle sum of 180 degrees; a square has 360 degrees; a pentagon has 540 degrees. The more interior angles, the greater the interior sum. Can you figure out a pattern?

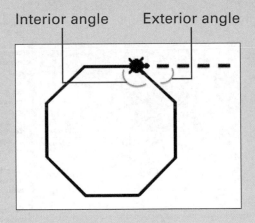

Interior angle   Exterior angle

Procedures you create in a project exist only within that project — they can only be used in other projects if you copy and paste them into the new project.

Save, Test, and Debug

Choose File⇨Save Project from the menu bar to save your game. Your finished game should look similar to Figure 1-15.

Test each button in your toy to make sure it functions as you intend. If it doesn't, look for error messages in the Command Center — they provide clues about how to correct your code. If you find a *bug,* meaning a problem with your code, look at each line of code carefully and check for misspelled primitives and missing quotes. Also check that new procedures you have written begin with to and end with end.

 If a button is executing Forever, you can always stop execution by clicking the Stop All button on the MicroWorlds EX toolbar.

Once finished, play with the Art Toy and ask friends to play with it, too!

Enhance your game

Consider enhancing your project with new features:

✔ **New buttons:** Add new buttons for favorite colors, both for the background and for the turtle.

✔ **New angles:** Create new turn angles for the turtle. You can even use a one degree turn angle if you want to provide Art Toy users fine control over their drawings!

✔ **New pen sizes:** Make buttons to create larger pen sizes to provide the turtle thicker lines when drawing.

✔ **Pen erase:** Add a button with a pen erase (pe) command. In pen erase mode, a turtle will erase a previously drawn line that it walks over.

✔ **Teleport:** Add a teleport command (setx random 640 sety random 480) to instantly send the turtle to a random coordinate in the workspace. If the pen is down and you set teleport to forever, the turtle will create some crazy kinetic art!

Mini Golf

One of the many cool things you can do when learning to code is making a game or toy. This project guides you in creating your own miniature golf game that you can share with friends.

In the role of game-maker, you are in control of graphics tools as you paint a golf hole, and then create ball and obstacle objects. You put your button-making skills to use as you code motion and direction commands. Next, you code how the ball reacts to the environment — falling in a water trap or the hole, as well as reflecting off an obstacle.

Several new primitive commands are used in this golf course, plus a couple of easy-to-write procedures. When complete, consider adding new features to make your game even more challenging and fun to play!

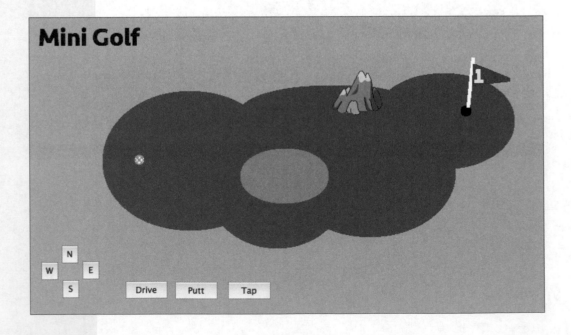

Brainstorm

Miniature golf courses can be crazy! You can make a themed hole with all sorts of decorations and colors, as well as weird bumpers and traps. Explore the Painting/Clipart palette and go a little wild with your game theme:

- ✔ Tropical

- ✔ Spacey

- ✔ Sports

In my hometown of Las Vegas, there's a miniature golf course featuring Kiss — the 70s rock band — where you can golf *and* rock and roll all night!

Start a New Project

Begin creating Mini Golf by starting a new project as follows:

1. Start MicroWorlds EX.

2. On the yellow MicroWorlds EX startup screen, select Free Mode.

   A new project opens.

3. From the menu bar, choose File⇨New Project Size⇨MicroWorlds Standard.

Draw a Golf Green, Water Trap, and Hole

Paint a golf green where the player will play. Include a water trap and a target hole. Follow these steps:

1. On the toolbar, click the Hide/Show Painting/Clipart button.

   The Painting/Clipart palette opens.

2. Select the Painting Tools on the Painting/Clipart Palette.

Painting with the Painting/ Clipart palette

The Painting/Clipart palette has tools for drawing and painting in the workspace and for making new shapes for turtles. It also has premade backgrounds, single shapes, and animation shapes for use in your projects. Access the Painting/Clipart palette by clicking the Hide/Show Painting/Clipart button on the toolbar. To see the painting tools, click the button in the upper-left corner of the palette.

Drawing brush tips

Drawing and Painting tools

Textures   **Paint color palette**

The row of small buttons includes the drawing and painting tools (from left to right in the figure): Pencil for free-form drawing; Pen for lines; Paint Can for fills; Spray; Rectangle; Filled Rectangle; Oval; Filled Oval; Selector for selecting rectangular regions; Lasso for selecting free-form areas; Color Picker for sampling a color; Eraser; and Undo.

Below the painting tools are the drawing brush tips. Each brush is a different shape, diameter, fade, and style. You can also double-click on an empty spot to open the Brush Editor and create your own brush!

The middle of the palette consists of the paint colors. Each color has a number from 0 to 139. Each column of colors is a family. Grays are in the first family, followed by reds, and so on. Below the color families is the Opacity slider. Set at 100%, a selected color is opaque (not see-through). Set at 0%, a color is transparent (see-through). The bottom of the palette consists of textures.

3. Select a background color in the color palette by clicking it.

4. Click the Paint Can tool and then move into the workspace. Click in the workspace to fill the background.

In Figure 2-1, a solid shade of lime green is used.

5. Now, create the grass for Hole 1. Select a different color in the color palette by clicking it. Click the Filled Oval tool and select a dot-sized drawing brush. Move into the workspace and draw two or three overlapping ovals, as shown in Figure 2-1.

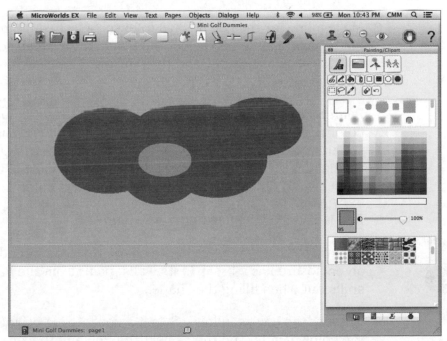

Figure 2-1

If you make a mistake while painting, you can undo each step by clicking the Undo button in the Painting/Clipart palette, or by clicking Ctrl-Z (Windows) or Command-Z (Mac).

6. Next, create the water trap. Click a shade of blue in the color palette. Continue painting with the Filled Oval tool and brush you selected in Step 4. Move into the workspace and paint a blue oval onto the grass (refer to Figure 2-1).

   This blue oval will be the water trap.

7. Now create the target hole. Select black in the color palette, and then select the Pencil and the small circle drawing brush. Move into the workspace and click one time near an edge of the putting green to create a circle where the golf ball will fall, as shown in the title figure (the figure at the beginning of this project).

8. Make a line for the flag post as follows: Select white in the color palette, and then select the Pen and the small square brush. Click in the hole, and then drag and release to make a line (refer to the title figure).

9. Paint a flag on the pole as follows: Select a bright color in the color palette, and then select the Pen or Pencil and the small square drawing tip. Make three lines to create a triangle for the flag on the post. Make sure the triangle is closed. Use the Paint Can to fill the inside of the triangle with color.

   Red is used for the flag in the title figure.

Be sure to completely enclose a shape that you intend to fill. If an enclosure has a break in its walls, paint from the Paint Can spills out when filling the shape.

10. Number the flag as follows: Select a contrasting bright color in the color palette, and then select the Pen and the small square brush. Make lines to draw the number of the hole on the flag.

    The title figure shows a yellow number 1 drawn on the flag.

Leave the Painting/Clipart palette open. You will use it again soon.

Create a Title Text Box

Add a title to the page as follows:

1. On the toolbar, click the Create a Text Box button; move into the workspace and draw a rectangle for the text box; type a title — Mini Golf — in the white area of the text box.

2. Select the text inside the text box. From the menu bar, select the Text menu options and format the text.

   See Project 1 for details on formatting text.

   You can resize text boxes at any time. Ctrl-click (Windows) or Command-click (Mac) an opaque text box. Sizing dots appear — click and drag any of them to resize the text box.

3. Right-click (Windows) or Ctrl-click (Mac) inside the text box and select Transparent from the pop-up menu.

Create a Golf Ball and an Obstacle

The golf game needs two turtle objects: one to serve as a golf ball, and another to be the obstacle. Follow these steps to create the two turtles:

1. On the toolbar, click the Create a Turtle button. Move into the workspace and click to hatch a turtle.

2. Drag the turtle to a position on the putting green. Right-click (Windows) or Ctrl-click (Mac) the turtle and select Open Backpack from the pop-up menu.

   The turtle backpack opens, as shown in Figure 2-2. For more details on the backpack, see the nearby sidebar, "Exploring the turtle backpack."

Exploring the turtle backpack

In MicroWorlds EX, each turtle object carries a *backpack*. The backpack holds important information, organized into six tabs (sort of like pockets):

- **State tab:** Like a wallet, the State tab includes the turtle Name, where it is located (its Xcor and Ycor), the direction it is pointed (Heading), Size, Shape, Animation mode (SetShape or SetRotate), Pen state (Up, Down, or Erase), and Visibility. Variable values known only to a specific turtle are stored in the lower I Have Value section of its State tab.

- **Procedures tab:** Holds procedures that only its turtle owner knows. This differs from the project Procedures tab, which holds procedures known by all turtles in the project. If a project procedure and backpack procedure have the same name, the turtle uses its backpack procedure.

- **Shapes tab:** Holds shapes that the turtle wears, similar to a closet of clothes. This differs from the project Shapes tab, which holds shapes wearable by all turtles in the project. If a project shape and backpack shape have the same name or same number, the turtle wears its backpack shape.

- **Notes tab:** Holds turtle-specific notes you want to keep.

- **Audio tab:** Holds music and sounds unique to the individual turtle.

- **Rules tab:** One of the most frequently used tabs in the turtle backpack. The Rules tab tells the turtle what to do when clicked on (OnClick), how to behave when walking over colors (OnColor) or bumping into other turtles (OnTouching), what to do at specific times (OnTick), what do to when hearing a message (OnMessage), and how to react to User Defined Events (When This Do That).

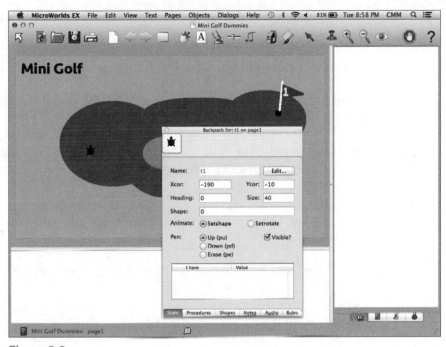

Figure 2-2

3. On the backpack State tab, click the Edit button beside the Name field.

The Name dialog box appears.

4. Type golfball in the Name field, as shown in Figure 2-3. Click OK to close the Name dialog box.

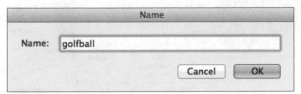

Figure 2-3

 5. Time to find a shape for the ball turtle to wear! Return to the Painting/Clipart palette. Click the Singles button to show a collection of shapes you can use in your projects.

Shapes in the Singles area can be worn by turtles or stamped onto the background.

6. Scroll down to the ball shape located beside the star.

   This ball shape looks similar to a golf ball, but it needs some recoloring.

7. You can recolor the golf ball on the project Shapes pane. Click the project Shapes tab (located in the lower-right corner of the window).

   The project Shapes pane holds the collection of shapes used in your project.

8. Drag the ball shape from the Painting/Clipart palette to any spot on the project Shapes pane.

   Your screen now looks similar to Figure 2-4.

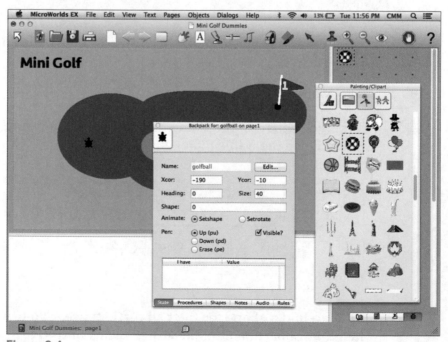

Figure 2-4

9. Double-click the shape spot with the ball.

   The Shape Editor opens. The Shape Editor contains the same painting tools as the main Painting/Clipart palette.

 10. Select a medium shade of gray and select the Pencil and dot-sized brush. Paint the gray over the black areas to make it look more like a golf ball.

   Figure 2-5 shows the painting in progress.

Figure 2-5

11. When you're finished, click OK at the top of the Shape Editor.

   The recolored ball appears at the shape spot.

12. Click the ball at the shape spot, and then move into the workspace and click the turtle.

The golfball turtle now wears the ball shape. Your screen now looks similar to Figure 2-6. Leave the backpack open for later.

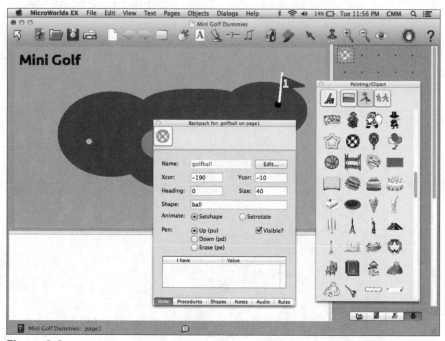

Figure 2-6

Don't click a shape and attempt to drag it onto the turtle's back — you'll end up placing it on the background of the workspace. Just click-release the shape in the Shapes tab or Singles, and then click-release the turtle's back. If you accidentally place the shape on the background, right-click (Windows) or Ctrl-click (Mac) the shape and select Cut from the pop-up menu to get rid of it.

13. Repeat Steps 1–5 to create a new turtle and name it obstacle. Select any shape from the Singles area of the Painting/Clipart palette to put on the turtle.

   You don't have to recolor this shape unless you want to — just click the shape and then click the turtle to apply the shape. Figure 2-7 shows how the screen looks now. In this example, the obstacle turtle wears the mountain shape.

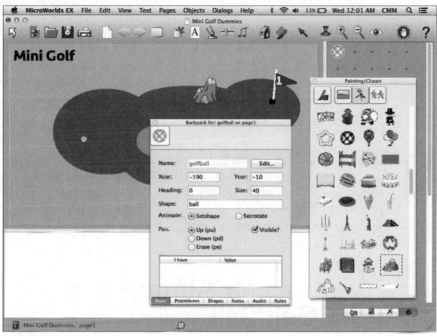

Figure 2-7

Set the Starting Position of the Golf Ball

At the start of the game, the golf ball must be set to the position where the player will tee off. The ball will also be set to this starting position following a fall into the water trap or a successful drop into the hole.

Follow these steps to set the starting position of the ball:

1. Drag the golf ball to a starting position.

2. Look at the State tab of the `golfball` turtle backpack, and note the Xcor and Ycor fields.

Figure 2-6 shows that the Xcor equals -190 and the Ycor equals -10. This means that the golf ball is positioned at the coordinates (-190, -10). Note that your Xcor and Ycor values may be different depending on what makes sense in your game. You will need these coordinates later in the "Write a Watertrap Procedure" section and the "Write a Win Procedure" section. Leave the backpack open.

Coordinates are the mathematical way of naming a position on a graph. René Descartes is credited with the method. Coordinates in two dimensions, like your MicroWorlds EX workspace, are listed as a pair (x, y). The first number is the x-coordinate (position right to left) and the second number is the y-coordinate (position top to bottom).

Create Controls for Aiming and Hitting the Golf Ball

Aiming the golf ball means pointing it in the direction you want it to travel. Hitting the golf ball can be done in one of three ways:

✔ Driving it (hitting a long way)

✔ Putting it (hitting a short distance)

✔ Tapping it (hitting a tiny distance)

As the game designer and coder, you want to provide easy-to-use controls for both aiming and hitting the ball. Create buttons for pointing the ball North, East, South, or West. Then create buttons to Drive, Putt, and Tap the ball.

Pointing a turtle in a direction requires turning it. Right turn (rt) and left turn (lt) are relative turn commands because they turn the turtle relative to where it currently points. Set heading, or seth, is an absolute turn command because it causes the turtle to point to the selected heading regardless of where it was pointing before the turn. To use the seth command, you must indicate the degree angle around a circle where the turtle should point; for example, seth 90 points east. See Figure 2-8.

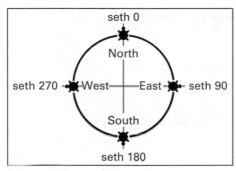

Figure 2-8

Create buttons for aiming the ball

Follow these steps to create the four buttons — N, S, E, and W — for aiming the ball:

1. First, create a button to point the golf ball turtle north. On the toolbar, click the Create a Button button. Then click the workspace anywhere.

2. In the Button dialog box, fill in the following information (see Figure 2-9):

   • *Label:* Type N (for north) in the Label field to name the button.

   • *Instruction:* Type golfball, seth 0 in the Instruction field. Here's what the instruction does. The command golfball, (including the comma) says "I'm speaking to the golf ball." Commands that follow are executed by only the golf ball turtle. The command that follows is seth 0. So the entire instruction tells just the golf ball to set its heading to 0, meaning to point north.

   • *Do It:* Select the Once radio button. When the *N* button is clicked, it will execute its instruction one time.

   • *Visible:* Select this check box to leave the button visible.

button	
Name:	button1
Label:	N
Instruction:	golfball, seth 0
Do It:	⦿ Once ☑ Visible ◯ Forever
	Cancel OK

Figure 2-9

3. Click OK to close the Button dialog box.

   The N button is added to the workspace.

4. Drag the button to the lower-left corner of the workspace.

Arrange player/user controls such as buttons, sliders, and drop-down lists in a clear and understandable layout. Your graphical user interface, or GUI, should allow the player/user to easily operate your game, toy, or simulation!

5. Test the N button by clicking it.

   Although nothing appears to happen to the golf ball, you should see that the State tab of the golf ball backpack shows a Heading of 0.

6. Repeat Steps 1–5 to create and test one button each for aiming the ball E (east), S (south), and W (west). Refer to Figure 2-8 for help in writing the instruction for each direction.

7. Arrange your N, E, S, and W buttons to match real compass headings as shown in the title figure.

Create buttons for hitting the ball

Now it's time to create buttons to get that golf ball moving! Follow these steps to create three buttons for hitting the ball:

1. On the toolbar, click the Create a Button button. Then click the workspace anywhere.

2. In the Button dialog box, fill in the following information (as shown in Figure 2-10):

   - *Label:* Type Drive in the Label field to label the button.

   - *Instruction:* Type golfball, glide 100 0.2 in the Instruction field.

     The instruction begins with the command golfball, meaning that only the golf ball turtle will execute the command that follows. The command that follows is glide 100 0.2, which tells the turtle to move 100 pixels at a speed of 0.2.

     The glide primitive is similar to the fd primitive in that both commands cause the turtle to move. But glide is followed by two numbers — a distance and speed — whereas fd is followed by only one number — a distance. The glide command creates the appearance of smoother movement than fd.

   - *Do It:* Select the Once radio button. When the Drive button is clicked, it executes its instruction one time.

   - *Visible:* Select this check box to leave the button visible.

button
Name: button5
Label: Drive
Instruction: golfball, glide 100 0.2
Do It: ⦿ Once   ☑ Visible
○ Forever
Cancel   OK

Figure 2-10

Your button label doesn't know whether your button instruction makes sense. The button Label field could read something that in no way relates to the Instruction field! Additionally, the button Label field does not define a procedure. For example, creating a button with the label Drive and the instruction `glide 100 0.2` does not define a new procedure named `drive`. To define a procedure, write the procedure on the project Procedures pane or on the Procedures tab of a turtle backpack.

3. Click OK to close the Button dialog box.

   The Drive button is added to the workspace.

4. Drag the button to the bottom of the workspace.

5. Test your Drive button by clicking it.

   Your game's ball should mimic the motion of a real golf ball that has been hit hard! Note that the direction is not set in this command — the player must set the direction by clicking a heading button before clicking Drive.

6. Repeat Steps 1–5 to create and test one button each for Putt and Tap.

   One possible instruction for Putt is `glide 20 0.02`, but you can decide for yourself what distance and speed make sense for putt. One possible instruction for Tap is `glide 5 0.02`. Ultimately, you decide what commands work best!

7. Arrange your Drive, Putt, and Tap buttons in logical positions, as shown in the title figure.

8. Test your Putt and Tap buttons by clicking each one.

If you want to edit the instructions you wrote, simply right-click (Windows) or Ctrl-click (Mac) a button and select Edit from the pop-up menu. The Button dialog box reappears, and you can revise your commands.

Code the Ball to Bump Off the Obstacle

Part of what makes a miniature golf game fun is the challenge of getting past the obstacles between the tee and hole. In this game, there is one obstacle, a mountain. The player may want to hit around the obstacle, or else hit the obstacle so that the ball bounces or reflects off the obstacle.

In MicroWorlds EX, you can code an object to react to other objects that it touches. This is done in the OnTouching field of the Rules tab of the turtle backpack. Any commands or procedures in the OnTouching field of a turtle are executed when the turtle bumps into another turtle.

Make the golf ball turtle bounce off the obstacle turtle as follows:

1. In the `golfball` backpack, switch to the Rules tab.

2. At the OnTouching field, type `rt 90 glide 20 0.05`, as shown in Figure 2-11.

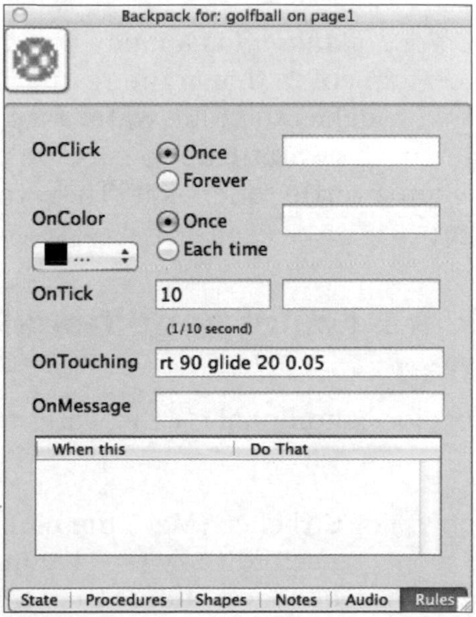

Figure 2-11

Here's how the commands work. The rt 90 command turns the golf ball turtle to the right 90 degrees. Then glide 20 0.05 moves the ball away from the obstacle by a short distance at a slow speed. The motion should look as though the golf ball is bouncing off the obstacle (the mountain).

3. Test your commands by deliberately driving, putting, or tapping the golf ball into the obstacle and looking at the result. Revise your commands as needed to create the bounce motion you want. After you are satisfied with the motion, close the turtle backpack by clicking its X button.

Collisions — two turtles bumping into each other — are common in computer program execution, especially video games! Some collisions result in a bounce, others increase a score, and others reduce the number of lives. Throughout the projects in this book, there will be lots of opportunities to code collision outcomes.

Code Universal Color Conditionals

The term *universal color conditional* is a fancy way to say, "If anything touches a certain color, this is the result." In Mini Golf, you want anything that touches the blue water trap to fall in. You will code the blue of the water trap to execute a procedure called watertrap when a turtle touches it. Then you write the watertrap procedure.

Create the universal color conditional for the water trap

Create the universal color conditional for the water trap as follows:

1. Right-click (Windows) or Ctrl-click (Mac) the blue water trap. From the pop-up menu, select Edit Sky (see Figure 2-12). Note that if you chose a different shade of blue than this example, your pop-up menu may show Edit Turquoise, Edit Cyan, or Edit Blue.

Figure 2-12

The Instructions for Color dialog box appears and allows you to set the universal color conditional. Because this example uses the color Sky, the name of the dialog box is Instructions for Sky.

2. In the dialog box, fill in these options, as shown in Figure 2-13:

- *Mouse:* Leave the Mouse text box blank for this project. This option means that when the user clicks on the color, the associated instruction is executed.

- *Turtle:* In the Turtle field, type `watertrap`. (You will write the `watertrap` procedure later in this project.)

- *Once:* Select this radio button.

This means that when a turtle is on the color sky, the `watertrap` procedure is executed once.

Instructions for: sky
Mouse: [   ]
Turtle: [watertrap   ]
⦿ Once   ◯ Each Time
[Cancel] [OK]

Figure 2-13

If you select the Each Time radio button in the dialog box, the turtle will execute the associated instruction with every step in the color until you move the turtle somewhere else. Be careful with choosing Each Time because it can cause your turtle to get stuck. There are some instances when you will select Each Time, but usually, the preferred choice is Once. Once does not mean "one time ever"; it means, "one time until you exit the color and then return again later."

3. Click OK to save your changes.

When a universal color conditional is coded, all locations on the background with that color possess the associated instruction. Be careful to look at the entire background to see where a color appears, and be especially careful of colors that appear in patterned backgrounds. If a turtle touches any instance of that color, the associated instruction is executed.

Create the universal color conditional for the hole

Create the universal color conditional for the hole as follows:

1. Right-click (Windows) or Ctrl-click (Mac) the black hole. From the pop-up menu that appears, select Edit Black (see Figure 2-14).

Figure 2-14

The Instructions for Black dialog box appears and allows you to set the universal color conditional.

2. In the dialog box, fill in these fields (as shown in Figure 2-15):

- *Mouse:* Leave this text box blank.

- *Turtle:* In the Turtle field, type win.

- *Once:* Select this radio button.

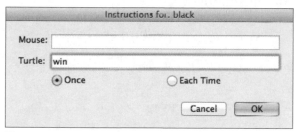

Figure 2-15

This means that when a turtle is on the color black, the win procedure is executed one time. This occurs when the player has sunk the ball in the hole! You will write the win procedure in the next section.

3. Click OK to save your changes.

Universal color conditionals function only on background colors, not turtle colors and not colors in shapes worn by turtles.

Universal means that any turtle walking across the color or mouse clicking the color will cause the instructions to be executed. Conditional means that MicroWorlds EX treats the command as an IF-THEN command, even though the command isn't written using IF-THEN structure. There are also turtle-specific color conditionals: With these, each turtle is coded to individually respond to (or ignore) certain colors on the background. Universal color conditionals are coded on the background, while turtle-specific color conditionals are coded on the OnColor tab of the turtle backpack. Because there is only one moving turtle in Mini Golf, the color conditionals can just as easily be programmed in the turtle backpack.

Write a Watertrap Procedure

The watertrap procedure is executed when a turtle touches the water. Note that the only turtle moving in the workspace is the golf ball turtle. Follow these steps to write this procedure:

 1. Click the project Procedures tab (located in the lower-right corner of the window).

2. Type the watertrap procedure as shown:

```
to watertrap
ht
announce [Water trap!]
wait 3
setpos [-190 -10]
st
end
```

Here's how this procedure works:

- This procedure starts with the to primitive in order to define the new command watertrap.

- In the next line, it uses the ht (hide turtle) primitive to make it appear that the golf ball has plunged into the water.

- The procedure then uses the announce primitive to issue an on-screen announcement to the player. Type the announcement you want to make between the two square brackets: [Water trap!]. Figure 2-16 shows an example of this announcement.

- After the player dismisses the announcement, the procedure pauses briefly using the wait primitive. wait is followed by a number that is in tenths of a second — the bigger the number, the longer the wait. The purpose of the wait is to set the pacing of the game.

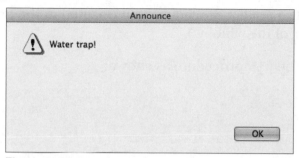

Figure 2-16

- Next, the procedure sets the position of the golf ball back to the starting tee-off position using `setpos [-190 -10]` (or whatever coordinates you chose for your game). Note that because the golf ball is hidden, the player does not see it move back to the tee.

- Finally, the procedure uses the `st` (show turtle) primitive to make the ball visible again.

- As with all procedure definitions, `end` is the final primitive.

3. Drag the ball into the water and check that the `watertrap` procedure works as expected. If not, look at the Command Center for clues about possible errors.

Be sure to look carefully at the example code when deciding whether to use square brackets or parentheses in MicroWorlds EX. Other languages, such as Java, make extensive use of curly braces and parentheses. Each type of punctuation is understood differently by each computer language, very much like commands themselves. Incorrect usage of punctuation will cause program code to fail in execution.

Write a Win Procedure

The `win` procedure is executed when a turtle touches the hole. Note that the only turtle moving in the workspace is the golf ball turtle. Follow these steps to write the `win` procedure:

1. Click the project Procedures tab (located in the lower-right corner of the window).

2. Type the `win` procedure as shown:

```
to win
ht
announce [You win!]
wait 3
setpos [-190 -10]
st
end
```

You can type the `win` procedure above or below the preceding procedure in the project Procedures pane. Figure 2-17 shows the `win` procedure following the `watertrap` procedure.

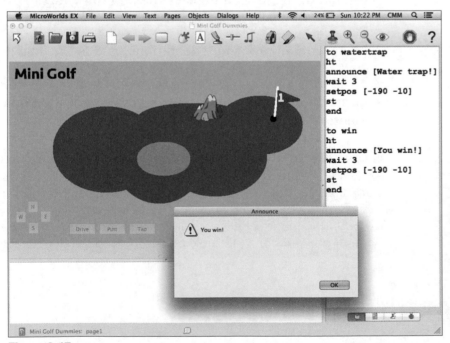

Figure 2-17

Note that the win procedure is nearly identical to the watertrap procedure. Only the word between the square brackets in the announcement differs: [You win!]. Type the announcement you want to make between the two square brackets to tell the player he has won.

3. Drag the ball into the hole and check that the win procedure works as expected. Figure 2-17 shows the completed game, as well as the successful execution of the win procedure.

In MicroWorlds EX, the order of the procedures entered in the Procedures pane does not matter. This is true for both the project Procedures pane and turtle backpack Procedures. However, the order in which procedures are sequenced for execution *does* matter. As an analogy, think about a pile of clothes — order doesn't matter until you need to get dressed, then it matters a great deal. Shirts go on your body before jackets, socks then shoes, and pants then belts — otherwise, your outfit receives a big error message!

Save, Test, and Debug

Choose File⇨Save Project from the menu bar to save your game. Test each button to make sure it functions as you intended. Check for error messages in the Command Center to determine where any bugs may exist in your code. When you're finished, play several times and share it with friends!

Freeze the golf ball turtle, buttons, and obstacle by right-clicking (Windows) or Ctrl-clicking (Mac) it and then selecting Freeze from the pop-up menu for each element. This prevents the player from manually moving the ball and other elements of your game. Unfreeze a frozen element by selecting Unfreeze from the pop-up menu.

To view your game as a player will see it — viewing only the work-space — click the Presentation Mode button on the toolbar. The game should appear similar to the title figure. Press Esc to leave Presentation Mode.

Enhance your game

Consider enhancing your project with new features:

- **New obstacles:** Create new bumpers and other obstacles to obstruct the path of the golf ball to the hole.

- **New traps:** Consider a sand trap or a lava trap! Write a new universal color conditional procedure for each trap such as `sandtrap` or `lavatrap`.

- **New directional buttons:** Write in-between directions to aim the ball. Northeast (NE) would have an associated instruction of `seth 45`. What would the instructions be for SE, SW, and NW? Position these buttons logically with the existing direction buttons.

- **New golf holes:** In the `win` procedure, add a `nextpage` command before the `end` command. From the menu bar, choose Pages⇨New Page to draw Hole 2! Be sure that the ball tees off from the same coordinates as Hole 1. You can make an entire 9- or 18-hole mini golf course.

Sketcher Etcher

Etch A Sketch is a toy that first appeared in 1960 and is still around today. In this project, you code your own Sketcher Etcher. The Sketcher Etcher toy has a red frame and a light gray drawing area. Controls at the bottom of the toy allow a player to draw horizontally (left or right) and vertically (up and down) using straight lines. The player can only draw in the gray area — if the drawing pen, or *stylus,* reaches the red frame, it encounters a boundary the pen can't go past. After drawing for a while, the player can erase the screen, returning to a clean gray slate, ready to draw again.

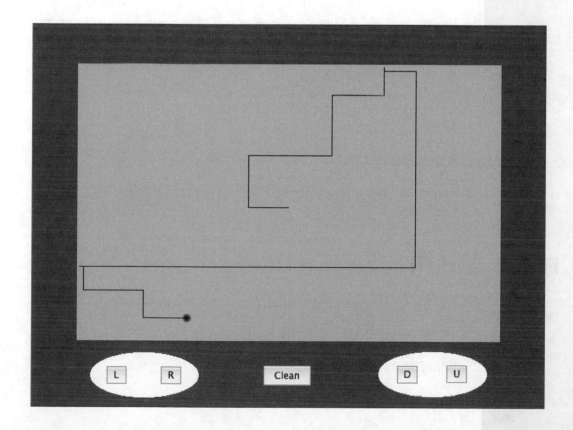

Brainstorm

During one of my first years teaching coding, I had a student named Matthew who made every project into a Whoopi project in honor of actress Whoopi Goldberg. Even his Sketcher Etcher featured a little Whoopi drawing stylus. Other students changed their styluses to characters and objects you might consider using for your project:

- Footballs, basketballs, and other balls
- Penguins
- Abstract shapes

Start a New Project

Begin creating your Sketcher Etcher toy by starting a new project as follows:

1. Start MicroWorlds EX.

2. From the yellow MicroWorlds EX startup screen, select Free Mode.

   A new project opens.

3. From the menu bar, choose File⇨New Project Size⇨Full Screen 640 x 480.

Paint and Freeze the Background

Follow these steps to paint and freeze the background:

1. From the toolbar, click the Hide/Show Painting/Clipart button.

   The Painting/Clipart palette opens.

2. Open the Painting Tools.

3. From the color palette, select any color of your choosing, click the Paint Can tool, and then click the workspace to fill it with that color. Figure 3-1 shows a fill using the color red.

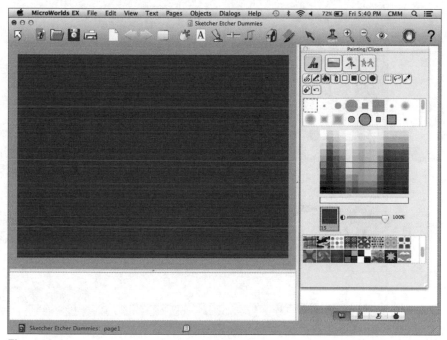

Figure 3-1

This color becomes the frame for your Sketcher Etcher.

4. Select a light shade of gray from the color palette, click the Filled Rectangle tool, and then draw a filled rectangle over the red workspace, leaving a thick red frame at the edges, as shown in Figure 3-2.

Make sure the bottom edge of the frame is wider than the other edges.

5. Select the color white from the color palette. Select the Filled Oval tool and choose a dot-sized brush. Draw two ovals on the bottom section of the red frame, as shown in Figure 3-2.

These ovals serve as dials for drawing with the Sketcher Etcher. Close the Painting/Clipart palette by clicking its X button.

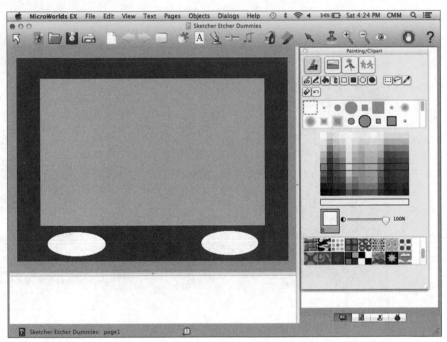

Figure 3-2

6. Freeze the background so that it cannot be erased: Right-click (Windows) or Ctrl-click (Mac) the background and select Freeze Background from the pop-up menu.

On an unfrozen background, the clean command (which you create later in this chapter) erases both lines drawn with the Sketcher Etcher and also the background itself. Be sure to freeze the background!

Create a Drawing Stylus

Follow these steps to create a drawing stylus for your Sketcher Etcher and put the stylus down so that it will leave a mark as it draws:

1. From the toolbar, click the Create a Turtle button. Then in the workspace, click to hatch a turtle.

2. In the Command Center, type the command pd and press the Enter (Windows) or Return (Mac) key to set the turtle pen down.

   Now, whenever the stylus turtle draws, it will leave behind a mark.

3. Next, you need to paint a shape for the stylus. Click the project Shapes tab (located in the lower-right corner of the window).

4. On the project Shapes tab, double-click any shape spot.

   The Shape Editor opens.

5. In the Shape Editor, click the Pencil tool and a small, faded brush. Then click in the center of the drawing area to create an Etcher drawing stylus, as shown in Figure 3-3, and click OK.

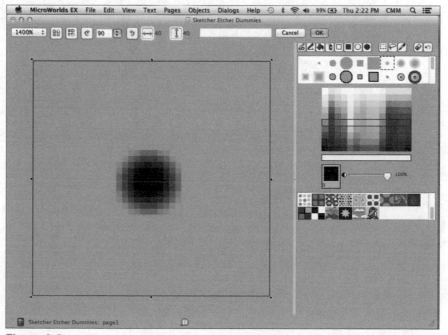

Figure 3-3

The completed Etcher drawing stylus appears on the project Shapes pane.

6. Click the stylus on the project Shapes pane and then click the turtle in the workspace.

The turtle now wears the shape, as shown in Figure 3-4.

Figure 3-4

If you accidentally click somewhere other than the turtle, the stylus shape appears on the background. To remove it, simply right-click (Windows) or Ctrl-click (Mac) the shape and select Remove from the pop-up menu.

Add Horizontal and Vertical Drawing Controls

Just like a real Etch A Sketch, your Sketcher Etcher needs a way to control drawing horizontal lines and vertical lines. Follow these steps to create four buttons — left, right, down, and up — to control the drawing stylus:

1. On the toolbar, click the Create a Button button. Then click anywhere on the workspace.

   The Button dialog box appears.

2. In the dialog box, type L (for left) in the Label field and seth 270 fd 5 in the Instruction field. Leave the Once radio button and Visible check box selected.

   The dialog box should look like Figure 3-5.

button		
Name:	button1	
Label:	L	
Instruction:	seth 270 fd 5	
Do It:	● Once	☑ Visible
	○ Forever	Cancel OK

Figure 3-5

The seth 270 command points the drawing stylus to the left (or west), and the fd 5 command moves the stylus forward 5 pixels. Because the stylus pen is down, it leaves a short mark on the Sketcher Etcher screen.

3. Click OK.

   The L button is added to the workspace.

4. Drag the L button to reposition it to the left dial control of your Sketcher Etcher.

You may want to resize the button to reduce its size so that it fits on the background dial. To do so, Ctrl-click (Win) or Command-click (Mac) on the button. Sizing dots appear on the corners of the button — drag one of those dots to resize your button, and then release.

5. Repeat Steps 1–3 three more times to create the Right, Down, and Up buttons. Use these commands for each button:

   - *Label:* R *Instruction:* `seth 90 fd 5`

   - *Label:* D *Instruction:* `seth 180 fd 5`

   - *Label:* U *Instruction:* `seth 0 fd 5`

The unit of circular measurement is the degree. There are 360 degrees in a circle. In MicroWorlds EX, the top of the circle is 0 degrees (this is north on a compass). East is 90 degrees; the bottom of the circle is 180 degrees (this is south on a compass). West is 270 degrees.

6. Reposition the new buttons so the arrangement looks similar to Figure 3-6.

   These buttons represent your Sketcher Etcher control dials.

Figure 3-6

7. Click each button a few times to make sure it functions as expected:

   - Clicking the L button causes the drawing stylus to move left, drawing a line as it moves.

   - Clicking the R button causes the drawing stylus to draw as it moves right.

- Clicking the U button causes the stylus to draw as it moves up.

- Clicking the D button causes the stylus to draw as it moves down.

Set Up Horizontal Boundary Conditions for the Stylus

The Sketcher Etcher stylus must be prevented from drawing in the red frame when moving horizontally — left and right. You will write a *When This Do That* rule (a rule that is always running) so it can continuously check whatever its rule says to check. Here, it checks whether the turtle runs into the frame. Follow these steps to set up horizontal boundary conditions:

1. First, you need to find the x-coordinates of the left boundary between the gray drawing area and the red frame. To do so, drag the stylus turtle to where these two areas intersect on the left side of the workspace.

2. Open the stylus backpack by right-clicking (Windows) or Ctrl-clicking (Mac) the stylus turtle and choosing Open Backpack.

3. On the State tab, find the Xcor value.

   In Figure 3-7, the Xcor value is −260, but your value may be slightly different.

The left side of the x-axis has negative values, and the right side of the x-axis has positive values.

4. Switch to the Rules tab of the stylus turtle backpack.

5. On the Rules tab, find the When This . . . Do That section, and then in the blank space below that, right-click (Windows) or Ctrl-click (Mac), and select Add from the pop-up menu, as shown in Figure 3-8.

   The User-Defined Event dialog box opens.

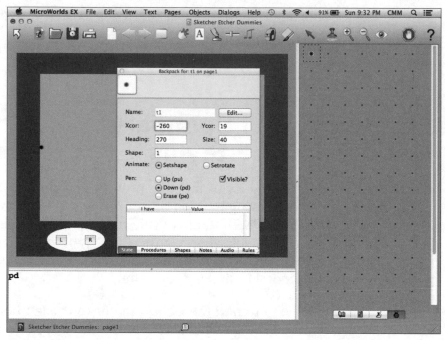

Figure 3-7

Figure 3-8

6. Type xcor < -260 (or whatever value you found in Step 3) in the When field, and type bk 5 in the What field, as shown in Figure 3-9. Click OK.

User–Defined Event	
When:	xcor < –260
What:	bk 5
	Cancel OK

Figure 3-9

These two commands — xcor < -260 and bk5 — mean that if the user clicks the L button and the x-coordinate of the stylus is less than –260, the stylus moves backward 5 pixels. Because the L button command — seth 270 fd 5 (see the preceding section) — moves the stylus forward 5 pixels, this has the net effect of not moving the stylus at all — and it does not move left into the red frame.

7. Click OK to close the dialog box.

8. Repeat Steps 1–4 for the right boundary between the gray drawing area and the red frame. Be sure to check the Xcor value at this boundary.

9. In the User-Defined Event dialog box, type xcor > 260 (or whatever xcor value you have) in the When field, and bk 5 in the What field. Click OK.

The Rules tab of the stylus turtle backpack now looks something like Figure 3-10.

If you need to edit a When This . . . Do That command, click the command to select it. Then right-click (Windows) or Ctrl-click (Mac) and select Edit from the pop-up menu. Then make your changes in the dialog box.

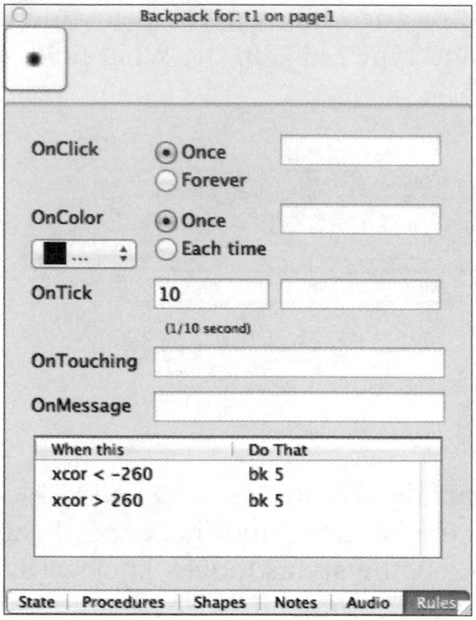

Figure 3-10

Set Up Vertical Boundary Conditions for the Stylus

The stylus of the Sketcher Etcher must be prevented from drawing in the red frame when moving vertically — down and up. To set up vertical boundary conditions using another When This Do That rule, follow these steps:

1. First, you need to find the y-coordinates of the bottom boundary between the gray drawing area and the red frame. Drag the stylus turtle to that boundary.

2. Open the stylus backpack by right-clicking (Windows) or Ctrl-clicking (Mac) the stylus turtle and choosing Open Backpack.

3. On the State tab, find the Ycor value.

   In Figure 3-11, the Ycor value is −150, but your value may be slightly different.

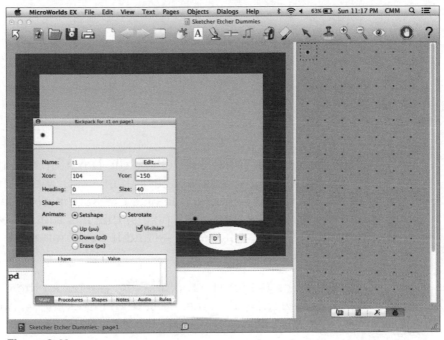

Figure 3-11

The bottom half of the y-axis has negative values, and the top half of the y-axis has positive values.

4. Switch to the Rules tab of the stylus turtle backpack.

5. Right-click (Windows) or Ctrl-click (Mac) in the When This . . . Do That area of the Rules tab and select Add from the pop-up menu.

   The User-Defined Event dialog box opens.

6. In the dialog box, type ycor < -150 (or whatever value you have) in the When field and bk 5 in the What field, as shown in Figure 3-12. Click OK.

User-Defined Event	
When:	ycor < –150
What:	bk 5
	Cancel　OK

Figure 3-12

This means that if the user clicks the D button and the y-coordinate of the stylus is less than –150, the stylus will move backward 5 pixels. Because the button command moves the stylus forward 5 pixels, this has the net effect of not moving the stylus at all — and it does not move down into the red frame.

7. Repeat Steps 1–4 for the top boundary between the gray drawing area and the red frame. Be sure to check the y-coordinate value at this boundary.

8. In the User-Defined Event dialog box, type ycor > 185 (or whatever value you have) in the When field, and bk 5 in the What field. Click OK.

The Rules tab of the stylus turtle backpack now has a complete set of rules and looks something like Figure 3-13.

Boundary conditions are important constructs in mathematics, business, and science. You will see the math of Sketcher Etcher in an algebra course, but the deeper ideas will pop up again in calculus, physics, economics, and other advanced courses!

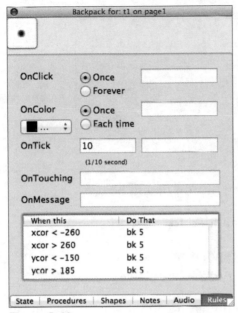

Figure 3-13

Make a Button to Clean Drawings

A Clean button allows users to erase a drawing they make with the Sketcher Etcher. To create a Clean button, follow these steps:

1. Click the Create a Button button, and then click anywhere in the workspace.

2. In the Button dialog box, fill in the following information, as shown in Figure 3-14:

   - *Label:* Type Clean in the Label field to name the button.

   - *Instruction:* Type clean in the Instruction field.

   - *Do It:* Select the Once radio button.

   - *Visible:* Select this check box so the button is visible.

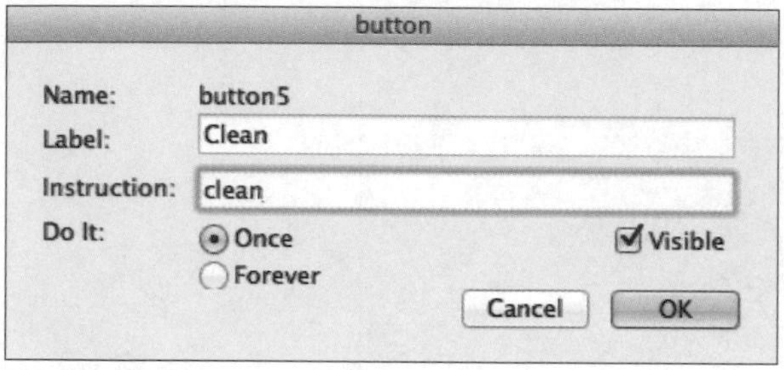

Figure 3-14

3. Click OK to close the Button dialog box.

   The Clean button is added to the workspace.

4. Drag the button to reposition it at the bottom of the workspace, between the drawing controls.

   Note that the pd command is no longer needed in the
   Command Center and is now removed. Once the pen is down,
   it requires no additional commands to remain down.

When coding, there are many occasions when different commands or
programming strategies can accomplish the same task. This project
could also have used a universal color conditional (refer to Project 2)
to constrain the drawing stylus. While universal color conditional commands work well with solid colors, the When This Do That method of
using inequalities presented here provides a more general solution for
handling boundaries.

Save, Test, and Debug

To save your toy, click the Save Project button on the toolbar. Test
all the buttons to ensure they work correctly.

Troubleshoot and fix bugs until the toy looks just the way you
want!

Enhance your game

Consider enhancing your Sketcher Etcher toy with new features. Here are some suggestions:

- Add buttons to allow drawing in diagonal directions, using commands such as `seth 45 fd 5`.

- Add buttons to change the drawing color of the stylus, using commands such as `setc "red`

- Add a button to change the pen size of the stylus using a command such as `setpensize 5`.

- Set the drawing stylus in constant motion! Just right-click (Windows) or Ctrl-click (Mac) the stylus and select Animate from the pop-up menu. If desired, you can halt the motion of the stylus by clicking the Stop All button on the toolbar.

Week 2
Motion, Animating Shapes, and Reacting to Input

This week you'll build . . .

If you're a teacher using this book in the classroom, check out the Action Plans available via www. dummies.com/extras/codingforkids. Each project has an Action Plan with a checklist for each step in the project. You will also find a list of key ideas students learn as they complete the project.

Horse Race

It's a day at the races! And you can construct your own horse derby, complete with animated horses, trotting sounds, and a photo finish.

Horse Race is a simulation featuring a racetrack you paint, as well as animated horses available in the MicroWorlds EX Animation collection. You'll add commands for setting the horses at the starting line and then moving the horses along the track at random speeds. As with any horse race, the horses all run at the same time — in coding terms, this means that the commands controlling their racing motion execute in *parallel*. Every race is unique, so you never know which horse will win! You'll also add object-specific color under commands to each horse object, and announce (via an alert box) which horse reaches the finish line first. Finally, you'll use the Create a Melody feature to make a simple trotting sound that plays throughout the race.

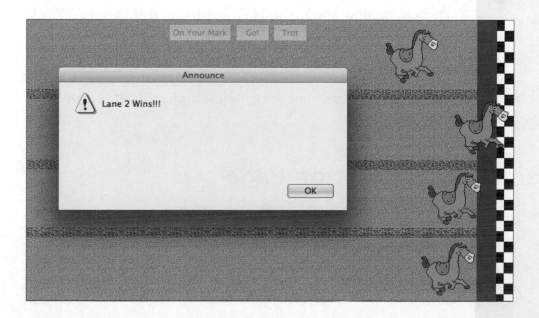

Brainstorm

There are numerous options for objects that can be raced down the lanes of the track. MicroWorlds EX has a wide variety of characters in the Animation collection that are fun to race:

- Kids on a track team

- Dogs

- Kangaroos

- Fire-breathing monsters

- Ghosts

Start a New Project

Begin creating your Horse Race simulation by starting a new project as follows:

1. Start MicroWorlds EX.

2. From the yellow MicroWorlds EX startup screen, select Free Mode.

   A new project opens.

3. From the menu bar, choose File⇨New Project Size⇨MicroWorlds Standard.

Paint the Simulation Page

The *simulation page* is where the Horse Race is viewed. Paint a racetrack on the simulation page, adding four lanes and two vertical finish lines (one of which is decorative). Follow these steps:

1. On the toolbar, click the Hide/Show Painting/Clipart button.

The Painting/Clipart palette opens.

2. Open the Painting Tools.

3. Select the speckled, gray texture and use the Paint Can tool; click to fill the workspace with that texture, as shown in Figure 4-1.

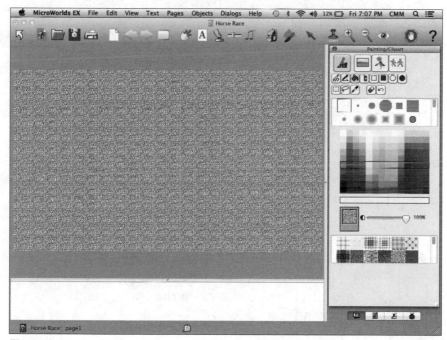

Figure 4-1

4. Select a medium shade of brown from the color palette and drag the slider to set the opacity to 70%. Select the Filled Rectangle tool and a medium brush; then draw a filled rectangle over the entire workspace, as shown in Figure 4-2.

TIP

Use a medium brush (the brush with a diameter of 5 pixels) when drawing with the Filled Rectangle tool to make it easier to fill the entire workspace without gaps.

Figure 4-2

5. Next, you need to create four lanes. Select the grass texture, and drag the slider to set the opacity at 100%. Use the Pen tool and a large brush (the brush with a diameter of 15 pixels) to draw three lane dividers on the track, creating four lanes, as shown in Figure 4-3.

Draw the center divider first to make it easier to space the lanes equally.

6. Select the checkerboard texture. Use the Pen tool and a very wide brush (the brush with a diameter of 29 pixels) to draw a vertical finish line at the far right side of the track, as shown in Figure 4-4.

This line is just for decoration.

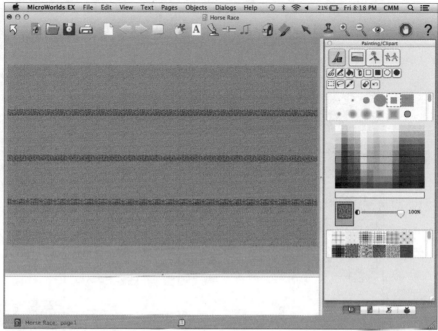

Figure 4-3

7. Select the red color. Use the Pen tool and a very wide brush to draw another vertical finish line touching the left side of the checkerboard line, as shown in Figure 4-4.

This red line will be used to determine which horse wins the race.

TIP

After you've finished painting a background, it's a good idea to freeze it so that there's no possibility of erasing it. Just right-click (Windows) or Ctrl-click (Mac) the background and select Freeze Background from the pop-up menu.

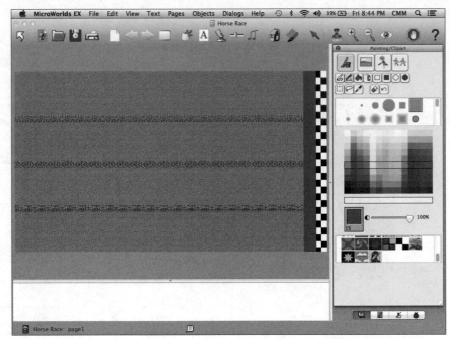

Figure 4-4

Create a Racing Horse Character

Follow these steps to create one horse character and then add primitive commands to the OnClick field to create its racing motion:

1. On the toolbar, click the Create a Turtle button. Click on the workspace to hatch a turtle. Drag the turtle to the start of Lane 1.

2. At the Command Center, type the command seth 90 and click the Enter (Windows) or Return (Mac) key on the keyboard.

   This command sets the turtle heading (seth) — the direction it points — to east (90), as shown in Figure 4-5. (See Project 2 for details on setting the heading.)

Turtle facing east

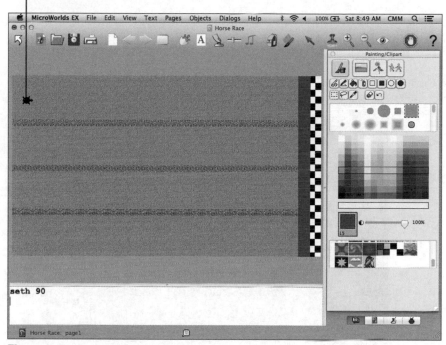

Figure 4-5

 3. In the Painting/Clipart palette, click the Animation button.

The Animation button offers animated shapes for your turtle to wear.

4. Next, you need to add the three animated horses to the turtle. Scroll down to the brown horse shapes. Click the first horse shape and then hold down the Shift key and click the last horse shape.

All the horse shapes are selected, as shown in Figure 4-6.

Figure 4-6

5. In the workspace, click on the turtle.

The turtle now wears the animated sequence of horses. Note that when the horse is not moving on the screen, you see only one shape, as shown in Figure 4-7.

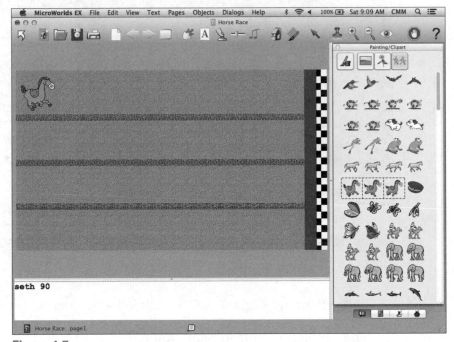

Figure 4-7

6. Close the Painting/Clipart palette by clicking its X button.

7. Although you can't see all three horses, you can check that all the horse shapes are in the turtle backpack. Right-click (Windows) or Ctrl-click (Mac) on the turtle and select Open Backpack from the pop-up menu. On the backpack State tab, the Shape field shows the shape names horse5, horse6, and horse7, as shown in Figure 4-8.

Note that the backpack also shows that the horse turtle's heading is 90 (degrees) from the command you issued in Step 2.

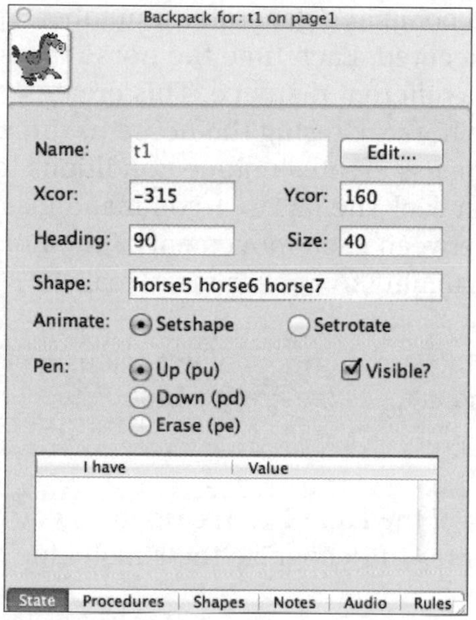

Backpack for: t1 on page1

Name:	t1 Edit...
Xcor:	−315 Ycor: 160
Heading:	90 Size: 40
Shape:	horse5 horse6 horse7
Animate:	⦿ Setshape ○ Setrotate
Pen:	⦿ Up (pu) ☑ Visible?
	○ Down (pd)
	○ Erase (pe)

I have	Value

State | Procedures | Shapes | Notes | Audio | Rules

Figure 4-8

8. With the horse's backpack still open, switch to the Rules tab. Type `fd random 10 wait 1` in the `OnClick` field and set it to Forever, as shown in Figure 4-9.

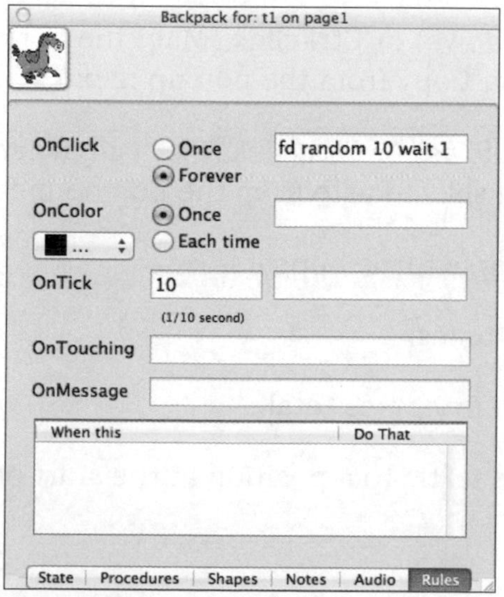

Backpack for: t1 on page1

OnClick	○ Once	fd random 10 wait 1
	⦿ Forever	
OnColor	⦿ Once	
◼ ... ⇕	○ Each time	
OnTick	10	
	(1/10 second)	
OnTouching		
OnMessage		

When this	Do That

State | Procedures | Shapes | Notes | Audio | Rules

Figure 4-9

The `random 10` command generates a number from 0 to 9 each time it's executed. Each time the horse takes a step, it moves forward a different distance. This creates variation in the speed of the horse, causing the horse to run each race differently. Randomness creates unique conditions for each race, so any horse can win! The `wait 1` command inserts a 0.01 second pause between each movement of the horse, and slows the pace of the running to appear more realistic.

Random number generation is important in coding and is used in all sorts of programs and games. See Project 1 for details on using the `random` command.

Leave the backpack of the Lane 1 horse open — you'll get back to it in the "Set Up Horses to Recognize the Finish Line" section, later in this project.

Make Copies of the Horse

Three more horse turtles are needed to occupy the race track. Create them as follows:

1. Right-click (Windows) or Ctrl-click (Mac) the horse turtle in Lane 1 and select Copy from the pop-up menu.

2. Right-click (Windows) or Ctrl-click (Mac) anywhere on the background and select Paste from the pop-up menu.

   A copy of the horse turtle appears.

3. Paste two more times.

   There are now four horses total.

4. Drag each horse turtle to a position at the start of a lane.

Line Up the Horses at the Starting Gate

At the start of a race, the horses need to be lined up vertically so that the race is fair. The horses must all have the same x-coordinates.

Objects aligned vertically all have the same x-coordinate, like a vertical line on a graph.

Follow these steps to create a button to line up the horses at the starting gate:

1. Find the x-coordinate of the horse in Lane 1 by opening its backpack and viewing the State tab.

   In this example, the Xcor value is −315 (refer to Figure 4-8).

2. On the toolbar, click the Create a Button button. Then click anywhere in the workspace.

   The Button dialog box opens.

3. Fill in the following information:

   - *Label:* Type On Your Mark in the Label field to name your button.

   - *Instruction:* In this field, enter everyone [setx -315] (or replace -315 with whatever Xcor value you found in Step 1). This causes all horse turtles to set their x-coordinates to the same value, lining them up vertically.

   - *Do It:* Select the Once radio button.

   - *Visible:* Leave this check box selected.

   The dialog box for the example looks like Figure 4-10.

4. Click OK to close the Button dialog box.

   The On Your Mark button is added to the workspace.

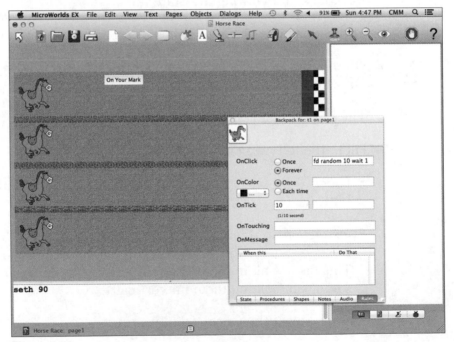

Figure 4-10

5. Drag the button to reposition it at the top of the workspace (see Figure 4-11).

Figure 4-11

If the Label text is longer than the button length, resize the button: Ctrl-click (Windows) or Command-click (Mac) on the button. Sizing dots appear — drag them to resize your button, and then release.

6. Click the On Your Mark button to make sure it functions as expected.

All four horse turtles should line up close to the left edge of the workspace, as shown in Figure 4-11.

Set Up Horses to Recognize the Finish Line

There are two different types of color detection in MicroWorlds EX:

- **Universal color detection** is set on the background color so that every turtle object reacts to the color in the same way.

- **Local color detection** lets you set a different reaction of each turtle to a color.

You will use local color detection to determine which horse crosses the red finish line first. Set up local color detection for each horse turtle as follows:

1. Return to the backpack Rules tab of the horse turtle in Lane 1.

The backpack should still be open from earlier.

2. From the OnColor drop-down list, select the red color swatch to match the red finish line

3. In the OnColor field, add the command announce [Lane 1 Wins!!!] stopall and set it to Once, as shown in Figure 4-12.

When the horse in Lane 1 touches the red finish line, its OnColor command for red is executed. This command announces that the horse in Lane 1 is the winner. The stopall command halts further program execution.

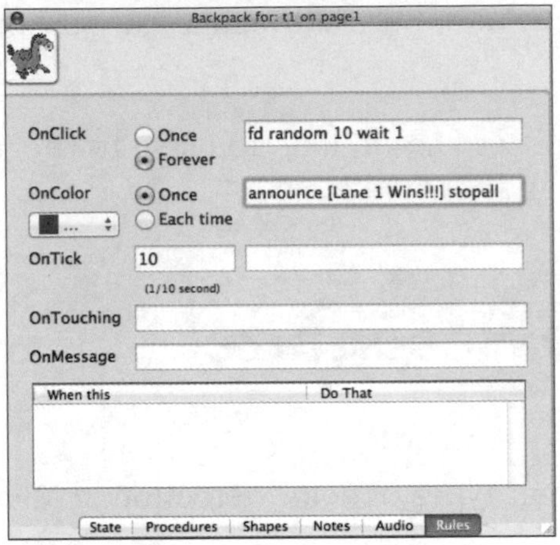

Figure 4-12

4. In the workspace, drag the horse turtle in Lane 1 over to the red finish line to check that the expected onscreen announcement is made.

   During actual operation of the simulation, the `stopall` command you added in Step 3 will stop all code from executing — otherwise, the horses would continue racing after you dismissed the announcement!

5. Right-click (Windows) or Ctrl-click (Mac) the horse turtle in Lane 2 and select Open Backpack from the pop-up menu.

6. From the OnColor drop-down list, select the red color swatch. Add the command `announce [Lane 2 Wins!!!] stopall` to the `OnColor` field and set it to Once.

7. Drag the horse turtle in Lane 2 over to the red finish line to check that the expected announcement is made.

8. Repeat Steps 5–7 for the horse turtles in Lane 3 and in Lane 4, changing each announcement accordingly.

9. Close all the horse turtle backpacks. They are no longer needed.

Create a Button to Start the Race

Each horse contains commands for simulating racing motion in its OnClick field. You need to create a button that activates that command in all four horses at the same time to start the race. Follow these steps:

1. From the toolbar, click the Create a Button button. Click anywhere in the workspace.

2. In the Button dialog box, fill in the fields as follows:

   - *Label:* Type Go! in the Label field to name the button.

   - *Instruction:* In this field, enter everyone [clickon]. This command "clicks on" all the horse turtles simultaneously; they execute the commands in their OnClick fields at the same time.

   - *Do It:* Select the Once radio button.

   - *Visible:* Leave this check box selected.

   The dialog box for the example looks like Figure 4-13.

button	
Name:	button2
Label:	Go!
Instruction:	everyone [clickon]
Do It:	⦿ Once ☑ Visible
	◯ Forever
	Cancel OK

Figure 4-13

3. Click OK to close the Button dialog box.

   The Go! button is added to the workspace.

4. Drag the button to reposition it at the top of the workspace near the On Your Mark button you made previously.

5. Click the Go! button to make sure it functions as expected.

All four horse turtles should begin racing.

Parallel versus serial execution

Some aspects of coding in MicroWorlds EX can be considered *object-oriented* — each object does its thing according to rules established within the object. Those things can happen in parallel, meaning that multiple objects can be executing their own commands at the same time. It's like a rock band in which five instruments are playing different parts of the music simultaneously. Parallel execution of commands is contrasted with *serial execution,* in which commands execute one at a time, including commands associated with different objects.

Here's an example that helps you visualize the difference between parallel and serial execution. Create two turtles and issue the command `forever [everyone [fd 1 wait 1]]` in the Command Center. Note that the turtles take turns moving, one after the other; this is serial execution. Now, start over and create two turtles with each turtle possessing the command `fd 1 wait 1` set to forever in its OnClick field. Issue the command `everyone [clickon]` in the Command Center. Note that the turtles move simultaneously; this is parallel execution.

The horses in Horse Race are coded to execute their movements in parallel with one another, which is what real horses would do at the track. Additionally, the trotting sounds execute in parallel with the racing horses to create the impression that the horses are stomping their hooves into the dirt as they run.

Add Trotting Sounds

Racing horses produce a lot of noise with all those hooves clomping on the ground! MicroWorlds EX features several options for adding audio to your project so that you can re-create sounds of the racetrack. One option is using the Melody dialog box to create a simple tune or sound effect. Create your own trotting sounds to play during the simulation as follows:

 1. From the toolbar, click the Create a Melody button.

2. Move the cursor into the workspace and click the background.

   The Melody dialog box appears.

3. Click the marimba, the last instrument in the instrument collection of the dialog box.

   The *marimba* is a percussion instrument that most closely mimics the sound of clomping.

4. Click any two keys on the large keyboard, followed by a rest to create a horse trot sound (see Figure 4-14).

   The "Making melodies" sidebar, later in this chapter, goes into more detail about using this dialog box.

5. Adjust the Volume and Tempo sliders and then click Play to hear your sound. Use the cursor to select and cut notes, or insert new notes into your sound until you are satisfied that it sounds like a trot.

6. In the Name text box, type trotsound for the sound name. Leave the Show Name and Visible check boxes selected. Click OK to dismiss the dialog box.

   The trotsound icon now appears in the workspace — click it to make sure it sounds the way you want it to.

7. Right-click (Windows) or Ctrl-click (Mac) the trotsound icon and click Hide.

Audio icons are usually executed from procedures and buttons, so they don't need to be visible in the workspace. Leaving the icon in the workspace clutters the graphical user interface and may cause the user to assume it performs a needed function.

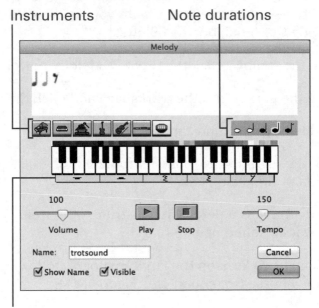

Figure 4-14

If you want to show any hidden object, switch to the main Project pane and then click the triangular arrow next to any page in the project. This will list all objects on the page. Right-click (Windows) or Ctrl-click (Mac) any object and select Show from the pop-up menu. The object will now show in the workspace.

Many computer programs, especially games, feature theme music, background music, or sound effects. Sometimes the audio takes the form of recorded sound (see Project 12 for details on recording sound in MicroWorlds EX). Other times the audio is created digitally, in much the same way as the MicroWorlds EX Create a Melody interface operates.

Making melodies

The Melody dialog box (refer to Figure 4-14) features seven instruments: a piano, an electronic keyboard, a xylophone, an electric guitar, a cello, a flute, and a marimba. Clicking the icon of an instrument selects that instrument to play a score, or series of notes and rests you create. Here's how to create your melody:

✔ **Add notes:** Create your series of notes by clicking each note in order on the large keyboard.

✔ **Specify the duration of a note:** Select the note and then click the icon for whole note, half note, dotted quarter note, quarter note, or eighth note.

✔ **Add rests:** You can also add rests of different durations by clicking a rest symbol (located below the large keyboard). Like editing a text document, you can click anywhere in your score and add new notes or rests at the insertion point; delete notes and rests; or select a note or series of notes and change their instrument.

✔ **Adjust volume and tempo:** The Volume slider and Tempo slider control the volume and tempo during playback.

✔ **Control playback:** The Play and Stop buttons allow you to play back or halt playback while editing.

✔ **Change name of score:** The default name of your score is `melody1`, but you can enter a different name in the Name text box. Just be sure there are no spaces in the name.

Finally, selecting the Show Name check box shows the name of your audio creation with its icon when displayed in the workspace, and selecting the Visible check box makes the icon visible in the workspace.

Make a Button to Play the Trotting Sounds

Clicking the trotsound icon plays the sound you created just once, but you want to hear the sound of horses racing until one racer crosses the finish line. Follow these steps to create a button to continue to play the trot sound until the race is over:

1. From the toolbar, click the Create a Button button. Then click anywhere in the workspace.

2. In the Button dialog box, fill in the following information:

   • *Label:* Type Trot in the Label field to name the button.

   • *Instruction:* Type trotsound (which is the sound you created in the preceding section) in this field.

   • *Do It:* Select the Forever radio button.

   • *Visible:* Select this check box to leave the button visible.

   The dialog box for the example looks like Figure 4-15.

Figure 4-15

3. Click OK to close the Button dialog box.

   The Trot button is added to the workspace.

4. Drag the button to reposition it at the top of the workspace, near the On Your Mark and Go! buttons you made previously, as shown in Figure 4-16.

5. Click the Trot button to make sure the sound plays as expected. Click the button again to stop the playback.

   Note that the seth 90 command that set the heading of the Lane 1 horse is no longer needed in the Command Center. You can now remove the command.

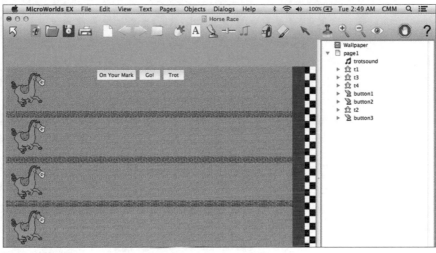

Figure 4-16

Save, Test, and Debug

 Click the Save Project button on the toolbar to save your simulation. Test your simulation by clicking On Your Mark, then Go!, and then Trot to ensure it runs the way you want.

Click the Stop All button on the toolbar at any time to stop simulation procedures and processes from executing.

Troubleshoot and fix bugs until the simulation looks just the way you want!

TIP

Enhance your game

Consider enhancing your Horse Race simulation with new features:

✔ Add additional randomness to racing speeds by changing the `wait 1` command to `wait random 2` in each horse turtle OnClick field.

✔ Increase the number of lanes from four to five or six.

✔ Create and add an "Off to the Races" piece of music to the Go! button to start the race.

Winter Wonderland

Depending on what part of the world you live in, you may see a Winter Wonderland every year — or not at all! Regardless of whether such a scene exists outside your window, you can bring it to life on your computer screen.

Winter Wonderland is an animated scene featuring blinking tree lights, gently falling snowflakes, imported music, and a sky that cycles between night and day. You'll create your own shapes for the blinking light bulbs and use a `pick` command to change the bulbs. You'll also make your own animated shapes for the snowflakes and write a procedure that makes them appear to fall. One thing you won't need to do — shovel the driveway!

Brainstorm

Winter Wonderland is just one option for your animated scene. You can choose virtually any season, holiday, or place to set your scene, such as

- An autumn scene with falling leaves and a spooky Halloween jack-o-lantern with flashing eyes

- A city street scene with glowing neon signs and gently sprinkling rain

- A birthday party scene with rising helium balloons and flickering flames on the cake candles

Start a New Project

Begin creating your Winter Wonderland scene by starting a new project as follows:

1. Start MicroWorlds EX.

2. From the yellow MicroWorlds EX startup screen, select Free Mode.

   A new project opens.

3. From the menu bar, choose File⇨New Project Size⇨ MicroWorlds Standard.

You can customize project sizes to take advantage of larger screen sizes and high resolutions. An alternative to selecting a standard project size is to create a custom size by typing `newprojectsize [width height]` in the Command Center. For example, the command `newprojectsize [1200 800]` creates a workspace of 1200 pixels by 800 pixels.

Paint the Scene Page

The *scene page* is where you view the Winter Wonderland scene. You will paint a tree and snow on the ground, but you will leave the sky unpainted. By leaving the sky unpainted, you can write the `day_and_night` procedure (later in this project) to change the color of the sky from black to blue to cyan.

Paint the scene page as follows:

1. At the Command Center, type the command `setbg "black` and then press Enter (Windows) or Return (Mac).

   The `setbg` command sets the background color, which in this case is black, as shown in Figure 5-1.

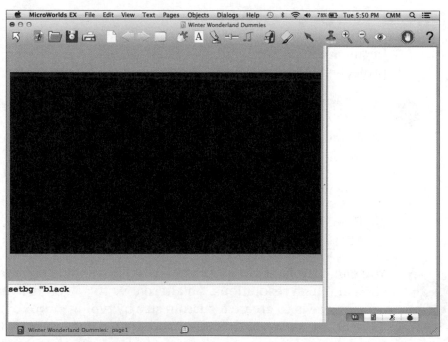

Figure 5-1

When using the set background color command in MicroWorlds EX, you use quotation marks before the color name, but not after the color name.

2. On the toolbar, click the Hide/Show Painting/Clipart button.

   The Painting/Clipart palette opens.

3. Use the Painting Tools to paint your own tree in the black workspace, and then add snow to cover the ground, as shown in Figure 5-2.

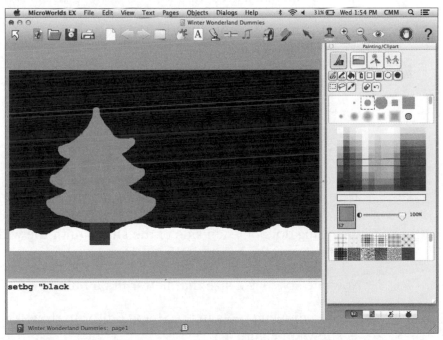

Figure 5-2

Don't paint any lights or snowflakes — those will be turtle objects!

4. When you're finished, close the Painting/Clipart palette by clicking its X button.

Create Bulb Characters

In this section, you create a red bulb character, add the `blink` procedure (which you write later in the project) to it, and then make multiple copies of the bulb that you place on the tree. You also create several shapes for bulbs of different colors.

Follow these steps:

1. On the toolbar, click the Create a Turtle button. Move into the workspace and click to hatch a turtle. (Avoid hatching the turtle over the black area, or it will be difficult to see.)

2. Drag the turtle to a position on the tree.

3. Now, you need to paint a shape for the bulb. Click the project Shapes tab (located in the lower-right corner of the window).

4. On the project Shapes tab, double-click a shape spot.

   The Shape Editor opens.

5. The default shape size of the shape is 40 pixels by 40 pixels. This size is too large for bulb shapes and needs to be decreased. Increase the zoom to 1600%. Then pull and adjust the sizing dots on each side of the shape until the width is 15 pixels and the height is 15 pixels.

   Now the space is a size that better fits a bulb.

6. Use the drawing tools in the Shape Editor to draw a red bulb, as shown in Figure 5-3.

7. Name the bulb shape `redbulb` (in the empty white field at the top of the Shape Editor) and then click OK.

   The Shape Editor closes, and the redbulb shape appears in a spot at the project Shapes tab.

Zoom   Width | Height | Shape name

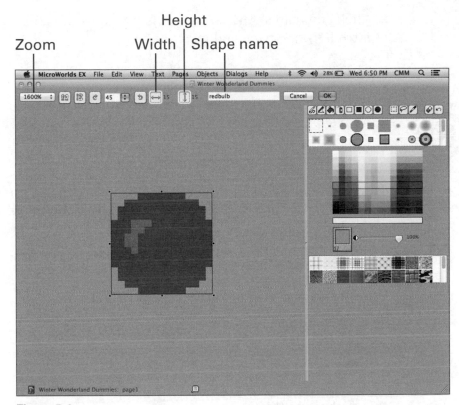

Figure 5-3

8. Repeat Steps 4–7 to create several shapes for bulbs of different colors. Name the bulbs `goldbulb`, `bluebulb`, `silverbulb`, and `violetbulb`.

The completed bulb shapes now appear on the project Shapes pane, as shown in Figure 5-4.

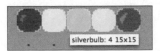

silverbulb: 4 15x15

Figure 5-4

9. Click any bulb shape on the project Shapes tab and then move into the workspace and click the turtle.

The turtle now wears the bulb shape.

If you accidentally click somewhere other than the turtle, the bulb shape will appear on the background — simply right-click (Windows) or Ctrl-click (Mac) the shape and select Remove from the pop-up menu to remove it.

10. Next, you need to add the `blink` procedure to the turtle. Right-click (Windows) or Ctrl-click (Mac) on the turtle wearing the bulb shape and select Open Backpack from the pop-up menu.

11. On the backpack Rules tab, type 5 in the first field, and `blink` in the second field of OnTick, as shown in Figure 5-5.

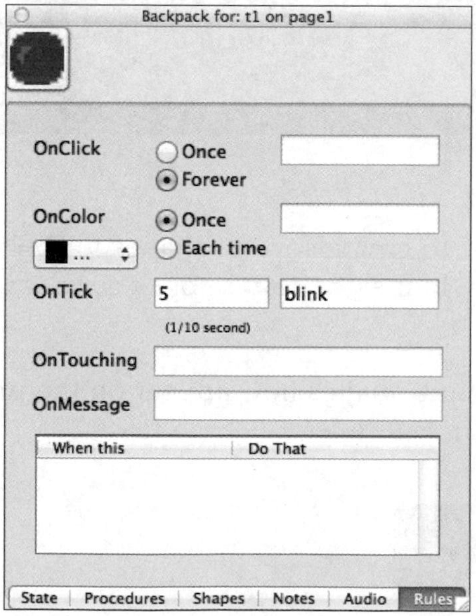

Figure 5-5

The blink procedure (which you write later in the project) changes the color of the bulb shapes on the tree, creating a blinking effect. The blink procedure executes every 5/10 of a second, but you can increase or decrease this rate by typing a different number in the first OnTick field.

OnTick commands begin executing immediately when entered into the second OnTick field. If the command is a procedure that doesn't exist yet, you will receive error statements in the Command Center. For example, you may see I don't know how to blink appear repeatedly. Click the Stop All button on the toolbar to halt the execution of the OnTick commands in the project. You can toggle back to executing the OnTick commands by clicking the Stop All button again.

12. Close the turtle backpack by clicking its X button.

13. Make a copy of your blinking light bulb turtle: Right-click (Windows) or Ctrl-click (Mac) the turtle and select Copy. Click the background and select Paste.

   A copy of the light bulb turtle appears in the workspace.

14. Click Paste again to drop another light bulb turtle on the background. Repeat several more times until you have around 8 to 12 bulb turtles.

15. Click and drag the light bulb turtles, one at a time, into positions on the tree. Note that all the bulbs are currently red.

Create Snowflake Characters

Follow these steps to create a snowflake character, add the fall procedure (which you create later in this project) to it, and make multiple copies of the snowflake:

1. From the toolbar, click the Create a Turtle button. Move to the snow area of your workspace and click to hatch a turtle.

2. Now, you need to paint a shape for the snowflake. On the project Shapes tab, double-click a shape spot.

   The Shape Editor opens.

3. Use the drawing tools in the Shape Editor to draw a snowflake:

   • Use gray, not white, to draw the snowflake so it can be seen against the white of the snowy ground.

   • Move the opacity slider to 70% so that the snowflake is slightly transparent.

   The Shape Editor closes, and the snowflake shape appears in a spot on the project Shapes tab.

4. Make copies of the snowflake. Right-click (Windows) or Ctrl-click (Mac) the snowflake shape and select Copy. Move to the next empty shape spot and right-click (Windows) or Ctrl-click (Mac) and choose Paste. Paste the snowflake on each of the next two shape spots.

   In the example, you should now have four identical snowflake shapes on the project Shapes tab, as shown in Figure 5-6.

Figure 5-6

5. Now, you create animated snowflake shapes. Double-click the second snowflake shape.

   The Shape Editor opens.

6. Click the Angle drop-down button to change the angle to 90 degrees and then click the Rotate Clockwise button, as shown in Figure 5-7.

Rotate Clockwise

Angle

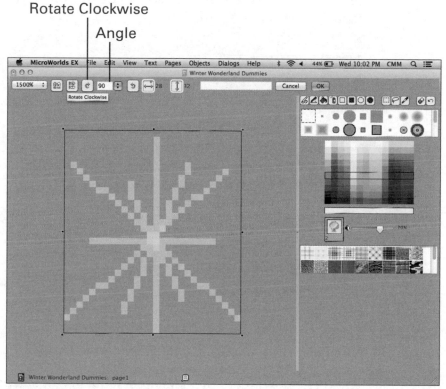

Figure 5-7

The shape rotates.

7. Click OK.

The Shape Editor closes and the rotated snowflake shape appears in a spot on the project Shapes tab.

8. Repeat this process for the third snowflake, rotating it clockwise 180 degrees. Repeat again for the fourth snowflake, rotating it clockwise 270 degrees.

   Once complete, the animated sequence of snowflakes for the example looks like Figure 5-8.

Figure 5-8

9. Next, you add the animated snowflakes to the turtle. Click the first snowflake shape, and then hold down the Shift key and click the last snowflake shape.

   All the snowflake shapes are selected, as shown in Figure 5-9.

Figure 5-9

10. Move into the workspace and click the turtle.

   The turtle now wears the animated sequence of snowflakes.

When the snowflake is not moving, you see only one snowflake in the workspace. But you can check that all the snowflake shapes are in the turtle backpack. Right-click (Windows) or Ctrl-click (Mac) the turtle and select Open Backpack. On the State tab, the Shape field shows the shape numbers of four shapes — these are the four snowflakes (see Figure 5-10). The snowflake shapes don't have names because you left them unnamed in the Shape Editor. Because these shapes will not be referenced by name, there is no need to name them.

Backpack for: t9 on page1

Name:	t9		Edit...
Xcor:	78	Ycor:	85
Heading:	0	Size:	40
Shape:	6 7 8 9		

Animate: ⦿ Setshape ◯ Setrotate

Pen: ⦿ Up (pu)   ☑ Visible?
     ◯ Down (pd)
     ◯ Erase (pe)

I have	Value

State | Procedures | Shapes | Notes | Audio | Rules

Figure 5-10

Each shape has a default name, which you can change. If you use a shape from the Painting/Clipart palette, MicroWorlds EX has already assigned it a default name, for example penguin. If you create a new shape, its default name is the position number of the shape spot it occupies in the project Shapes pane. You can rename a new shape by opening it in the Shape Editor and typing a new name. Naming shapes helps you write and read code more easily; however, you aren't required to name every shape. Shape names should not have spaces in them.

Like shapes, turtles are given default names when they are created. Default turtle names take the form t1, t2, and so on. You can rename a turtle on the State tab of its backpack. Naming turtles helps you write and read code more easily; however, you aren't required to name every turtle. Turtle names should not have spaces in them. Avoid using the same name for a shape and a turtle.

11. Next, you need to add a `fall` procedure to the turtle. With the backpack still open, switch to the Rules tab. Type `fall` in the OnClick field and set it to Forever, as shown in Figure 5-11.

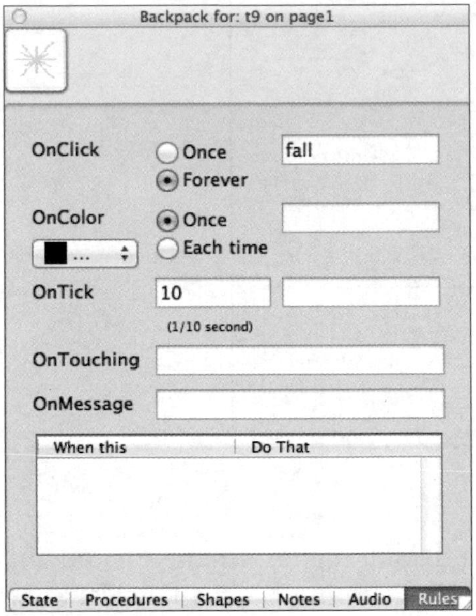

Figure 5-11

The `fall` procedure, which you write later in the project, makes the snowflakes fall to the ground in a gentle, irregular pattern.

12. Close the turtle backpack by clicking its X button.

13. Make a copy of your animated snowflake turtle as follows. Right-click (Windows) or Ctrl-click (Mac) the turtle and select Copy from the pop-up menu. Click the background and select Paste.

A copy of your animated snowflake turtle appears.

14. Click Paste again to drop another animated snowflake turtle on the background. Repeat this step 8 to 12 times to add multiple copies.

15. Click and drag the animated snowflake turtles, one at a time, into the sky area of the workspace, as shown in Figure 5-12.

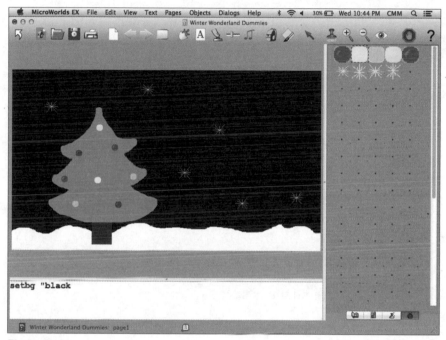

Figure 5-12

Add Music

It wouldn't be a festive Winter Wonderland without a little music to set the mood. You can include audio in MicroWorlds EX projects several ways, including creating your own music using the built-in Melody feature (discussed in detail in Project 4).

Another way to add music to your scene is to import it from the web as follows:

1. Using any search engine, find a winter-themed song on the web.

The file format may be WAV (.wav) or MIDI (.mid). WAV files are actual recorded music or sounds, whereas MIDI files are digitally-created music.

Files in .wav format tend to be larger — and may eat up more processing power — than files in .mid format, which are usually smaller.

2. Right-click (Windows) or Ctrl-click (Mac) the name of the sound file. Select Save Link As from the pop-up menu.

The Save As dialog box appears, as shown in Figure 5-13.

Figure 5-13

3. Click Save.

The sound file is saved.

4. From the menu bar, choose File⇨Import. You can select either Import Sound to import a .wav file (actual recorded music or sounds) or Import Music(Midi) to import a digitally created .mid music file. (See Figure 5-14.)

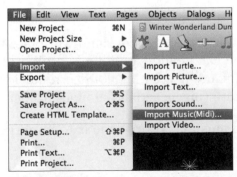

Figure 5-14

5. Navigate to locate your saved sound file and select the file-name. Select the Embed in Project option to embed the file; otherwise, the file will be linked to your project.

Your sound is imported and added to the scene, as shown in Figure 5-15. In the example, the sound name is `winter-wonderland`.

Figure 5-15

6. Click the sound to hear it play. Click it again to stop the music playing.

Embedded sound files can make your project size very large, with .wav files increasing project size more than .mid files. If you choose to link a sound file (or any auxiliary file, including video), you must be sure to include the file with your project. This is especially important when uploading and posting your projects to the web for online distribution (as described in the Appendix).

Write a Blink Procedure

Your scene will use the `blink` procedure to change the color of the bulb shapes worn by the turtles on the tree, creating a blinking effect.

In the Procedures pane, write a `blink` procedure as follows:

```
to blink
setsh pick [redbulb goldbulb bluebulb silverbulb
    violetbulb]
end
```

The `blink` procedure is executed in the bulb turtle's OnTick field according to the timing frequency you set previously. To confirm that it functions properly, make sure that the Stop All button is *not* clicked in the toolbar.

The `blink` procedure sets the shape (`setsh`) of the turtle to a shape picked randomly (`pick`) from the shape names inside the square brackets — [redbulb goldbulb bluebulb silver bulb violetbulb].

Write a Fall Procedure

Your scene will use a `fall` procedure to make the snowflakes fall with a gentle, irregular pattern to the ground.

In the Procedures pane, write a `fall` procedure as follows:

```
to fall
seth 180
rt random 45
glide 100 0.2
lt random 45
glide 100 0.2
end
```

The `fall` procedure is executed forever from each snowflake turtle's OnClick field when the turtle is clicked. (This will be completed in "Make a Let it Snow Button.")

The `fall` procedure sets the snowflake turtle heading (`seth`) to south (`180`), and then turns the heading slightly to the right (`rt`) by a random quantity (`random 45`). The turtle then glides 100 pixels at a slow pace of 0.2 (`glide 100 0.2`). Finally, the turtle performs a slight left turn (`lt`) by a random quantity (`random 45`), followed by the same `glide` command it executed previously (`glide 100 0.2`).

Make a Let it Snow Button

When you click any snowflake turtle, the `fall` procedure in its OnClick field executes, causing the turtle to look like a falling snowflake.

But rather than click each snowflake turtle individually to turn it on, you can make a button that clicks all the turtles at once by using the `everyone [clickon]` command. Follow these steps to make this button:

1. On the toolbar, click the Create a Button button and then click the workspace anywhere.

2. In the Button dialog box, fill in the following information:

   * *Label:* Type `Let It Snow` in this field to name the button.

   * *Instruction:* Type `everyone [clickon]`, which makes all the turtles turn on at once. Any turtle with an OnClick instruction will execute the instruction.

   * *Do It:* Select the Once radio button.

   * *Visible:* Select this check box to leave this button visible.

   The dialog box for the example looks like Figure 5-16.

button
Name: button1
Label: Let it Snow
Instruction: everyone [clickon]
Do It: ⦿ Once ☑ Visible
○ Forever
Cancel   OK

Figure 5-16

3. Click OK to close the Button dialog box.

   The Let it Snow button is added to the workspace.

4. Drag the button to an out-of-the-way position in a corner of the workspace.

The Let it Snow button can serve additional functions beyond clicking on the snowflakes to make them fall. For example, you can also make it play the music you imported. Just place the name of your music at the end of the current instruction: everyone [clickon] winter-wonderland (or whatever your music name is). When the Let it Snow button is clicked, it executes both commands! You can then hide the music icon so that it doesn't clutter up the scene. Hidden objects can be made visible again on the Project pane.

Write a Day and Night Procedure

A day_and_night procedure slowly changes the background color of the scene, cycling among daytime, dusk, and night colors.

 In the Procedures pane, write a day_and_night procedure as follows:

```
to day_and_night
setbg "black
wait 30
setbg "blue
wait 30
setbg "cyan
wait 30
end
```

The day_and_night procedure is executed when you click the Day and Night button, which you create in the next section. This procedure cycles among black, blue, and cyan background colors with 3-second wait periods (wait 30) in between.

Remember that procedure names made of more than one word must not have spaces! Either place all the words together without spaces, or use a dash (-) or underscore (_) symbol to connect words.

Make a Day and Night Button

The Day and Night button will execute the day_and_night procedure forever. Follow these steps to create this button:

 1. On the toolbar, click the Create a Button button and then click the workspace anywhere.

2. In the Button dialog box, fill in the fields as follows:

   - *Label:* Type Day and Night in the Label field to name the button.

     While procedure names must not have spaces, it's okay for Label names to have spaces.

   - *Instruction:* Type day_and_night in the Instruction field.

   - *Do It:* Select the Forever radio button.

   - *Visible:* Select this check box to leave the button visible.

   The dialog box for the example looks like Figure 5-17.

button	
Name:	button2
Label:	Day and Night
Instruction:	day_and_night
Do It:	○ Once ☑ Visible
	⦿ Forever
	Cancel OK

Figure 5-17

3. Click OK to close the Button dialog box.

The Day and Night button is added to the workspace.

Resize buttons to better fit long labels. Ctrl-click (Windows) or Command-click (Mac) button. Sizing dots appear — click and drag any of them to resize the button.

4. Drag the button to an out-of-the-way position in a corner of the workspace.

The completed Winter Wonderland scene for the example looks similar to Figure 5-18.

Note that the `setbg "black` command is no longer needed in the Command Center and can now be removed.

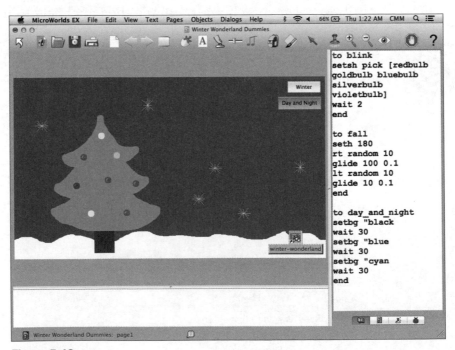

Figure 5-18

Save, Test, and Debug

Click the Save Project button on the toolbar to save your scene. Test your scene by clicking the two buttons and the music icon to ensure it runs the way you want. Because the blinking lights execute via OnTick, they should function automatically unless the Stop All button is clicked.

Click the Stop All button on the toolbar at any time to stop game procedures and processes from executing. Click it again to reactivate the blinking lights.

Troubleshoot and fix bugs until the scene looks just the way you want!

TIP

Enhance your game

Consider enhancing your Winter Wonderland scene with new features:

✔ A snowman, gifts, candy canes, or gingerbread houses

✔ Candles or luminarias with animated, flickering flames

✔ Animals such as polar bears, penguins, or reindeer

✔ Bells that ring

✔ A selection of several music choices

Sports Vote

Voting is a tool for determining relative popularity and can be used for everything from family members deciding on a restaurant to electing a president! It's easy to code a simple voting booth that presents candidates and invites voters to pick their favorite, and then shows the results.

In Sports Vote, you code a voting booth that asks voters to choose their favorite of three sports, but you can customize the voting booth to feature any theme and any candidates. Each vote registers a sound to indicate the vote has been cast. But, instead of showing the number of votes received, the icon for each candidate changes in size according to its relative popularity — the largest candidate wins!

Brainstorm

Expressing our opinions through voting is something you probably do every day informally among friends, in the classroom, and on Facebook. You can't watch television without a news or entertainment station posting the results of their latest poll. So ask yourself, what do want to vote on?

- ✔ Favorite foods

- ✔ Best athletes

- ✔ Political candidates

- ✔ Who will win *America's Got Talent* or *American Idol*

Start a New Project

Start a new project for your voting machine as follows:

1. Start MicroWorlds EX.

2. On the yellow MicroWorlds EX startup screen, select Free Mode.

    A new project opens.

3. From the menu bar, choose File⇨New Project Size⇨Web Player.

Add a Sports-Themed Background

Create a background for your voting machine that relates to the voting theme. For the theme of Favorite Sports, a sports-themed background is appropriate. Follow these steps to add a background and then paint a semi-opaque rectangle over the background:

1. From the toolbar, click the Hide/Show Painting/Clipart button.

   The Painting/Clipart palette opens.

2. Click the Backgrounds button to show the backgrounds, and then click a background image you want to apply to your voting machine. Click in the workspace to drop the background image onto your machine.

   For example, I selected the basketball court background.

3. Right-click (Windows) or Ctrl-click (Mac) the background image. From the pop-up menu, select Stamp Full Page.

   The image is stamped to fill the entire workspace, as shown in Figure 6-1.

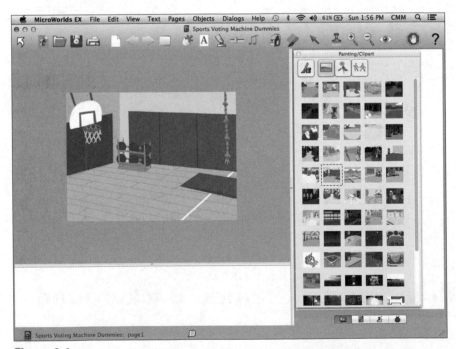

Figure 6-1

4. Switch to the Painting Tools on the Painting/Clipart palette.

5. Select a shade of orange and set the opacity to 80%. Use the Filled Rectangle and a small brush size to draw a rectangle over most of the workspace, as shown in Figure 6-2.

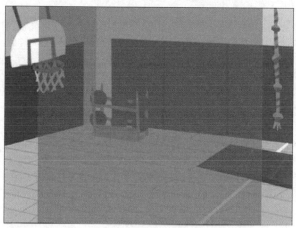

Figure 6-2

The partially opaque orange background will allow you to more easily see the text boxes and turtles you will be adding to the workspace.

 If you don't like the way your rectangle turns out, you can undo the painting and try again. Undo the last step by choosing Edit⇨Undo from the menu bar, or clicking Ctrl-Z (Windows) or Command-Z (Mac) on the keyboard. You can also undo your action by clicking the Undo button in the Painting/Clipart palette.

Leave the Painting/Clipart palette open because you will be using it again soon.

Add Text for the Title and Directions

Use text boxes to add the title, directions, and information on how to read the voting results.

1. From the toolbar, click the Create a Text Box button; move into the workspace and draw a long rectangle for the text box; type the title of your voting machine (for example, Voting Machine) in the white area of the text box.

2. Select the text inside the text box. From the menu bar, select the Text menu options and format the text.

   For the title text in the example, I selected Rockwell font, bold style, 35-point size, and cyan color. See Project 1 for details on formatting text.

3. Right-click (Windows) or Ctrl-click (Mac) the title text box and select Transparent from the pop-up menu. Drag the title text to reposition it to where you want it located, as shown at the top of Figure 6-3.

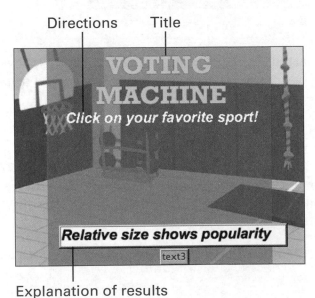

Figure 6-3

4. Repeat Steps 1–3 to create directions for using your voting machine.

   For example, add `Click on your favorite sport!`, as shown below the title in Figure 6-3.

5. Repeat Steps 1–3 to explain how the voting machine indicates which candidate wins or what the difference in size of each candidate means.

   For example, add `Relative size shows popularity`, as shown at the bottom of Figure 6-3, or `The bigger the candidate, the more votes it received`.

   You can edit text in transparent text boxes, but you must first make the text box opaque. Right-click (Windows) or Ctrl-click (Mac) a text box and select Opaque from the pop-up menu. Then edit your text as desired.

   You can resize text boxes at any time as long as the text box is opaque. To make a text box opaque, right-click (Windows) or Ctrl-click (Mac) a text box and select Opaque. Then Ctrl-click (Windows) or Command-click (Mac) the text box. Sizing dots appear — click and drag any of them to resize the text box.

To make sure that users don't accidentally move your text labels, simply right-click (Windows) or Ctrl-click (Mac) any label and select Freeze from the pop-up menu to freeze it in place.

Create Candidates

Create three turtles to serve as candidates in your voting machine. The turtles will eventually wear shapes to indicate the theme of your voting machine. Follow these steps:

1. From the toolbar, click the Create a Turtle button. Move into the workspace and click to hatch a turtle.

2. Name the turtle that will be your first candidate as follows: Right-click (Windows) or Ctrl-click (Mac) the turtle and select Open Backpack. On the backpack State tab, click the Edit button next to the Name field.

3. In the Name dialog box that appears, type `candidate1` in the Name field, as shown in Figure 6-4. Click OK to close the dialog box.

```
                          Name
  Name:  candidate1

                              Cancel      OK
```

Figure 6-4

4. Repeat Steps 1–3 to create a second candidate and name it `candidate2` in the Name field.

5. Repeat Steps 1–3 to create a third candidate and name it `candidate3` in the Name field.

6. Drag the three turtles into a horizontal line in the center of the workspace, as shown in Figure 6-5.

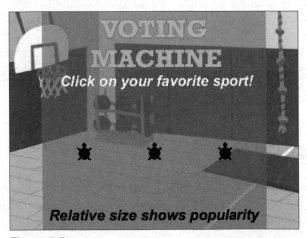

Figure 6-5

Add Shapes to the Turtle Candidates

Each turtle candidate needs a shape. You can create your own original shapes on the project Shapes tab, or you can use one of the MicroWorlds EX shapes available in the Painting/Clipart palette.

Follow these steps to add shapes to the three turtle candidates:

1. In the Painting/Clipart palette, click the Singles button.

2. Scroll down to the sports shapes. Click a sports shape and then move into the workspace and click the turtle named `candidate1`.

   In the example, the `candidate1` turtle now wears the baseball shape, as shown on the left in Figure 6-6.

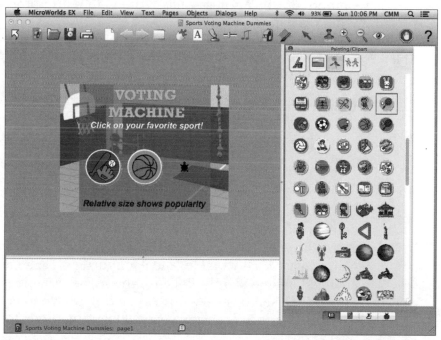

Figure 6-6

3. Repeat Step 2, choosing a different sports shape for the turtle named `candidate2`.

   The example in Figure 6-6 shows the baseball and basketball shapes placed on turtle `candidate1` and turtle `candidate2`.

4. Repeat Step 2, choosing a different sports shape for the turtle named `candidate3`.

5. When you're finished, close the Painting/Clipart palette.

When selecting or creating shapes for each candidate, they should be similarly sized.

Write a Startup Procedure

A startup procedure is a procedure that runs automatically as soon as you open a MicroWorlds EX project. The name startup is reserved for this purpose only. Write a startup procedure for the voting machine as follows:

1. Click the project Procedures tab (located in the lower-right corner of the window).

2. Type the startup procedure as follows:

```
to startup
everyone [setsize 20]
end
```

This startup procedure sets the initial size of all turtle candidates to 20. Because size is a variable, it can have different values as votes are cast for a candidate. Each turtle candidate has its own size variable, and each turtle's size can be changed independently. Because the size variable is an attribute possessed by every turtle, you don't have to create this variable. In other projects, you will learn methods for creating new variables.

3. Type startup in the Command Center to execute the startup procedure and determine whether it works the way you want.

All candidate turtles should set their size to 20. Because their default size was 40, the turtles should appear to shrink in the workspace.

You can tinker with the value of size until you find a good starting value for your machine. The minimum value of size is 5, and the maximum value is 160.

You may have heard of the term *variable* in a math class. Variables are quantities that can have different values at different times. In MicroWorlds EX, size is a built-in variable possessed by every turtle. Size can start out as one value and then change to a different value at a later time. Variables can increase or decrease in value according to instructions provided by the code you create. By contrast, *constants* are numbers such as –9 or 0.102003. Constants never change in value.

Make a Bell Sound to Ring When a Vote Is Cast

Each time a voter casts a vote by clicking on a candidate, a small bell sound plays. Create your own unique bell sound using the Create a Melody feature as follows:

1. From the toolbar, click the Create a Melody button. Then click anywhere on the workspace.

   The Melody dialog box opens.

2. Click a button for an instrument.

   Options consist of piano, keyboard, xylophone, electric guitar, cello, flute, and marimba. (See Project 4 for more on the Create a Melody dialog box options.)

3. Create a sequence of notes resulting in a sound indicating a vote has been cast:

   • *To produce a note:* Click a key on the large keyboard to produce a note.

   • *To specify a note duration:* You can select a note duration before clicking a key, or you can select a note and then select a note duration. Note durations consist of whole, half, quarter, dotted quarter, and eighth.

- *To add a rest duration:* You can also include rests of various durations by clicking the buttons immediately below the keys on the large keyboard.

4. Adjust the Volume and Tempo sliders and then click the Play button to hear the adjustments to your bell sound.

5. When you're satisfied with your bell sound, type the name `bell` in the Name field.

6. Leave the Show Name check box and the Visible check box unselected, as shown in Figure 6-7.

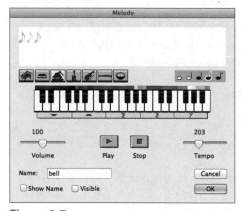

Figure 6-7

7. Click OK to add the bell sound to the project and close the Melody dialog box.

   The icon representing the `bell` sound does not appear in the workspace because the Visible check box was not selected.

8. Click the Project tab (located in the lower-right corner of the window).

   The Project tab opens and shows all pages and elements in your project.

9. Click the plus symbol or gray triangle next to page1 to expand the list and see all elements on page1. Verify that the bell sound has been added to the project, as shown in Figure 6-8.

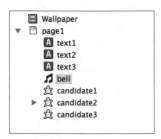

Figure 6-8

 You can edit or show a hidden project element by right-clicking (Windows) or Ctrl-clicking (Mac) the element on the Project tab, and then selecting Edit or Show from the pop-up menu that appears. Alternatively, you can click the Eye Tool button on the toolbar to make all objects visible.

Write a Get Vote Procedure and Add It to the Candidates

When voters click on the candidates they want to vote for, a bell rings, and those candidates grow in size. The more votes (clicks) a candidate receives, the larger it grows in size. Create a procedure called getvote to play the bell and increase the size of the candidate as follows:

 1. Click the project Procedures tab.

2. Type the getvote procedure:

```
to getvote
bell
setsize size + 1
end
```

3. Right-click (Windows) or Ctrl-click (Mac) on the `candidate1` turtle and select Open Backpack. On the Rules tab, type `getvote` into the OnClick field, as shown in Figure 6-9. Leave the radio button set to Once.

Figure 6-9

Now, whenever the voter clicks on the `candidate1` turtle, the `getvote` procedure is executed. The `getvote` procedure plays the bell sound (`bell`) that you created in the preceding section, and then increases the size of the selected turtle by one (`setsize size + 1`).

The size increase command works by setting the size of the turtle (`setsize`) to whatever size it was previously (`size`) plus one more (`+ 1`). This has the effect of increasing the turtle candidate's size a little bit each time it is clicked.

4. When you're finished, close the `candidate1` backpack.

5. Repeat Steps 3–4 for `candidate2` and `candidate3`.

Save, Test, and Debug

 Click the Save Project button on the toolbar to save your voting machine. The final machine should look similar to Figure 6-10.

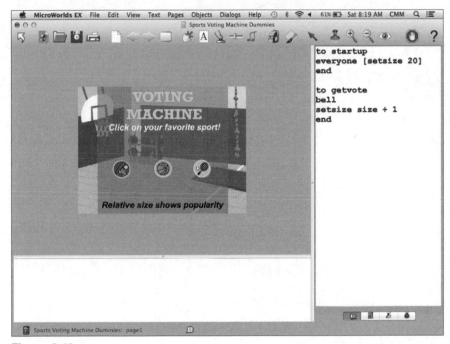

Figure 6-10

Note that the startup command is no longer needed in the Command Center and you can remove it.

Test the voting machine by clicking each candidate several times. Each time you click a candidate, the bell should ring, and the candidate should grow in size. After many votes, you should see a visual representation of candidate popularity in relative terms: Larger candidates received more votes, and smaller candidates received fewer votes. Troubleshoot and fix bugs until the simulation functions just the way you want. Note that a turtle candidate cannot exceed its maximum turtle size.

Enhance your voting machine

Consider enhancing your vote machine with new features:

✔ Add a fourth or fifth candidate.

✔ On the project Shapes tab, create your own original shapes in the Shape Editor, or add small pictures from the web to shape spots, ensuring that shapes are similarly sized.

✔ Add a vote counter for each candidate and a total votes counter (see Project 7 for an example).

Week 3

Variables: Counting and Conditionals

This week you'll build . . .

Would you like to share your projects with friends who don't have MicroWorlds EX? All you have to do is output your project to HTML and share it on the web. For help sharing your projects online, check out www.dummies.com/extras/codingforkids.

Happy Birthday

Real-world events like counting how many babies are
born means collecting lots of data. Sometimes, this can take too
long. Creating a *simulation* helps you to understand an event in
less time. A simulation is a pretend version of the real event. In
this project, you will create a maternity ward simulation — a
model of a hospital room where babies are born and celebrate
their "zero birthdays."

Instead of taking nine months for a baby to arrive, this simulation makes a pretend newborn boy or girl by clicking a button.
Then, using the `repeat` command, you can make hundreds of
babies (or more) to represent all the births in a state or country.
Using the simulation, you can quickly look at the *distribution* of
births, meaning how many boys and girls are born in a large
population of babies. Say "Happy Birthday!"

Brainstorm

The Happy Birthday simulation does not have to feature babies being born. Consider simulating the birth of any creature, particularly those that produce only one offspring at a time:

- ✔ Elephants

- ✔ Whales

- ✔ Hippos

- ✔ Gorillas

    . . . or fantasy creatures you invent!

Also consider alternatives for where the "baby" is born:

- ✔ A meadow or forest

- ✔ A zoo or circus

- ✔ The ocean

- ✔ A space station!

You can even change the entire project to represent any other two-outcome scenario, such as flipping a coin (heads or tails), evaluating the state of a radioactive atom (decayed or not decayed), lighting a lamp (on or off), or monitoring the health of Schrödinger's cat (dead or alive).

Start a New Project

Begin creating Happy Birthday by starting a new project as follows:

 1. Start MicroWorlds EX.

2. From the yellow MicroWorlds EX startup screen, select Free Mode.

   A new project opens.

3. From the menu bar, choose File⇨New Project Size⇨Full Screen 640 x 480.

Apply a Hospital Theme to the Workspace

Because babies are often born in a maternity ward, apply a background to your simulation that conveys a hospital theme:

 1. From the toolbar, click the Hide/Show Painting/Clipart button.

   The Painting/Clipart palette opens.

 2. Click the Backgrounds button to show the backgrounds, as shown in Figure 7-1.

Figure 7-1

3. Click on a background image you want to apply to your Happy Birthday simulation. (I used the hospital room background in the example.) Then click in the workspace to apply the background image.

4. Right-click (Windows) or Ctrl-click (Mac) the background image. From the pop-up menu, select Stamp Full Page.

   The image is stamped to fill the entire workspace.

5. Switch to the Painting Tools. Use the Painting Tools to draw a filled rectangle at the bottom of the background.

   This area will be used to feature the buttons of the graphical user interface (refer to the figure at the beginning of this project).

6. Close the Painting/Clipart palette by clicking its X button.

Create a Title Text Box

Add a title to the page as follows:

1. From the toolbar, click the Create a Text Box button; move into the workspace and draw a rectangle for the text box; type a title — Happy Birthday — in the white area of the text box.

2. Select the text inside the text box. From the menu bar, select the Text menu options and format the text.

   See Project 1 for details on formatting text.

3. Right-click (Windows) or Ctrl-click (Mac) inside the text box and select Transparent from the pop-up menu.

Text boxes can be resized at any time. Ctrl-click (Windows) or Command-click (Mac) an opaque text box. Sizing dots appear — click and drag any of them to resize the text box.

Your can edit text only when the text box is opaque (not transparent). To change a text box from transparent to opaque, click the text; then right-click (Windows) or Ctrl-click (Mac) and select Opaque from the pop-up menu.

Create Boy and Girl Characters

The simulation requires only one turtle object. The turtle will represent the newborn baby. At each birth, the baby turtle will wear a shape indicating whether it is a girl baby or a boy baby. Create girl and boy characters for your simulation as follows:

 1. From the toolbar, click the Create a Turtle button. Move into the workspace and click to hatch a turtle.

2. Drag the turtle to a position just above the hospital bed.

   Your workspace now looks similar to Figure 7-2.

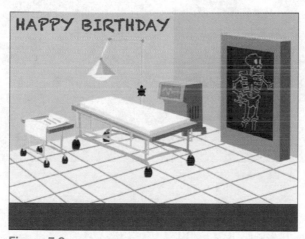

Figure 7-2

 3. Now you're ready to paint shapes for the girl baby and the boy baby. Click the project Shapes tab (located in the lower-right corner of the window).

4. On the Shapes pane, double-click a shape spot.

   The Shape Editor opens.

5. In the top-left corner, reduce the zoom to 500%. Then stretch the sizing dots on each side of the shape until the width is 135 pixels and the height is 125 pixels.

6. Use the drawing tools in the Shape Editor to draw a newborn girl shape, as shown in Figure 7-3. You can draw any female baby you want — human, zombie, alien — anything!

Figure 7-3

7. Name the girl shape pink (in the empty white field at the top of the Shape Editor) and then click OK.

   Feel free to call the shape any name you want; just be sure to keep track of the name you use when coding procedures. It's easiest to name the shape by its color.

   The Shape Editor closes, and the pink shape appears in a spot on the project Shapes tab.

8. Repeat Steps 4–6 to create a boy shape, as shown in Figure 7-4. Again, create any type of male baby you want.

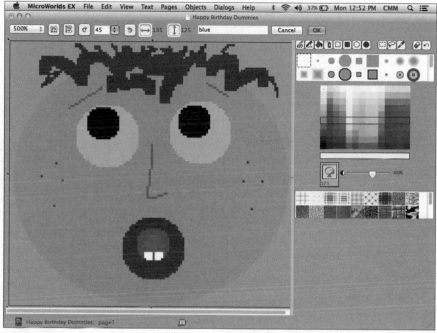

Figure 7-4

9. Name this shape blue at the top of the Shape Editor and then click OK.

   Again, call the shape any name you want; just keep track of the name you use when coding procedures.

   The Shape Editor closes, and the blue shape appears in a spot on the project Shapes tab.

10. Click either the pink or blue shape on the project Shapes tab and then move into the workspace and click the turtle.

    The turtle now wears the shape.

If you accidentally click somewhere other than the turtle, the pink or blue shape will appear on the background — simply right-click (Windows) or Ctrl-click (Mac) the shape and select Remove from the pop-up menu to get rid of it.

Create Variables

The Happy Birthday simulation needs a way to show whether a newborn baby is a boy or a girl. It also needs a way to count how many total boys and how many girls are born in a large population. Variables will be used for all three of these.

Variables are quantities that can have different values at different times. You will probably first learn about variables in a pre-algebra course. Math often uses single letters like *a* or *x* for a variable — and sometimes coding does, too — but coding also uses a whole word like "gender" or "boys" or "girls" for a variable name.

Create a variable as follows:

1. From the toolbar, click the Create a Text Box button; move into the workspace and draw a rectangle for the text box.

   Now, instead of showing a title, this text box will be used to show the value of a variable.

2. Right-click (Windows) or Ctrl-click (Mac) inside the text box and select Edit from the pop-up menu.

3. Name the text box gender. The Show Name and Visible check boxes should be selected.

   This text box will be used to show a *discrete variable* value — a value that can only be a certain number such as 0 (for a girl) or 1 (for a boy). Like flipping a coin, there is no "in-between" value — it's either heads or tails, boy or girl.

   Text boxes used as variables must remain opaque for the variable values to change.

4. Repeat Steps 1–3 to make two more text boxes to show variable values; name one girls and the other boys.

These will be *counting variables* or *counters* that count the total number of girls and the total number of boys. (*Counting variable* is not a formal mathematical term, just a description of how this variable is functioning in your program.)

To create a new text box with the same size and shape as an existing text box: Right-click (Windows) or Ctrl-click (Mac) inside the text box you want to duplicate and select Copy Box from the pop up menu. Then right-click (Windows) or Ctrl-click (Mac) in the workspace and select Paste from the pop-up menu. A duplicate text box appears.

5. Drag the text boxes to where you want them positioned.

Your workspace should look similar to Figure 7-5.

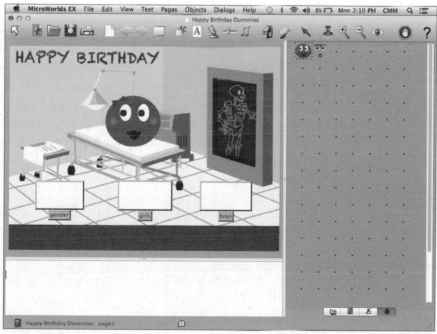

Figure 7-5

Write an Initialize Procedure and Make an Associated Button

Like any simulation, the maternity ward needs a starting point. A procedure is needed to start, or initialize, the model. The procedure represents starting a new shift at a hospital or starting a new day when the number of babies born is zero.

Follow these steps to write an `initialize` procedure and create a button to execute it:

1. Click the project Procedures tab (located in the lower-right corner of the window).

2. Type the `initialize` procedure as shown:

```
to initialize
setgirls 0
setboys 0
end
```

This procedure sets the value of the `girls` and `boys` variables to zero. Remember, each of these variables counts how many girls and how many boys are made with the model. Now that you have written the `initialize` procedure, MicroWorlds EX recognizes it as a new command that you can use!

3. Next, you need to create a button to run the procedure. From the toolbar, click the Create a Button button. Then click anywhere in the workspace.

4. In the Button dialog box, fill in the following information (as shown in Figure 7-6):

   • *Label:* Type `Initialize` in the Label field to name the button.

   • *Instruction:* Type `initialize` in the Instruction field.

- *Do It:* Select the Once radio button.

- *Visible:* Select this check box to leave the button visible.

Figure 7-6

5. Click OK to close the Button dialog box.

The Initialize button is added to the workspace.

6. Drag the button to the lower-left corner of the workspace.

7. Test your Initialize button by clicking it.

A zero should appear in the `girls` text box, and a zero should appear in the `boys` text box.

Programming languages often require you to set the *initial value* of a variable. That's because you must know how much of a quantity you have initially (at the beginning) so that you can figure out how much you end up with when you add to the quantity, or subtract from the quantity.

Besides calling a procedure from a button, you can also add it to the rules of a turtle backpack, or embed it another procedure.

Write a Reproduce Procedure and Make an Associated Button

My students always ask me, "What does reproduce mean?" In our computer simulation, it means to make a new baby. (In biology, it means that, too, but I won't explain those details. There may be a stork involved.)

You probably know from simple genetics that if a baby has certain genes, it's a girl. If it has different genes, it's a boy. Notice that I used the words *if* and *then* when writing those sentences. You will use the same structure to create IF-THEN commands in your program code. These commands let you show the gender of the newly made baby. Gender means boy or girl.

Write a procedure to make a baby and show its gender as follows:

1. In the Procedures pane, type the `reproduce` procedure as shown:

```
to reproduce
setgender random 2
if gender = 0 [setsh "pink setgirls girls + 1]
if gender = 1 [setsh "blue setboys boys + 1]
end
```

This procedure sets the value of `gender` randomly to 0 or 1. The number 0 means that a girl is born, and the number 1 means that a boy is born. Each number has an equal probability of appearing, so there is a 50% chance of creating a girl and a 50% chance of creating a boy.

The procedure then uses two IF-THEN conditional statements. Each statement affects the shape worn by the turtle and a counter variable:

- The first IF-THEN says that if the `gender` variable value is 0, then set the turtle shape to `pink` (the girl baby shape) and add 1 to the current value of the `girls` variable.

- The second IF-THEN says that if the gender variable value is 1, then set the turtle shape to blue (the boy baby shape) and add 1 to the current value of the boys variable.

Here, the girls variable and the boys variable serve as counters by keeping track of the total number of girls and the total number of boys.

IF-THEN conditionals are logic statements that are common in coding. The general form is IF *condition* THEN *consequence*. However, different computer languages format IF-THEN conditionals in different ways. In MicroWorlds EX, the format is IF *condition* [*consequence*]. The commands in the consequence are executed when the condition is true; otherwise, the consequence is ignored. See Project 8 for additional information on IF-THEN conditionals.

2. Create a button to run the procedure. From the toolbar, click the Create a Button button. Then click anywhere in the workspace.

3. In the Button dialog box, fill in the following information (as shown in Figure 7-7):

   - *Label:* Type Reproduce in the Label field to name the button.

   - *Instruction:* Type reproduce in the Instruction field.

   - *Do It:* Select the Once radio button.

   - *Visible:* Select this check box.

button	
Name:	button2
Label:	Reproduce
Instruction:	reproduce
Do It:	⦿ Once ☑ Visible
	○ Forever
	Cancel OK

Figure 7-7

4. Click OK to close the Button dialog box.

The Reproduce button is added to the workspace.

5. Drag the button to the bottom of the workspace, to the right of the Initialize button.

6. Test the Reproduce button by clicking it.

A 0 or 1 should appear in the gender text box, and the shape worn by the baby turtle object should change to match the gender. The associated girls or boys variable value should increase by 1.

If needed, you can resize a button (assuming it is not frozen) to better fit the labels it displays. Ctrl-click (Windows) or Command-click (Mac) a button. Sizing dots appear — click and drag any of them to resize the button.

Write a Make 10 Babies Procedure and Make an Associated Button

After you have written both the initialize procedure and the reproduce procedure, you can put them together in new ways. For example, you can combine these two procedures with a repeat command to write a procedure to make ten babies.

Follow these steps to write the make_10_babies procedure and make a button to execute it:

1. In the Procedures pane, type the make_10_babies procedure as shown:

```
to make_10_babies
initialize
repeat 10 [reproduce]
end
```

This procedure might represent the births at a single hospital in a single day, assuming that ten births occur. It allows you to see each newborn baby appear — really fast — and count the total number of boys born and the total number of girls born.

Note that both the `initialize` procedure and the `reproduce` procedure are nested in the `make_10_babies` procedure.

2. Next, create a button to run the procedure. From the toolbar, click the Create a Button button. Then click the workspace anywhere.

3. In the Button dialog box, fill in the following information (as shown in Figure 7-8):

   - *Label:* Type `Make 10 Babies` in the Label field to name the button.

   - *Instruction:* Type `make_10_babies` in the Instruction field.

   - *Do It:* Select the Once radio button.

   - *Visible:* Select this check box.

Figure 7-8

4. Click OK to close the Button dialog box.

   The Make 10 Babies button is added to the workspace.

5. Drag the button to the bottom of the workspace to the right of the Reproduce button.

Each time you click the button, the make_10_babies procedure is executed. The girls and boys counters allow you to
see the frequency distribution of gender in the baby population.

MATH CONNECTIONS
1
+1
2

A *frequency distribution* describes how many of each possible outcome appears in a small sample or large population. Sometimes the
Happy Birthday simulation produces 5 girls and 5 boys; other times, it
makes 8 girls and 2 boys; and rarely, it produces 0 girls and 10 boys.

Save, Test, and Debug

Choose File⇨Save Project from the menu bar to save your simulation. Your finished simulation should look similar to the title figure,
and your procedures should look similar to Figure 7-9. Note that
this figure includes procedures suggested in the nearby "Enhance
your simulation" sidebar.

```
to initialize
setgirls 0
setboys 0
end

to reproduce
setgender random 2
if gender = 0 [setsh "pink setgirls girls + 1]
if gender = 1 [setsh "blue setboys boys + 1]
end

to make_10_babies
initialize
repeat 10 [reproduce]
end

to make_100_babies
initialize
repeat 100 [reproduce]
end

to make_1000_babies
initialize
repeat 1000 [reproduce]
end
```

Procedures Project Processes Shapes

Figure 7-9

Test each button to make sure it functions as you intend. Check for error messages in the Command Center to help you determine where any bugs may exist in your code. When you're finished, run the simulation several times and evaluate how well you believe it models the real world.

Enhance your simulation

Now that you know how to build the basic procedures and buttons in the Happy Birthday maternity ward simulation, consider enhancing your project with these new features:

✔ **Simulate citywide births:** Write a `make_100_babies` procedure and make an associated button.

✔ **Simulate statewide births:** Write a `make_1000_babies` procedure and make an associated button. (Refer to Figure 7-9.)

✔ **Simulate national births in a given country:** What would this look like?

✔ **Make the baby grow:** Write a `grow` procedure to make the baby grow when the associated button is clicked. Use `setsize size + 1`.

What real-world scenarios would these new procedures model?

Number Guessing Computer

The Number Guessing Computer may look like a clunky chunk of technology from years gone by, but it serves a useful function — it plays a good game of "Guess My Number!" Using a slider, the player tells the Number Guessing Computer a maximum value. The computer then randomly generates the secret number, a variable that changes from one game to the next. A player is asked to input a guess at the secret number, and IF-THEN conditionals are used to compare the guess to the secret number. A procedure based on the law of trichotomy tells the player whether the guess is too low, too high, or correct. If the guess is too low or too high, the procedure uses *recursion* to execute again, checking the player's next guess until a correct guess is reached.

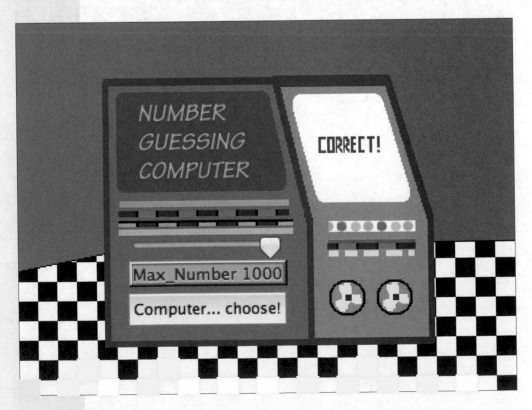

Brainstorm

This game doesn't have to feature a computer thinking of a secret number. Change the character to an opponent against whom a player might enjoy guessing. Create any type of device or character to think of a number:

✔ A genie in a bottle

✔ A super-intelligent alien

✔ Your favorite celebrity

✔ Your pet

✔ Your best friend

Start a New Project

Start a new project for your game as follows:

1. Start MicroWorlds EX.

2. From the yellow MicroWorlds EX startup screen, select Free Mode.

   A new project opens.

3. From the menu bar, choose File⇨New Project Size⇨Web Player.

Paint the Background

The background features the character thinking of the secret number. This character also communicates to the player how the player's guess compares with the secret number. Paint a background in the workspace as follows:

1. From the toolbar, click the Hide/Show Painting/Clipart button.

   The Painting/Clipart palette opens.

2. Open the Painting Tools.

3. Select any color and then use the Paint Can tool to fill the background.

   In the example, the background is a dark pink color.

4. Draw lines to define the floor or ground region, and then use the Paint Can tool to fill in the region with color or texture.

   In the example, the floor has a checkerboard texture.

5. Draw a Number Guessing Computer or other character in the workspace, as shown in Figure 8-1.

   Be sure to reserve regions for a title text box, a slider, a button, and a turtle wearing message shapes.

6. Add decorative features as desired using the textures available from the Painting Tools.

Area for title   Area for turtle wearing message shapes

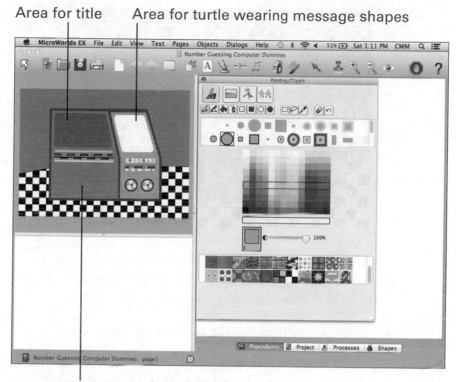

Area for slider and button
Figure 8-1

Create a Title Text Box

Add a title to the page as follows:

1. From the toolbar, click the Create a Text Box button; move into the workspace and draw a rectangle for the text box; type a title — *Number Guessing Computer* — in the white area of the text box, as shown in Figure 8-2.

Figure 8-2

2. Select the text inside the text box. From the menu bar, select the Text menu options and format the text.

   See Project 1 for details on formatting text.

3. Right-click (Windows) or Ctrl-click (Mac) inside the text box and select Transparent from the pop-up menu.

 Text boxes can be resized at any time. Ctrl-click (Windows) or Command-click (Mac) an opaque text box. Sizing dots appear — click and drag any of them to resize the text box.

Create a Secret Number Variable

The computer must generate a secret number for a player to guess. Follow these steps to create a secret number variable called secnum in the form of a text box:

 1. From the toolbar, click the Create a Text Box button; move into the workspace and draw a small rectangle for the text box.

2. Right-click (Windows) or Ctrl-click (Mac) inside the text box and select Edit from the pop-up menu.

   A Text dialog box appears.

3. In the Name field, type `secnum`. Select the check boxes for Show Name and Visible, as shown in Figure 8-3. Click OK to close the dialog box.

When the computer generates a secret number, `secnum`, it will appear in this text box.

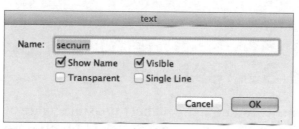

Figure 8-3

4. Drag the text box to an out-of-the-way position in the workspace, as shown in Figure 8-4.

Its position doesn't matter because this text box will eventually be hidden. Otherwise, it would reveal the secret number to the player! You will hide the `secnum` variable text box after all the testing and troubleshooting is complete.

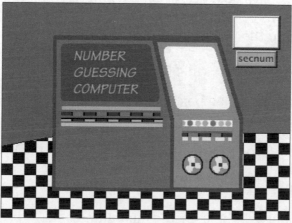

Figure 8-4

Leaving variable indicators visible during code development, even if they will later be hidden, is good coding technique. During testing and debugging, the visible indicators make it easy for programmers to look "behind the scenes" and see how the code is functioning. It may be helpful to know the value of the secret number when troubleshooting final code. After all code is debugged, the indicators can be hidden.

Make a Slider to Set the Maximum Value of the Secret Number

A player needs to know the highest possible value of the secret number. For example, if you say "Guess a number from 1 to 100," then 100 is the high value. Setting the high value of the secret number to a low number makes the game easier because there are fewer possible numbers to guess. Setting the high value to a high number makes the game more challenging.

Create a slider to allow the player to set the high value for each game.

 1. From the toolbar, click the Create a Slider button.

   Or, choose Objects⇨New Slider from the menu bar.

2. Move into the workspace and click.

   A Slider dialog box appears.

3. In the Slider dialog box, fill in the following information (as shown in Figure 8-5):

   - *Name:* Type Max_Number, which represents the maximum high value that the secret number — secnum — can ever have.

   - *Minimum:* Type 0 for the minimum value.

   - *Maximum:* Type 1000 for the maximum value.

- *Value:* Type 1000 for the starting value at which the slider is set. This value can be set at any number, but it may be helpful for the player to see the highest possible value for any game is 1000.

- *Show Name:* Select this check box.

- *Visible:* Select this check box.

- *Vertical:* If you want to make the slider vertical (up and down), check the Vertical check box.

slider		
Name:	Max_Number	
Minimum:	0	☑ Show Name
Maximum:	1000	☑ Visible
Value:	1000	☐ Vertical
		Cancel OK

Figure 8-5

4. Click OK to close the Slider dialog box.

   The Max_Number slider appears in the workspace.

5. Drag the slider to position it where you want it to appear in the workspace, as shown in Figure 8-6.

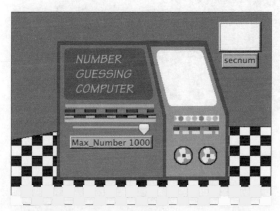

Figure 8-6

Sliders are variables to which you assign minimum and maximum values.

Create a Turtle and Paint Shapes for It

When a round of number guessing starts, the Number Guessing Computer displays a blank screen while it "thinks" of a new secret number. Then, when a player guesses at the secret number, the Number Guessing Computer displays the result of the guess on the screen: Too Low, Too High, or Correct!

A turtle wearing different shapes will be created for the computer display. Create the turtle and display shapes as follows:

1. From the toolbar, click the Create a Turtle button. Move into the workspace and click to hatch a turtle.

2. Drag the turtle to position it onto the computer screen of the Number Guessing Computer, as shown in Figure 8-7.

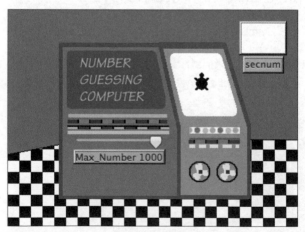

Figure 8-7

3. Now paint a `blank` shape for the turtle. Click the project Shapes tab (located in the lower-right corner of the window).

4. On the project Shapes tab, double-click a shape spot.

The Shape Editor opens.

5. You may want to draw a slightly larger shape than the default size of 40 by 40 pixels. To do so, resize the drawing area in the Shape Editor so that you have more room to draw:

   a. *Click the Zoom tab in the top-left corner and select 1200%.*

   b. *Drag the sizing dots of the drawing area until the shape dimension indicators each read approximately 50 by 50.*

6. Use the drawing tools in the Shape Editor to draw a blank, white square, as shown in Figure 8-8.

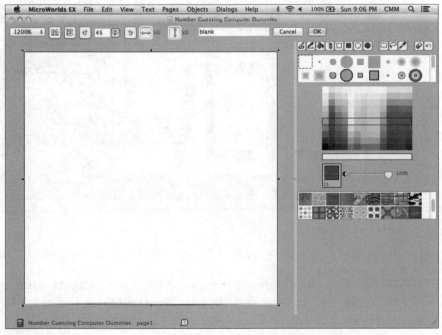

Figure 8-8

7. Name the shape `blank` in the empty white field at the top of the Shape Editor, as shown in Figure 8-8. Click OK.

   The Shape Editor closes, and the `blank` shape appears in a spot on the project Shapes tab.

8. Repeat Steps 3–7 to create three more shapes for the computer display. Use the Pen tool to draw straight lines, creating a `toolow` shape (see Figure 8-9), a `toohigh` shape, and a `correct` shape.

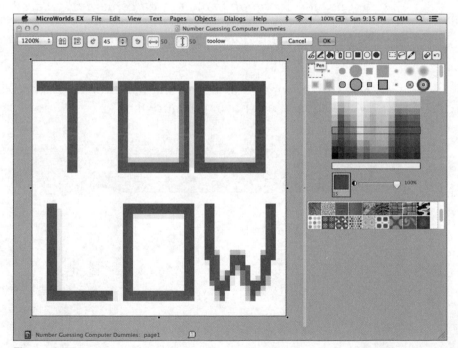

Figure 8-9

There are now a total of four shapes on the project Shapes tab.

9. Click any shape on the project Shapes tab and then move into the workspace and click on the turtle.

   It may be easier to choose a shape with words on it — the blank shape makes it appear that nothing is on the computer screen, and you may think you've lost the turtle.

The turtle now wears the shape, as shown in Figure 8-10.

Four shapes

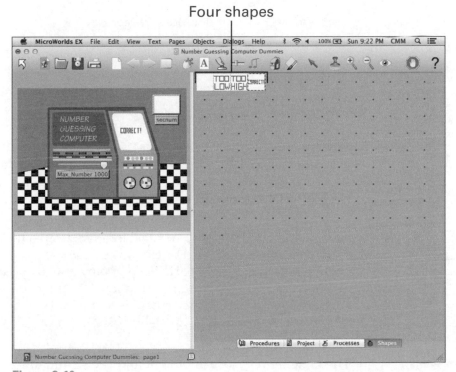

Figure 8-10

Write a Compchoosesecret Procedure and Make a Button

A `compchoosesecret` procedure is needed to start a new round of number guessing. Write a `compchoosesecret` procedure as follows:

 1. Click the project Procedures tab (located in the lower-right corner of the window).

2. Type the following procedure:

```
to compchoosesecret
setsecnum 1 + random Max_Number
setsh "blank
checkguess
end
```

Here's how the procedure works:

a. The `setsecnum 1 + random Max_Number` command
   sets the value of the `secnum` (secret number) variable to
   `1 + random Max_Number`. This means that `secnum`
   ranges from values of 1 to 1000.

The `random` command generates positive integers from 0 through
one less than the index number. For example, `random 6` can generate the numbers 0, 1, 2, 3, 4, or 5. However, many times, you will
want your random numbers to start at 1, not 0. Do so by adding 1 to
the `random` command: `1 + random 6`. This command can generate
the numbers 1, 2, 3, 4, 5, or 6.

The command `1 + random 6` and the command `random`
`6 + 1` are not equivalent. The command random `6 + 1` is
equivalent to random 7 and can generate the numbers 0, 1, 2,
3, 4, 5, or 6.

b. The procedure then sets the shape of the turtle to `blank`
   so that the computer display shows no message.

c. The final command is `checkguess`, a procedure you will
   write in the next section.

3. Create a Computer . . . choose! button to execute the `comp`
`choosesecret` procedure. From the toolbar, click the Create a
Button button.

4. In the Button dialog box, fill in the following information, as shown in Figure 8-11:

- *Label:* Type Computer. . .choose! in the Label field to name the button.

- *Instruction:* Type compchoosesecret in the Instruction field.

- *Do It:* Select the Once radio button.

- *Visible:* Select this check box so the button is visible.

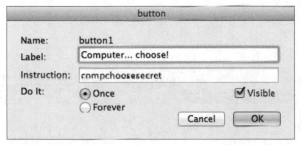

Figure 8-11

5. Click OK to close the Button dialog box.

Ctrl-click (Windows) or Command-click (Mac) your button to summon sizing dots. Click and drag any of them to resize your button. (Only unfrozen buttons can be resized.)

The Computer . . . choose! button is added to the workspace.

6. Drag the button to reposition it to where you want it located (see Figure 8-12).

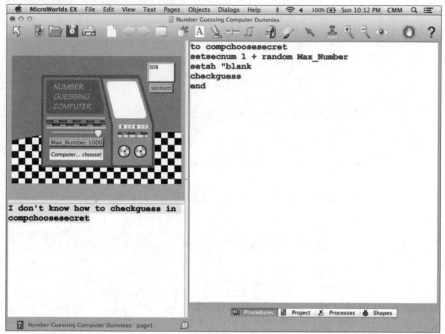

Figure 8-12

7. Test the Computer. . .choose! button by clicking it.

When clicked, the button runs the compchoosesecret procedure. The procedure should successfully generate a random
number in secnum, and then set the turtle shape to blank.
However, when it reaches the checkguess command (which
doesn't exist yet), an error message is issued at the Command
Center, as shown in Figure 8-12.

Write a Checkguess Procedure

A checkguess procedure checks how a player's guess compares
with the secret number. The checkguess procedure uses *conditional* statements, also called IF-THEN statements, to check
whether the player's guess is correct.

Conditionals, or IF-THEN statements, are logic statements that appear in math, computer programming, and philosophy. The first part of the IF-THEN statement is called the condition, or the IF. The second part is the consequence, or the THEN. The condition can be either TRUE or FALSE: When the condition is TRUE, the consequence is executed, and when the condition is FALSE, the program code skips to the next line. An example you may find familiar occurs in your house: IF it's later than 10pm, THEN your parents announce it's bedtime.

For this project, the checkguess procedure is first called from the compchoosesecret procedure, which you added in the preceding step. checkguess is then executed *recursively* (the procedure commands itself to run again) until the player guesses the correct number.

Recursion

Recursion is an important idea in both math and computer science. You may have heard of the word *recur,* which means to happen over and over:

✔ In everyday life, recursion can be thought of as a pair of mirrors that face each other and reflect an image over and over again. In mathematics, there is a field called fractal geometry in which an object is *self-similar* — it looks the same whether you look at it far away or zoomed in.

✔ In computer science, recursion is important because it allows a procedure to call itself from a line of code inside the procedure. By using recursion in a procedure, you can make the procedure execute over and over until a condition is met — at which point the procedure is exited. In a number guessing game, a recursive procedure allows the player to guess again and again until the player reaches the target number.

On the Procedures tab, type the following `checkguess` procedure:

```
to checkguess
question [What's your guess?]
if answer = secnum [setsh "correct tune stopall]
if answer > secnum [setsh "toohigh checkguess]
if answer < secnum [setsh "toolow checkguess]
end
```

Here's what happens when the `checkguess` procedure is executed:

1. `question` asks for input from the player.

   The question `What's your guess?` is displayed onscreen, as shown in Figure 8-13.

   The `question` command is a *primitive,* which means it's part of the MicroWorlds EX vocabulary and can be used to show a dialog box with a specific question.

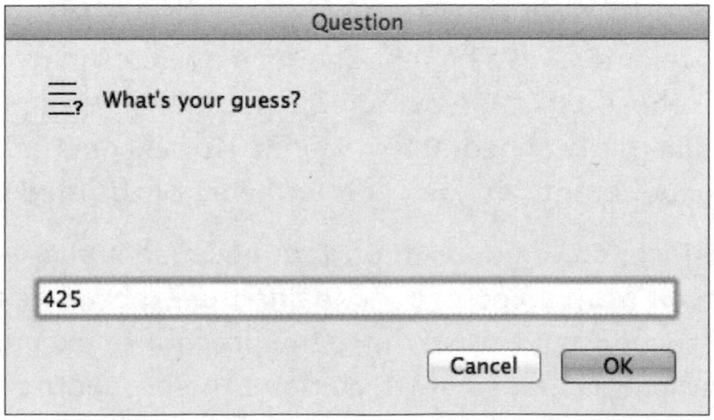

Figure 8-13

2. The player then types numerical input into the response field and clicks OK.

3. MicroWorlds EX names the player's input, `answer`, and the dialog box closes.

4. The player's answer is then compared to the secret number. This comparison has three possibilities:

   • *The player's answer equals the secret number.* If the player's answer equals the secret number (`answer = secnum`), the player has guessed correctly! The consequence is that the display turtle is set to the `correct` shape, a `tune` is played (you will create this later), and the `stopall` command halts all procedures from running.

   • *The player's answer is greater than the secret number.* If the player's answer is greater than the secret number (`answer > secnum`), the player has guessed too high. The consequence is that the display turtle is set to the `toohigh` shape, and the `checkguess` procedure is executed so that the player can guess again.

   • *The player's answer is less than the secret number.* If the player's answer is less than the secret number (`answer < secnum`), the player has guessed too low. The consequence is that the display turtle is set to the `toolow` shape, and the `checkguess` procedure is executed so that the player can guess again.

When comparing two numbers, a and b, there are three possibilities regarding their relationship: a=b, a>b, or a<b. In mathematics, this property of numbers is called the *law of trichotomy.* (And in computer science, this property leads to a great number-guessing game!)

Formatting conditionals

All programming languages use *conditionals,* or IF-THEN statements. However, each language formats the IF-THEN statement its own way. In English, here's an example of an IF-THEN statement: IF it is later than 10pm, THEN you announce it is bedtime.

MicroWorlds EX uses the IF but replaces the THEN with square brackets:

```
if time > 10 [announce [bedtime]]
```

JavaScript, a language used for making web pages, replaces the THEN with curly braces:

```
if (time > 10) {
greeting="bedtime";
}
```

The concept of working with IF-THEN statements is similar from one language to another — just be sure to check the exact syntax when coding in a new language.

Make a Tune Play When the Player Answers Correctly

Each time a player makes a correct guess, a short tune plays. Follow these steps to create your own tune using the Create a Melody feature of MicroWorlds EX. (*Note:* Additional details on creating a melody are provided in Project 4.)

 1. From the toolbar, click the Create a Melody button; then click in the workspace.

The Melody dialog box opens.

2. Click a button for an instrument.

3. Click a note duration and then click a key on the keyboard.

4. Repeat Step 3 to create a sequence of notes resulting in a sound indicating that the player is correct in guessing the secret number. You can also include rests.

5. Adjust the Volume and Tempo sliders and then click the Play to hear the adjustments to your tune.

6. When you're satisfied with your sound, type the name tune in the Name field.

7. Leave the Show Name and Visible check boxes unselected, as shown in Figure 8-14.

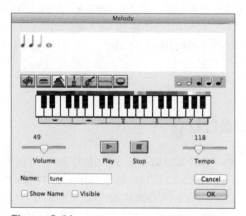

Figure 8-14

8. Click OK to add the sound to the project and dismiss the Melody dialog box.

   The icon representing the tune sound does not appear in the workspace because the Visible check box was not selected.

 9. Click the Project tab (located in the lower-right corner of the window).

   The Project tab opens and shows all pages and elements in your project.

10. Click the arrow next to page1 to see all elements on page1 and verify that the tune sound has been added to the project, as shown in Figure 8-15.

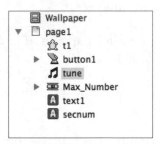

Figure 8-15

 You can edit or show a hidden project element by right-clicking (Windows) or Ctrl-clicking (Mac) the element on the Project tab, and then selecting Edit or Show from the pop-up menu that appears.

Save, Test, and Debug

 Click the Save Project button on the toolbar to save your Number Guessing Computer. Test the slider and the Computer. . .choose! button and run the guess-and-check game several times to ensure it runs the way you want. Troubleshoot and fix bugs until the game functions just the way you want.

When your game works well, right-click (Windows) or Ctrl-click (Mac) on the secnum variable text box and select Hide from the pop-up menu. That way, your player won't see the secret number, as shown in Figure 8-16.

 If you need to make secnum show again, just switch to the Project tab and right-click (Windows) or Ctrl-click (Mac) its icon on the Project tab, and then select Edit or Show from the pop-up menu that appears.

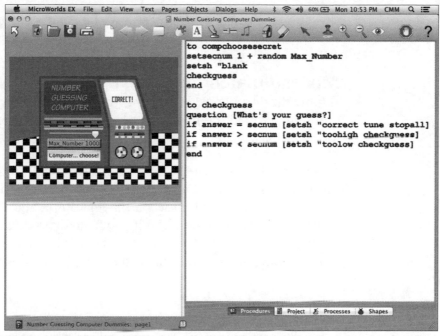

Figure 8-16

Enhance your game

Consider enhancing your guess-and-check game with new features:

✔ Increase the maximum value of the slider so that players have the option of choosing a higher value for the high number, making games more challenging.

✔ Add a counter variable (see Project 7) called guesses that counts how many tries it takes a player to guess the secnum. Set the initial value of guesses to 0 in compchoosesecret. Then add the command setguesses guesses + 1 on the line following the question command in checkguess.

✔ When reporting the results of a number comparison, add a storyline. For example, you can create a Three Bears story and report the temperature of the porridge as "too hot," "too cold," or "just right."

Monster Mashup

Mix-and-match toys take a variety of forms, from Mr. Potato Head to paper dolls. Now, you can create a virtual mix-and-match toy in the form of a monster generator called Monster Mashup.

Monster Mashup invites you to paint a collection of crazy monster parts — hair, faces, bodies, and feet — and then code an interface that allows a player to mix and match parts to create a new monster. You'll program drop-down lists and buttons to assign parts based on player choices, and build a Mashup button that randomly mashes parts together!

Brainstorm

Around Halloween, kids love coding Monster Mashup. But at other times of the year, they produce a wide variety of other mix-and-match toys. What are some options you can dream up?

✔ Potato people parts, similar to Mr. Potato Head

✔ Sports smashup featuring jumbled-up sports attire

✔ Fashionista diva dress-up doll

✔ School lunch smorgasbord (entrée, side, beverage, dessert)

✔ Celebrity family (mixed-up moms, dads, and kids)

Programs written for entertainment purposes take many forms, including games and toys. Games typically feature a goal the player strives to attain and some criteria for winning, while toys usually have no specific goal and are intended more for exploratory play.

Start a New Project

Begin creating your Monster Mashup toy by starting a new project as follows:

1. Start MicroWorlds EX.

2. From the yellow MicroWorlds EX startup screen, select Free Mode.

   A new project opens.

3. From the menu bar, choose File⇨New Project Size⇨MicroWorlds Small.

Feel free to create your project by using any size. Projects featuring many monster-part choices may require a larger workspace, so consider using a larger project size. Smaller spaces work well for smaller monsters, and require less resizing of the drawing area when creating parts in the Shape Editor.

Color the Background and Add a Title

Give the background a solid color and add a title for your toy as follows:

1. In the Command Center, type the command `setbg "violet` (or any other color) and click Enter (Windows) or Return (Mac). Remember to place the quotation marks in front of the color name, but not after.

   The command `setbg "colorname` sets the background color. In this case, the background color changes to violet.

2. From the toolbar, click the Create a Text Box button and then move into the workspace and create a medium rectangle for the text box; type the name of your toy — Monster Mashup — in the white area of the text box.

3. Select the text inside the text box. From the menu bar, select the Text menu and then use the menu options to format the text.

   In the example, I used the Haunt font. See Project 1 for details on formatting text.

4. Right-click (Windows) or Ctrl-click (Mac) in the white area of the text box and select Transparent from the pop-up menu.

5. Drag the title into a position where it will be out of the way from other toy components.

   For example, drag the title to the lower-right area of the workspace.

When you start to create an object, your mouse appears as a finger pointer. If you change your mind about creating the object, you'll want to switch back to the arrow pointer. Do so by clicking in the Command Center or clicking the Arrow Pointer button on the toolbar.

Create and Name Turtles for Different Monster Parts

Follow these steps to create four turtles — for the monster's hair, face, body, and feet — and then name each turtle for the monster part it will become:

1. From the toolbar, click the Create a Turtle button. Then in the workspace, click to hatch a turtle.

2. Repeat Step 1 three more times to create a total of four turtles.

3. Drag each turtle on the workspace to create a vertical lineup similar to Figure 9-1.

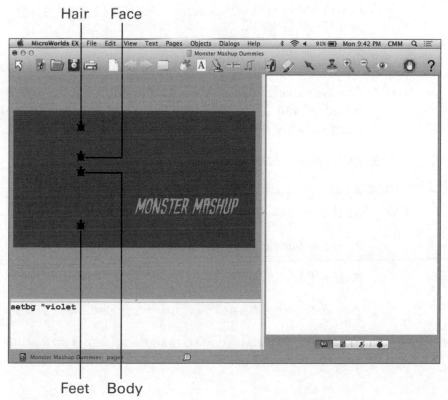

Figure 9-1

4. The turtle near the top of the workspace will be the monster head. Right-click (Windows) or Ctrl-click (Mac) on the top turtle and select Open Backpack from the pop-up menu.

5. On the State tab of the turtle backpack, click the Edit button.

   The turtle Name dialog box opens, as shown in Figure 9-2.

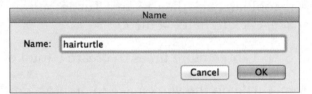

Figure 9-2

6. In the Name text box, type `hairturtle` for the turtle name and then click OK.

7. On the State tab, enter `60` in the Size field.

   The backpack now appears as shown in Figure 9-3. Note that other attributes on the State tab, such as your Xcor and Ycor, will probably differ from the figure.

8. Close the turtle backpack.

9. Repeat Steps 4–7 to name and size each of the remaining turtles as follows:

   • *Second turtle:* Name: `faceturtle`; Size: 60

   • *Third turtle:* Name: `bodyturtle`; Size: 40

   • *Fourth turtle:* Name: `feetturtle`; Size: 60

   Note that you may need to make additional size adjustments later to make all the body parts fit together.

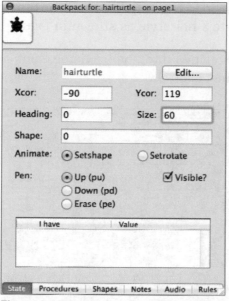

Figure 9-3

As your computer programs become more complex, it's a good idea to name all the turtles, shapes, and other elements. This helps you keep better track of everything in your code. Naming a turtle something like `feetturtle` — not just `feet` — lets you know that the element is a turtle when examining your code.

Create and Name Hair and Face Shapes

Follow these steps to create hair and face shapes for your monster:

1. Click the project Shapes tab (located in the lower-right corner of the window).

2. On the project Shapes tab, double-click a shape spot.

   The Shape Editor opens. The default shape size is 40 pixels by 40 pixels. This is a good size for the hair and face parts, so leave the size as is.

3. In the Shape Editor, in the empty white text box, use the drawing tools to create a hairstyle as shown in Figure 9-4.

4. At the top of the Shape Editor, type a name, such as `greenhair`, for the shape. Then click OK.

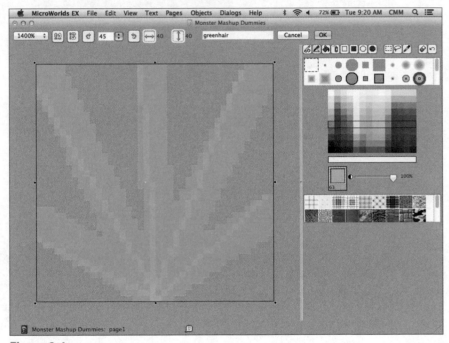

Figure 9-4

The shape appears in the Shapes pane.

5. Repeat Steps 2–4 to create three more hairstyles for your monster.

The hair shapes for the example — named `greenhair`, `goldhair`, `bluehair`, and `orangehair` — now look something like Figure 9-5 in the Shapes pane.

Figure 9-5

6. Click a hair shape on the project Shapes tab and then move into the workspace and click the `hairturtle`.

   The turtle now wears the shape.

7. Repeat Steps 2–4 to create four faces for your monster. Type a name for each shape (for example, `happyface`, `madface`, `worryface`, and `sadface`).

   The face shapes for the example now look like Figure 9-6 in the Shapes pane.

Figure 9-6

8. Click a face shape on the Shapes tab and then move into the workspace and click the `faceturtle`.

   The turtle now wears the shape.

If you accidentally click somewhere other than the turtle, the face shape will appear on the background — simply right-click (Windows) or Ctrl-click (Mac) the shape and select Remove from the pop-up menu to remove it.

Create and Name Body Shapes

Follow these steps to create body shapes for your monster:

1. On the project Shapes pane, double-click a shape spot.

   The Shape Editor opens. The default shape size is 40 pixels by 40 pixels. This size is too small for body shapes and needs to be increased.

2. From the top-left drop-down menu, select a zoom size of 200%. Then drag and adjust the sizing dots on each side of the shape until the width is 250 pixels and the height is 250 pixels.

Now there is sufficient room to draw a monster body.

3. In the Shape Editor, use the drawing tools to create a body.

4. At the top of the Shape Editor, type a name, such as bluebody, for the shape (see Figure 9-7). Click OK.

The shape appears in the Shapes pane.

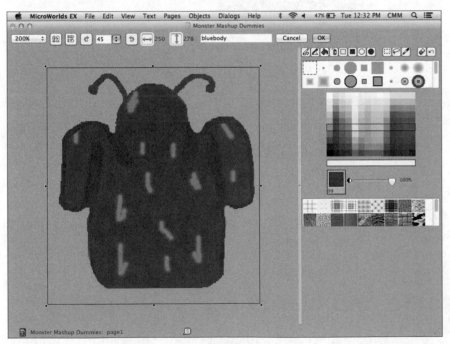

Figure 9-7

5. Repeat Steps 1–4 to create three more bodies for your monster.

The body shapes for the example — named bluebody, greenbody, orangebody, and pinkbody — now look something like Figure 9-8 in the Shapes pane.

orangebody: 39 250x250

Figure 9-8

6. Click one of the body shapes on the Shapes pane and then move into the workspace and click the `bodyturtle`.

   The turtle now wears the shape.

7. The body probably covers the face and needs to be moved behind the `faceturtle`. Right-click (Windows) or Ctrl-click (Mac) the `bodyturtle` and select Send to Back from the pop-up menu.

   The body should now be positioned behind the face.

 Turtle shapes may overlap each other depending on the size of the shapes and the coordinates of the turtles. To move a turtle to the front, right-click (Windows) or Ctrl-click (Mac) the turtle and select Bring to Front from the pop-up menu. To move a turtle to the back, right-click (Windows) or Ctrl-click (Mac) the turtle and select Send to Back.

Create and Name Feet Shapes

Follow these steps to create feet shapes for your monster:

1. Continue working on the project Shapes pane.

2. Double-click a shape spot.

   The Shape Editor opens. The default shape size is 40 pixels by 40 pixels. This size is too small for feet shapes and needs to be increased.

3. Change the zoom to 500 percent. Then drag and adjust the sizing dots on each side of the shape until the width is 120 pixels and the height is 60 pixels.

Now the dimensions are just right for creating a set of monster feet.

4. In the Shape Editor, use the drawing tools to create a set of feet.

5. At the top of the Shape Editor, type a name, such as `creepyfeet`, for the shape (see Figure 9-9). Then click OK.

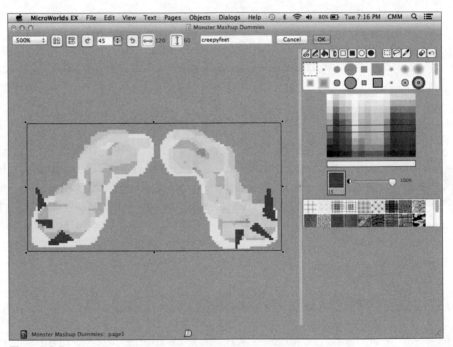

Figure 9-9

The shape appears in the Shapes pane.

6. Repeat Steps 2–5 to create three more sets of feet for your monster.

The feet shapes for the example — `creepyfeet`, `slipperfeet`, `birdfeet`, and `duckfeet` — now look something like Figure 9-10 in the Shapes pane.

birdfeet: 57 120x60

Figure 9-10

7. Click one of the feet shapes on the project Shapes pane and then move into the workspace and click the `feetturtle`.

The turtle now wears the shape.

If the size of a monster part requires adjustments, it is more efficient to make them by increasing or decreasing the size of the turtle, not the shape. In this way, you need only to make a change to a single turtle, not several shapes. Just open the turtle backpack and type a new number for the turtle size on the State tab.

Make Drop-Down Lists for Each Part

A user playing your Monster Mashup toy needs a way to select a shape for each body part. A drop-down list allows the user to see all the shape choices and then choose one. Make a drop-down list for each monster part as follows:

1. From the menu bar, choose Objects⇨New Drop Down.

   A drop-down dialog box appears.

2. In the Name field, type the name of the list, such as `hairdrop`.

3. In the Label field, type the name of the first shape in the collection, such as `orangehair`. Click Add (Windows) or Insert (Mac) to add the shape name to the list.

4. Repeat Step 3 to add three more labels — `greenhair`, `goldhair`, and `bluehair` — to the list (see Figure 9-11).

Figure 9-11

You can make additional adjustments to your drop-down list using the buttons in the Drop Down dialog box:

- To remove a label, select it and click Delete.

- To adjust the order of the labels, click any label and click Up or Down.

- To choose which label shows when the drop-down list appears in the workspace, click that label.

- To show a blank space when the drop-down list appears in the workspace, click Empty (Windows) or Unselect (Mac).

5. Leave the Visible option checked and the Show Name option unchecked.

6. Click OK to finish making the drop-down list.

   The drop-down list (shown in Figure 9-12) is added to the workspace.

   Check that the drop-down list names the shapes correctly by clicking the selection arrows on the right side of the drop-down list (see Figure 9-13).

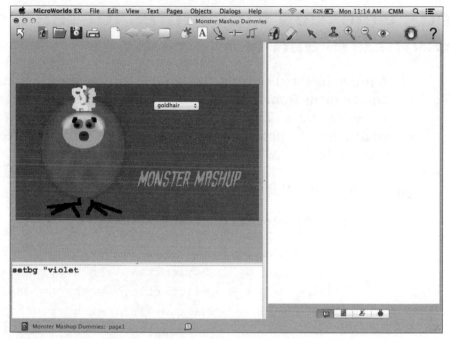

Figure 9-12

7. Drag the drop-down list to position it on your toy.

Figure 9-13

At this point, the shape on the monster might not match the shape showing in the drop-down list. That's because the function of the drop-down list is to show the choices for the monster part, not to change the shape. For each part, you will create a procedure and button to change the shape to a choice from the drop-down list.

Code Selection Procedures for the Drop-Down Lists and Make Buttons

A procedure and button allow the user to apply a monster part choice made from a drop-down list. These procedures are selecthair, selectface, selectbody, and selectfeet. You will write each procedure and then make a button to execute the procedure. Follow these steps:

1. Open the project Procedures pane.

2. Type the following selecthair procedure:

```
to selecthair
if hairdrop = 1 [hairturtle, setsh "greenhair]
if hairdrop = 2 [hairturtle, setsh "goldhair]
if hairdrop = 3 [hairturtle, setsh "bluehair]
if hairdrop = 4 [hairturtle, setsh "orangehair]
end
```

Here's how the procedure works:

- If the first shape, greenhair, in the Hair drop-down list is selected (if hairdrop = 1), the greenhair shape is applied to the hairturtle.

- If the second shape, goldhair, in the Hair drop-down list is selected (if hairdrop = 2), the goldhair shape is applied to the hairturtle.

- If the third shape, bluehair, in the Hair drop-down list is selected (if hairdrop = 3), the bluehair shape is applied to the hairturtle.

- If the fourth shape, orangehair, in the Hair drop-down list is selected (if hairdrop = 4), the orangehair shape is applied to the hairturtle.

An if-then conditional is written for each shape in the drop-down list. There are four hair shapes in the hairdrop, so there are four conditionals in the selecthair procedure.

 3. Next, you need to create a button that executes the selecthair procedure. On the toolbar, click the Create a Button button.

4. In the Button dialog box, fill in the following information:

 • *Label:* Type the name of the body part (Hair, for example) in the Label field.

 • *Instruction:* Type the name of the procedure that puts the selected shape on the monster (for example, selecthair).

 • *Do It:* Select the Once radio button.

 • *Visible:* Leave this check box selected.

The dialog box for the example looks like Figure 9-14.

5. Click OK to close the Button dialog box.

button		
Name:	button1	
Label:	Hair	
Instruction:	selecthair	
Do It:	⦿ Once	☑ Visible
	◯ Forever	Cancel OK

Figure 9-14

The Hair button is added to the workspace of the toy.

6. Drag the button to position it next to its drop-down list.

When the player clicks the Hair button, the selecthair procedure is executed. The hair shape selected at the hairlist drop-down list is applied to the hairturtle.

7. Follow the same pattern in Step 2 to create procedures for selectface, selectbody, and selectfeet. (See Figure 9-15.)

Here is the code for the selectface procedure:

```
to selectface
if facedrop = 1 [faceturtle, setsh "happyface]
if facedrop = 2 [faceturtle, setsh "madface]
if facedrop = 3 [faceturtle, setsh "worryface]
if facedrop = 4 [faceturtle, setsh "sadface]
end
```

Here is the code for the selectbody procedure:

```
to selectbody
if bodydrop = 1 [bodyturtle, setsh "orangebody]
if bodydrop = 2 [bodyturtle, setsh "greenbody]
if bodydrop = 3 [bodyturtle, setsh "bluebody]
if bodydrop = 4 [bodyturtle, setsh "pinkbody]
end
```

Here is the code for the selectfeet procedure:

```
to selectfeet
if feetdrop = 1 [feetturtle, setsh "creepyfeet]
if feetdrop = 2 [feetturtle, setsh "slipperfeet]
if feetdrop = 3 [feetturtle, setsh "birdfeet]
if feetdrop = 4 [feetturtle, setsh "duckfeet]
end
```

8. Follow the same pattern in Steps 3–6 to create buttons to execute the procedures for the selectface, selectbody, and selectfeet procedures that you created in Step 7.

Here is a complete list of all objects and instructions you create for Monster Mashup:

Turtle Name	Drop-Down List Name	Drop-Down List Labels	Button Name	Button Instruction (Selection Procedure)
hairturtle	hairdrop	greenhair, goldhair, bluehair, orangehair	Hair	selecthair
faceturtle	facedrop	happyface, madface, worryface, sadface	Face	selectface
bodyturtle	bodydrop	orangebody, greenbody, bluebody, pinkbody	Body	selectbody
feetturtle	feetdrop	creepyfeet, slipperfeet, birdfeet, duckfeet	Feet	selectfeet

The example shows four options for each body part, but you can use more or fewer parts. Just be sure to adjust your drop-down lists and selection procedures to match the number of shapes you create for each part.

Carefully match the order of shapes in the drop-down list with the order of shapes in the selection procedure. Also, be cautious to match the spelling of the shape name to its spelling in the procedure to minimize errors and reduce troubleshooting time.

Conditional statements, including the `IF-THEN` commands used in Monster Mashup are critical to any toy or game you code. See Projects 7 and 8 for additional details on working with `IF-THEN` commands.

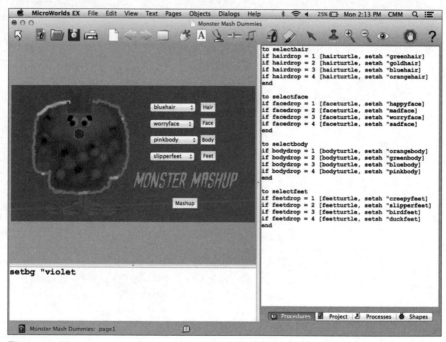

Figure 9-15

Code a Procedure and Add a Button for the Monster Mashup

A `mashup` procedure and button allow the user the wild and crazy option of randomly selecting all four monster parts at one time. In the Procedures pane, create the `mashup` procedure and button as follows:

1. Type the following `mashup` procedure:

```
to mashup
hairturtle, setsh pick [greenhair goldhair bluehair orangehair]
faceturtle, setsh pick [happyface madface worryface sadface]
bodyturtle, setsh pick [orangebody greenbody bluebody pinkbody]
feetturtle, setsh pick [creepyfeet slipperfeet birdfeet duckfeet]
end
```

The `pick` command randomly picks an item from the shapes listed inside the square brackets. The `setsh` command then applies that shape to the turtle identified at the beginning of the command line.

 2. Next, you need to create a Mashup button to execute the `mashup` procedure. From the toolbar, click the Create a Button button.

3. In the Button dialog box, fill in the fields as follows (see Figure 9-16):

- *Label:* Type `Mashup` in the Label field.

- *Instruction:* Type `mashup` in the Instruction field.

- *Do It:* Select the Once radio button.

- *Visible:* Select this check box to leave the button visible.

Figure 9-16

4. Click OK to close the Button dialog box.

The Mashup button is added to the workspace.

5. Drag the Mashup button to reposition it to where you want it.

Note that you can delete the `setbg "violet` command in the Command Center.

You can delete commands executed in the Command Center after your program is complete. Examples include initial setup commands, such as setting the initial heading of turtle objects or setting the background color. The purpose of deleting these commands is simply to tidy up your finished project.

Save, Test, and Debug

Click the Save Project button on the toolbar to save your toy. Test all the buttons to ensure it runs the way you want.

Troubleshoot and fix bugs until the toy looks just the way you want.

Enhance your toy

Consider enhancing your Monster Mashup toy with these new features:

🗸 **New parts:** Add new body parts by creating additional turtles, drop-down lists, selection procedures, and buttons for each part.

🗸 **Scary sounds:** Add monster sounds by importing .wav files and creating drop-down lists, selection procedures, and buttons for playing the sounds!

🗸 **Colorful backgrounds:** Provide the option to change the background color using `setbg` and creating a drop-down list, selection procedure, and button or slider and button to apply a new color.

Week 4
Multiturtles, Keyboard Control, Shooters

This week you'll build . . .

You can find an extra project online called Silly Story — a game where players fill in words for prompts you create, such as *adjective, celebrity,* and *exclamation.* But they don't know what the story is about! The program then transfers the words into a story template to create the silly story. In creating this story, you learn all about creating code that handles text. The bonus project is available via www.dummies.com/extras/codingforkids!

Viral Outbreak

No one likes to be sick, not even a turtle! Viral Outbreak is a simple simulation that models catching a cold in a population of turtles. You begin by coding a single turtle to move and react to the background and other turtles — and then clone that turtle, creating as many turtles as you want.

When a turtle gets sick, it infects other turtles that it bumps into. But if a sick turtle wanders into a hospital, it becomes well again. You can change how fast the turtles roam around and the size of the hospital, as well as add other new features to make your model even more realistic!

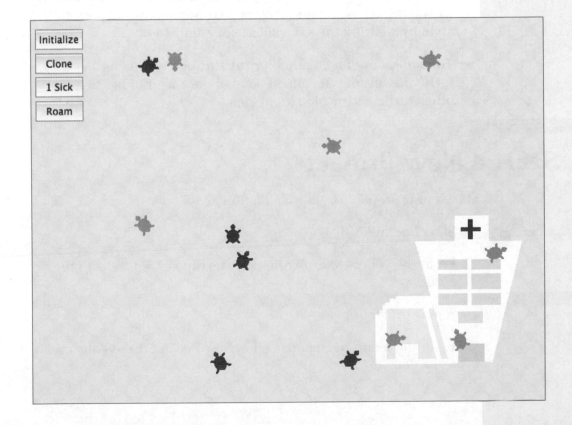

Brainstorm

We often hear of something going viral. Although the original meaning involved the rapid spread of a virus, these days "going viral" applies to anything that spreads through a network of people, places, or technology. Consider some of these ideas as your subject matter when building Viral Outbreak:

✔ Sharing of a YouTube video or Facebook post, with colliding turtles sharing a post, and the popularity of the post increasing as more turtles receive and share it

✔ Retweeting of a Twitter post, with an infected turtle tweeting, and every turtle it bumps into receiving the tweet; those recipients then retweet when they bump into other turtles, and so on

✔ Spreading popularity of a fashion accessory: an infected turtle wears an accessory, and any turtle it bumps into copies its style by wearing the same accessory, and so on

✔ Transmission of a computer virus through email, with each turtle possessing the infected email passing it along to any other turtle with which it collides

Start a New Project

Start a new project for your animation as follows:

1. Start MicroWorlds EX.

2. From the yellow MicroWorlds EX startup screen, select Free Mode.

   A new project opens.

3. From the menu bar, choose File⇨New Project Size⇨Full Screen 640 x 480.

Color the Background and Paint a Hospital

Give the background a solid (or nearly solid) color and paint a hospital as follows:

1. In the Command Center, type the command setbg 45 (which sets the background color as yellow) or any other color number except 0, which represents white. Click Enter (Windows) or Return (Mac).

   The workspace background changes color.

   Colors can be designated by either a number or a name. The command setbg 45 results in the same outcome as the command setbg "yellow: The background turns yellow. However, there are only a few named colors, so using a number gives you additional options. When you open the Painting Tools in the Painting/Clipart palette and click on any color in the color swatches, the color's number shows below it.

2. From the toolbar, click the Hide/Show Painting/Clipart button.

   The Painting/Clipart palette opens.

3. Open the Painting Tools.

4. Select any texture and set the opacity to 20%. Use the Paint Can tool to fill the workspace. The purpose of adding texture to the background is purely decorative and won't interfere with seeing the turtles in action.

5. Use the painting tools — including the Pen, Filled Rectangle, and Paint Can tools — to draw a simple hospital image (see Figure 10-1). Remember to set the Opacity back to 100% to draw the hospital.

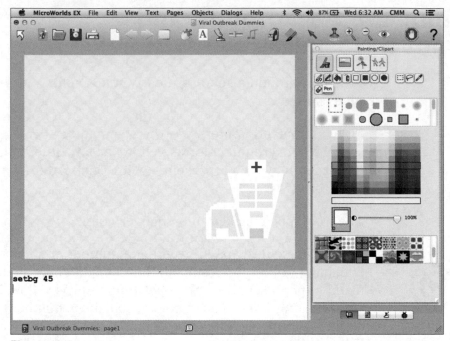

Figure 10-1

Be sure that most of the hospital image is the color white. The hospital can be any size and in any location in the workspace.

6. When you're finished, close the Painting/Clipart palette.

Create a Turtle

Follow these steps to create a turtle:

1. From the toolbar, click the Create a Turtle button.

2. Move into the workspace and click to hatch a turtle.

Later, you'll add information to this turtle and test that it works as expected. The turtle will then be cloned so that all clones will carry this information with them.

Write an Initialize Procedure and Make a Button

Although you have only one turtle in the workspace at this point, you will eventually have a large population of turtles. You need to create an initialize procedure that causes the turtle population to start out healthy by turning all of the turtles green. This procedure also distributes the turtles into random positions in the workspace.

Follow these steps to write the `initialize` procedure and then create an Initialize button to activate the procedure:

1. Click the project Procedures tab (located in the lower-right corner of the window) to open the project Procedures pane.

2. Type the following `reset` procedure:

   ```
   to initialize
   everyone [setc 57 setx random 640 sety random 480]
   end
   ```

   The `everyone` command causes all turtles in the workspace to execute the commands inside the square brackets, which are described in the following list:

   - `setc 57` sets the turtle color to green, the color being used to symbolize a healthy turtle.

   - `setx random 640` causes a turtle to randomly select an x-coordinate across the width of the screen.

   - `sety random 480` causes a turtle to randomly select a y-coordinate across the height of the screen.

3. Next, you need to create an Initialize button to execute the `reset` procedure. From the toolbar, click the Create a Button button. Then click the workspace anywhere.

Scattering the turtles

Games and simulations often require the random distribution or spreading out of objects across the field of action. The `setx random 640` command and the `sety random 480` command place the turtle at a random location in the 640 by 480 pixel workspace. You can use a similar structure for distributing objects in other programming languages by replacing 640 with the maximum dimension along the x-axis and replacing 480 with the maximum dimension along the y-axis.

One potentially confusing aspect of this is that the x-coordinates of the workspace go from −319 to +320, but the `setx random 640` command generates numbers from 0 to 639. You may be wondering why these two numbers don't match up! If `setx random 640` generates a number from 0 to 320, the turtle simply sets its x-coordinate to that value. But if `setx random 640` generates a number greater than 320, the turtle is pushed off the right side of the workspace to wrap around, reappearing on the left side of the workspace. If `setx random 640` generates an x-coordinate of 321, the turtle appears at an x-coordinate of −319. If `setx random 640` generates an x-coordinate of 421, the turtle appears at an x-coordinate of −219. In this way, the turtle can end up anywhere with any possible x-coordinate in the workspace. The y-coordinates of the workspace go from −239 to +240 and the `sety random 480` command works to position the turtle randomly in the y-direction in much the same way.

4. In the Button dialog box that appears, fill in the following information, as shown in Figure 10-2:

- *Label:* Type `Initialize` in the Label field to name the button.

- *Instruction:* Type `initialize` (the procedure name) in the Instruction field.

- *Do It:* Select the Once radio button.

- *Visible:* Select this check box to leave the button visible.

Figure 10-2

5. Click OK to close the Button dialog box.

   The Initialize button is added to the workspace.

6. Drag the button to reposition it to where you want it located.

   For example, drag the button to the upper-left corner of the workspace.

Make a Clone Button and Instruction

The Clone button is used to clone the current turtle so that many copies can be made of it. Make a Clone button as follows:

1. From the toolbar, click the Create a Button button. Then click the workspace anywhere.

2. In the Button dialog box, fill in the following information, as shown in Figure 10-3:

   - *Label:* Type Clone in the Label field to name the button.

- *Instruction:* Type `clone who` in the Instruction field. This command instructs the button to make a copy (`clone`) of the currently selected turtle (`who`), the turtle following instructions.

- *Do It:* Select the Once radio button.

- *Visible:* Leave this check box selected.

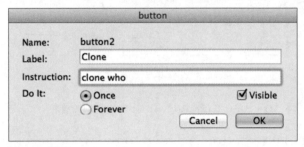

Figure 10-3

3. Click OK to close the Button dialog box.

   The Clone button is added to the workspace.

4. Drag the button to reposition it to where you want it located.

   For example, position this button below the Initialize button in the upper-left corner of the workspace.

5. Click the Clone button several times to make as many turtles as you want.

   Every cloned turtle has the same `OnTouching` and `OnColor` commands you added to the first turtle. Newly cloned turtles will appear on top of existing turtles. Click the Initialize button to scatter the turtles.

Cloning

Although the concept is slightly different in each programming language, *cloning* is a common coding process. For example, in Game Salad, you create *instances* (copies) of a prototype, and each instance has the same appearance and information as the prototype. In Java, the concept of *inheritance* is somewhat similar. Objects inherit traits from the parent, but may be altered to behave in a slightly different way if needed.

This ability to make object-specific alterations also exists in MicroWorlds EX. For example, say that you have an airplane turtle that runs a project-wide procedure called `fly`. If you clone that airplane turtle several times, all the clones possess the procedure `fly`. But if you want one airplane turtle to run a different `fly` procedure — maybe a kamikaze-style of flight — you can write a new `fly` procedure and place it in the backpack of that turtle. A local procedure of the same name will override the project-wide procedure.

Using cloning and related processes with a programming language allows you to reuse work you've invested in a project, especially when you need to create identical objects or procedures that vary slightly.

Make a 1 Sick Button and Instruction

The 1 Sick button is used to make a single turtle in the population sick. Make a 1 Sick button as follows:

1. From the toolbar, click the Create a Button button. Click anywhere on the workspace.

2. In the Button dialog box, fill in the following information, as shown in Figure 10-4:

- *Label:* Type 1 Sick in the Label field to name the button.

- *Instruction:* Type setc 15 in the Instruction field. The command setc 15 indicates that the 1 Sick button will set the color of the current turtle to 15, which is red.

The *current turtle* is the currently selected turtle. If only one turtle is present, that turtle is the current turtle. If multiple turtles are present, the current turtle is the turtle that has been clicked most recently. A turtle can also be made the current turtle with a command such as talk to (tto "*turtlename*). The who command reports the current turtle.

- *Do It:* Select the Once radio button.

- *Visible:* Select this check box to leave the button visible.

button
Name: button3
Label: 1 Sick
Instruction: setc 15
Do It: ⦿ Once   ☑ Visible
◯ Forever   Cancel   OK

Figure 10-4

3. Click OK to close the Button dialog box.

   The 1 Sick button is added to the workspace.

4. Drag this button to reposition it to where you want it located.

   For example, position this button so it's below the Clone button in the upper-left corner of the workspace.

Make an Infect Procedure and Add It to the Turtle

The infect procedure is used to cause a sick turtle to infect any other turtle it bumps into. Note that there should be only one turtle in the workspace to complete this step.

If you created multiple turtles when testing the Clone button in the earlier section "Make a Clone Button and Instruction," remove those turtles so that only one turtle remains in the workspace. To remove a turtle, right-click (Windows) or Ctrl-click (Mac) the turtle and select Remove from the pop-up menu.

Follow these steps to write an infect procedure and add it to the turtle. :

1. On the project Procedures pane, type this procedure:

   ```
   to infect
   if color = 15 [ask touchedturtle [setc 15]]
   end
   ```

   Here's how the infect procedure works. If a turtle is sick, its color is 15, or red. The infect procedure asks the touched turtle — the turtle with whom a sick turtle collides — to now also become sick by turning red (setc 15).

2. To cause the infect procedure to execute during a collision, you must add infect to the OnTouching field of the turtle backpack. Right-click (Windows) or Ctrl-click (Mac) the turtle and select Open Backpack.

3. On the backpack Rules tab, type infect in the OnTouching field, as shown in Figure 10-5.

   Leave the backpack open because you'll be using it again in the next step list.

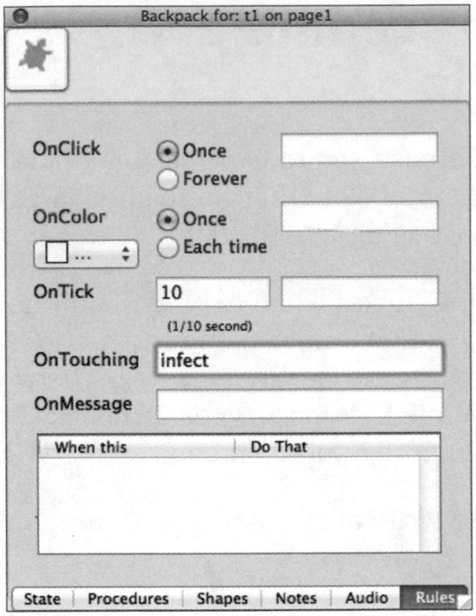

Figure 10-5

> **MATH CONNECTIONS**
> $\frac{1}{+1}$
> $\frac{}{2}$
>
> OnTouching commands are executed whenever the coordinates of a turtle intersect with the coordinates of another turtle. When some part of both turtles share the same coordinates, the turtles have *collided*.

Write a Health Command and Add It to the Turtle

A turtle visiting the hospital should exit healthy, represented by the color 57, or green. Create a health command at the open turtle backpack by following these steps:

1. On the Rules tab, select white from the OnColor drop-down list. Type setc 57 in the OnColor field and set it to Once, as shown in Figure 10-6.

The setc 57 command causes any turtles to turn green when they intersect with the color white (which is selected in the OnColor drop-down list).

2. Close the turtle backpack.

Figure 10-6

Write a Roam Procedure and Make a Button

The roam procedure and Roam button put the turtles in motion and make them walk around the screen so that they have the opportunity to bump into each other and sometimes visit the hospital. Write a roam procedure and make an associated button as follows:

1. On the project Procedures tab, type this procedure:

```
to roam
glide 50 0.5 rt random 360
end
```

The `roam` procedure instructs the turtles to move and turn so that they appear to be wandering around like real turtles. The command `glide 50 0.5` tells each turtle to walk 50 pixels at a speed of 0.5, and the command `rt random 360` tells each turtle to turn right by a random angle from 0 to 359 degrees.

Adjust the glide distance and speed as well as the turn angle to create the motion you prefer.

2. From the toolbar, click the Create a Button button and then click the workspace anywhere.

3. In the Button dialog box, fill in the following information, as shown in Figure 10-7:

- *Label:* Type `Roam` in the Label field to name the button.

- *Instruction:* Type `everyone [roam]` in the Instruction field. This command instructs `everyone`, meaning all turtles in the workspace, to execute the commands inside the square brackets, specifically the `roam` procedure.

- *Do It:* Select the Forever radio button.

- *Visible:* Leave this check box selected.

button	
Name:	button4
Label:	Roam
Instruction:	everyone [roam]
Do It:	○ Once ☑ Visible
	● Forever Cancel OK

Figure 10-7

4. Click OK to close the Button dialog box.

The Roam button is added to the workspace.

5. Drag the button to reposition it to where you want it located.

For example, place this button below the 1 Sick button in the upper-left corner of the workspace.

When clicked, the Roam button instructs all turtles in the workspace to exccute the `roam` procedure and to do so forever. Click the Roam button again to stop the Forever execution of the instruction.

 You can stop program execution at any time by clicking the Stop All button on the toolbar.

Save, Test, and Debug

 Click the Save Project button on the toolbar to save your simulation. The final simulation should look similar to Figure 10-8.

Note that the `setbg` command is no longer needed in the Command Center. You can remove it to tidy up the user interface.

Test all the buttons and run the simulation several times to ensure the simulation runs the way you want. Here's how to operate the simulation:

1. Start with a single turtle. This turtle carries instructions regarding infecting others, becoming infected, and regaining health in the hospital. If more than one turtle exists, right-click (Windows) or Ctrl-click (Mac) a turtle and select Remove from the pop-up menu.

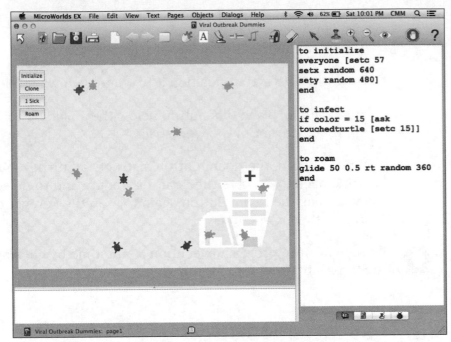

Figure 10-8

2. Click the Clone button to make additional turtles.

3. Click the Initialize button to make all the turtles healthy and then scatter them throughout the workspace.

4. Click the 1-Sick button to infect a single turtle.

5. Click the Roam button to put the turtles in motion.

Note the interaction between healthy turtles and also between turtles in which one turtle is sick. Also note what happens when turtles visit the hospital. Examine the rate at which an infection spreads in the turtle population. Troubleshoot and fix bugs until the simulation functions just the way you want.

If you decide you have cloned too many turtles, simply remove one or more turtles from the workspace. Right-click (Windows) or Ctrl-click (Mac) a turtle and select Remove from the pop-up menu.

Enhance your game

Consider enhancing your Viral Outbreak simulation with new features:

✔ Change the size of the turtle population to see how the number of turtles affects how long it takes for the virus to spread.

✔ Alter the size of the hospital to examine the impact of hospital size on the spread of the virus.

✔ Add smaller clinics at which the turtles can be "treated" and recover.

✔ Add randomness to virus transmission so that the virus transmits from a sick turtle to a healthy turtle only half the time (or some other fraction of the time).

✔ Slow down the movement of a sick turtle. Add conditionals into the roam procedure so that sick turtles (turtles with color = 15) move at a different speed than healthy turtles (turtles with color = 57).

✔ Add a button for automatically removing turtles using remove who as described in Project 14.

UFO Pilot

UFO Pilot is a side-scrolling game set in an asteroid field surrounding a distant planet. You'll use real space photos from the web to create your graphics. Then you'll write the code to let a player take on the role of a little alien piloting his UFO!

But now that you're becoming a master coder, you're not going to make this an easy game. You'll write commands to simulate gravity so that the UFO constantly falls towards the planet. And you'll build in single-key keyboard control so that the player can make his alien fire thrusters to counteract gravity. New coding concepts, including keyboard input, scoring, and mirrored motion apply here and in future programming!

Two background images courtesy of ESA/Hubble

Brainstorm

UFO Pilot is a side-scrolling style video game in the tradition of *Flappy Bird*. It can be adapted to a wide variety of formats including *Defender* (which includes shooting). Think about how you want to create your game:

✔ A ghost haunting a city as witches fly by on broomsticks

✔ A butterfly gliding through a rainforest full of flying insects

✔ Superman speeding through the air over rooftops and below toxic clouds

✔ A genie floating on a magic carpet, avoiding wild geese, meteor shower debris, and hostile missiles

Start a New Project

Start a new project for your UFO Pilot game as follows:

1. Start MicroWorlds EX.

2. From the yellow MicroWorlds EX startup screen, select Free Mode.

   A new project opens.

3. From the menu bar, choose File⇨New Project Size⇨MicroWorlds Standard.

Add a Space-Themed Background

Add a background for your UFO Pilot game that conveys a space theme. A great way to do this is to paste actual space and planet photos on your game background.

Follow these steps to create a space-themed background with images from the web:

1. In any web browser, navigate to the website of your favorite search engine. Search for space images to locate a background you like. One great source is the images category of the Hubble Space Telescope site (`http://spacetelescope.org/`), as shown in Figure 11-1. Go to the Images menu in the top-left corner and click any thumbnail image to open a full-size version of the image.

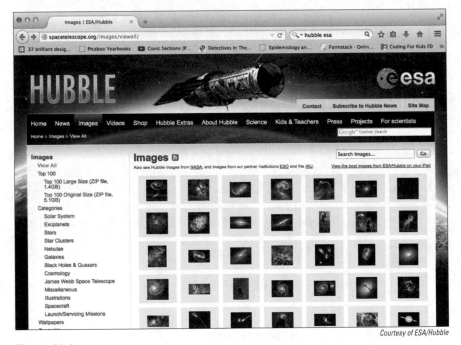

Courtesy of ESA/Hubble

Figure 11-1

TIP

An easy alternative to using real space images for your game background is to use one of the many space backgrounds provided by MicroWorlds EX. Open the Hide/Show Painting/Clipart palette and click the Backgrounds button to show the backgrounds. Scroll down to locate the three space backgrounds, shown in Figure 11-2. Click the background image you want to apply to your game, and then click in the workspace to apply the background image. Right-click (Windows) or Ctrl-click (Mac) the background image and select Stamp Full Page. The image is stamped to fill the entire workspace.

Figure 11-2

2. Copy a space background you like on the website by right-clicking (Windows) or Ctrl-clicking (Mac) the image and selecting Copy Image from the pop-up menu.

3. Move to the MicroWorlds EX workspace and paste the background by right-clicking (Windows) or Ctrl-clicking (Mac) the image and selecting Paste from the pop-up menu.

4. Right-click (Windows) or Ctrl-click (Mac) the pasted background image. From the pop-up menu, select Stamp or Stamp Full Page.

   The image is stamped to fill the entire workspace.

5. Return to the space images in your browser page. Now locate a moon or planet you like, for example in the Solar System category. Right-click (Windows) or Ctrl-click (Mac) the moon or planet image and select Copy Image from the pop-up menu.

6. Return to MicroWorlds EX and click the project Shapes tab in the bottom-right corner to open the Shape pane. Right-click (Windows) or Ctrl-click (Mac) a shape spot and select Paste from the pop-up menu.

   The moon or planet image is pasted into the shape spot, as shown in Figure 11-3.

Courtesy of ESA/Hubble

Figure 11-3

7. Double-click the shape spot where you pasted the moon or planet.

   The Shape Editor opens.

8. Decrease the Zoom percentage, in the top-right corner, to view as much of the moon or planet as possible. Select the Lasso tool in the Shape Editor. Click and hold down the mouse button as you drag to select a small wedge at the top of the moon or planet, as shown in Figure 11-4. Release the mouse button when you finish enclosing the wedge.

9. Choose Edit⇨Copy from the menu bar.

   The wedge is now copied. (Note that MicroWorlds EX may change the lassoed shape to a rectangular shape, even though only the lassoed region is actually copied.)

10. Click OK to close the Shape Editor.

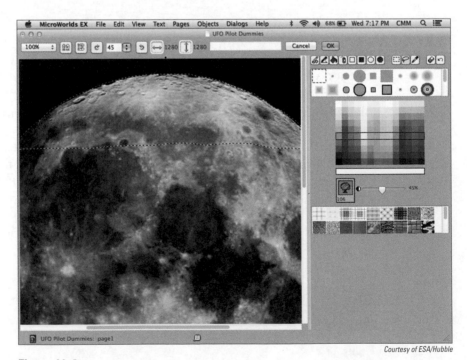

Courtesy of ESA/Hubble

Figure 11-4

11. Right-click (Windows) or Ctrl-click (Mac) an empty shape spot and select Paste from the pop-up menu.

    The wedge now occupies a shape spot, as shown in Figure 11-5.

Courtesy of ESA/Hubble

Figure 11-5

12. Click the wedge at the shape spot and then move into the workspace and click the background.

    The wedge appears on the background.

13. Drag the wedge near the bottom of the workspace.

14. Pull the sizing dots to resize the wedge as needed.

15. Right-click (Windows) or Ctrl-click (Mac) the wedge and select Stamp from the pop-up menu.

 16. On the toolbar, click the Hide/Show Painting/Clipart button.

    The Painting/Clipart palette opens.

 17. Use the Painting Tools area of the palette to add additional colors or make modifications to your space background.

    For example, use the Spray Can tool to spray additional white or blue stars across the background. Your completed background looks similar to Figure 11-6.

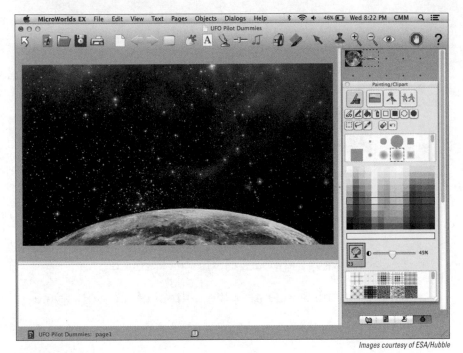

Images courtesy of ESA/Hubble

Figure 11-6

Create a UFO Character

The UFO character consists of a ship and an alien pilot. In this example, the alien ship is facing east. Create a UFO character for your game as follows:

1. On the toolbar, click the Create a Turtle button. Move into the workspace and click to hatch a turtle. Position the turtle at the center of the workspace.

2. Next, name the turtle that will be your UFO. Right-click (Windows) or Ctrl-click (Mac) the turtle and select Open Backpack from the pop-up menu.

3. On the backpack State tab, click the Edit button beside the Name field. In the dialog box that appears, type `ufo` in the Name field, as shown in Figure 11-7. Click OK to close the dialog box.

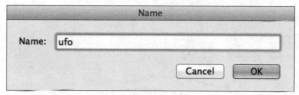

Figure 11-7

 4. With the Painting/Clipart palette still open, click the Singles button. Locate the shape of an alien spaceship — the choices are located near the planets, as shown in Figure 11-8.

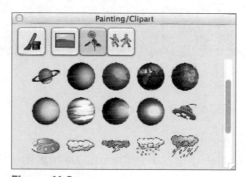

Figure 11-8

 5. Drag the alien spaceship shape into an empty shape spot next to the moon and wedge on the Shapes pane. Double-click the shape spot to open the Shape Editor where you can edit it, as shown in Figure 11-9.

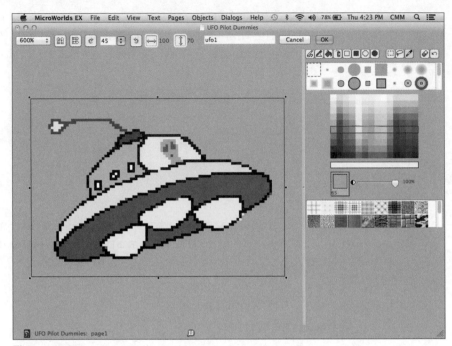

Figure 11-9

6. Modify the spaceship shape as desired.

You may want to use the vertical mirror image buttons near the zoom selector in the upper-left corner to flip the ship in the direction of flight. You can use the paint tools to recolor the ship or draw a little alien pilot at the helm.

7. When you're finished, click OK.

The edited alien spaceship shape now appears on the project Shapes tab, as shown in Figure 11-10.

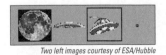

Two left images courtesy of ESA/Hubble

Figure 11-10

8. Move into the workspace and click the turtle. (In Windows, first click the shape at the shape spot and then click the turtle).

The ufo turtle now wears the alien spaceship shape.

TIP If desired, change the size of the ufo turtle. The default size is 40, but you can make the UFO bigger or smaller by typing a new number in the Size field of the backpack State tab. When finished, close the ufo turtle backpack by clicking its X button.

Don't worry about the heading of the UFO — this will be set in other places in the game.

Create Asteroid Cluster Characters

Asteroid clusters are the obstacles through which the player's UFO must navigate. Crash into an asteroid cluster and the mission is done! In this example, asteroid clusters appear to be moving west.

Creating asteroid cluster turtles

Create six asteroid cluster characters for your game as follows:

1. On the toolbar, click the Create a Turtle button. Move into the workspace and click to hatch a turtle.

2. Repeat Step 1 to create a total of six turtles for the asteroid clusters.

3. Drag the six turtles so that three are lined up across the top of the workspace and three are lined up across the bottom of the workspace, as shown in Figure 11-11.

Note that the background in the figure has been made mostly transparent so that you can see the turtles more easily. The turtles should not be perfectly lined up — variation in position makes the game more interesting.

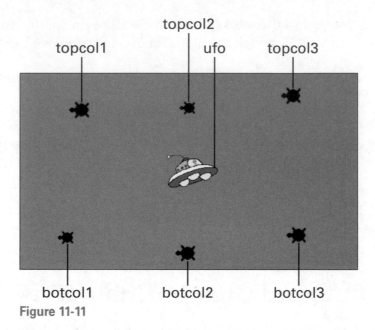

Figure 11-11

4. Next, name the turtles that will be your asteroid clusters. For each turtle, right-click (Windows) or Ctrl-click (Mac) the turtle and select Open Backpack. On the backpack State tab, click the Edit button. In the dialog box that appears, type the name for each turtle:

- `topcol1`, `topcol2`, and `topcol3` for the turtles that are the top columns

- `botcol1`, `botcol2`, and `botcol3` for the turtles that are the bottom columns

Click OK to close the Name dialog box for each turtle.

Although it's not required to name every turtle (object) or element in a project, it is easier to write and troubleshoot code with named objects. Give your objects simple, clear names, and give objects that are part of a group the same name followed by a number. Also, keep in mind that a turtle has a name, but the shape it wears has a different name.

5. Set the heading of all asteroid column turtles so that they move west (refer to Figure 11-11). To do so, type 270 in the Heading field of each backpack State tab.

6. If you want, adjust the size of the asteroid in the Size field on the State tab of each turtle backpack.

   The default value in the Size field is 40. Making turtles slightly larger or smaller will make the asteroid field look more varied and realistic.

7. When finished, close each asteroid column turtle backpack by clicking its X button.

Creating a cluster of asteroids for each turtle

Now, you need to create a cluster of asteroids in a column shape for each turtle. To do so, follow these steps:

1. Double-click an open shape spot next to the alien spaceship shape.

   The Shape Editor opens.

2. Reduce the zoom to 500%. Then pull and adjust the sizing dots on each side of the shape until the width is 50 pixels and the height is 120 pixels.

   Now there is sufficient room to paint!

3. Use the paint tools and the gray colors and textures to draw asteroids of different shapes and sizes. When you're finished, click OK.

   The asteroid column shape now appears on the Shapes tab, as shown in Figure 11-12.

Two left images courtesy of ESA/Hubble

Figure 11-12

4. Move into the workspace and click the `topcol1` turtle. (In Windows, first click the shape at the shape spot and then click the turtle.)

   The `topcol1` turtle now wears the cluster of asteroids column.

5. Click on the asteroid shape again and then click on `topcol2`. Repeat for `topcol3`, `botcol1`, `botcol2`, and `botcol3`.

   All asteroid turtles now wear the same shape (refer to the title figure at the beginning of the project).

An alternative strategy to "Create Asteroid Cluster Characters" is to complete one asteroid turtle in its entirely, and then copy and paste the asteroid turtle five times. Remember to name and size each asteroid turtle before proceeding.

When working with multiple turtles, it can be challenging to keep track of who's who. Just use the arrow pointer to hover over a turtle, and its name will appear. Or, in an open turtle backpack, click the icon of the turtle in the upper-left corner of the backpack and the associated turtle will magnify in the workspace as if to say, "Here I am!"

Create a Score Variable

A score variable allows someone playing your game to keep track of how many asteroid columns they pass without crashing. Follow these steps to create a score variable for the game:

1. On the toolbar, click the Create a Text Box button; move into the workspace and draw a small rectangle for the text box.

   This text box will be used to show the value of a variable.

2. Right-click (Windows) or Ctrl-click (Mac) inside the text box and select Edit from the pop-up menu.

3. In the Text dialog box, fill in the following information (see Figure 11-13):

- *Name:* Name the text box score.

- *Show Name:* Select this check box.

- *Visible:* Select this check box.

- *Transparent:* Deselect this check box so the text box is opaque.

A text box used as a variable must remain opaque (not transparent) for the variable value to change.

- *Single Line:* Deselect this check box.

4. Click OK.

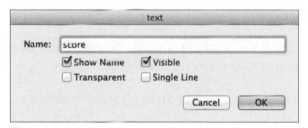

Figure 11-13

Write a Reset Procedure and Make a Button

A reset procedure sets the initial value of the score to zero and places the ufo at its starting position in the center of the workspace.

Write a reset procedure

Create a reset procedure as follows:

1. Click the project Procedures tab (located in the lower-right corner of the window).

2. Type the following reset procedure:

```
to reset
setscore 0
ufo, home
end
```

Here's how the `reset` procedure works:

- First, it sets the initial value of the score (`setscore`) to 0.

- Second, it gives the `ufo` the `home` command. `home` is a primitive that sets the position of a turtle to the coordinates (0, 0) and sets its heading to 0, pointing north.

During the game, you will change the heading of the `ufo`, so don't worry about its heading right now. The shape of the UFO appears to be facing east, although the heading of its turtle will always be either north (`seth 0`) or south (`seth 180`).

Also, if desired, you can set the starting position of every asteroid cluster, although this is not necessary.

In a side-scrolling game, the main character never actually moves side-to-side — it only moves up and down (north and south). The other objects in the game move from side to side, creating the appearance that the main character is actually moving horizontally, even though it isn't.

Create a Reset button

After you have written the `reset` procedure, MicroWorlds EX recognizes it as a new command that you can use. Create a button to run the procedure by following these steps:

1. On the toolbar, click the Create a Button button. Then click the workspace anywhere.

2. In the Button dialog box, fill in the following information, as shown in Figure 11-14:

   - *Label:* Type `Reset` in the Label field to name the button.

   - *Instruction:* Type `reset` in the Instruction field.

- *Do It:* Select the Once radio button.

- *Visible:* Select this check box so the button is visible.

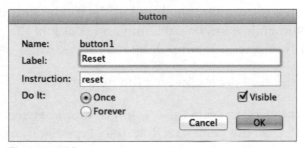

Figure 11-14

3. Click OK to close the Button dialog box.

   The Reset button is added to the workspace.

4. Drag the button to an out-of-the-way position in a corner of the workspace.

5. Test the Reset button to makes sure it functions as expected.

Code Gravity and Collisions

See that moon at the bottom of the game? The gravitational pull of that celestial body on the UFO is making it extra difficult for the alien to pilot his way through the asteroid field. If the alien fails to navigate safely, he crashes into the asteroids!

Follow these steps to code the constant fall of the UFO towards the moon and code the crash between the UFO and asteroids:

1. Right-click (Windows) or Ctrl-click (Mac) the ufo turtle and select Open Backpack from the pop-up menu.

2. On the backpack Rules tab, type seth 180 fd 5 wait 1 in the OnClick field and set it to Forever, as shown in Figure 11-15.

When the ufo is clicked on via the clickon command (in the Go! button that you will create later), this command sequence causes the ufo to point south (seth 180) and move in that direction at a moderate speed (fd 5 wait 1) forever. This simulates the gravitational pull of the moon. In the next section, you code a keyboard command that lets the player counteract this gravitational pull by moving north.

Leave the backpack open for the next step.

3. Next, you need to code the crash (collision) between the UFO and asteroids. On the backpack Rules tab, type announce [Crash!] stopall in the OnTouching field, as shown in Figure 11-15.

Here's how this code works: If the UFO touches any asteroid turtle, the announce command shows whatever text you type between the square brackets. Then, stopall ceases program execution — the entire game stops.

4. Close the ufo backpack.

Figure 11-15

Write a Keyboard-Controlled Fly Procedure

This is your first project that includes a keyboard-controlled interface. It uses a single key on the keyboard — the up arrow key — to execute the fly procedure by the UFO. The fly procedure lets a player fire the thrusters on the UFO to oppose the pull of gravity from the moon.

 On the project Procedures tab (located in the lower-right corner of the window), write a fly procedure as follows:

For a Windows game:

```
to fly
let [key readchar]
if (ascii :key) = 38 [seth 0 fd 20 wait 1]
end
```

For a Mac game:

```
to fly
let [key readchar]
if (ascii :key) = 30 [seth 0 fd 20 wait 1]
end
```

Simply put, the fly procedure reads the character of the key pressed by a player. If the key is the up arrow (ASCII code 38 in Windows, or ASCII code 30 on a Mac), the commands inside the square brackets are executed. Here, the example UFO has its heading set to north (seth 0) and then it moves in that direction 20 pixels (fd 20) with a wait of 1. You may need to tinker with the code to create the upward thrust you want.

Note that when the UFO turtle is clicked on, its OnClick commands constantly point and move it south. This fly procedure will be put into the Go! button, which you create later in this project.

See Project 12 for a more detailed explanation of how a keyboard-controlled procedure works.

 If you plan to distribute your game on both Windows and Mac platforms, you can put both sets of ASCII keyboard commands into the fly procedure so that the game operates everywhere. Just type the if line of code for Windows, followed by the if line of code for the Mac on the next line.

Write a Scoring Procedure for Navigating Asteroids

As the player successfully navigates the UFO past each column of asteroids, a point is scored. Write a checkpass procedure to check for this successful passage.

 On the project Procedures pane, write the checkpass procedure as follows:

```
to checkpass
if xcor = 0 [setscore score + 1]
end
```

Think about what is happening in checkpass. Because the UFO never moves horizontally, its x-coordinate is always 0. So if a moving asteroid column has an xcor of 0 and hasn't collided with the UFO, the score increases by 1 (setscore score + 1). Because checkpass is based on the motion of the asteroids relative to the UFO, it will be placed in the asteroid turtles.

Code the Motion of the Asteroids and Include the Scoring Procedure

The asteroids will move from east to west across the screen, barraging the little UFO and leaving only a small gap for the alien pilot to fly through. There are three columns of asteroids. Each column of asteroids has a top turtle and a bottom turtle; that's

why you named them `topcol1` and `botcol1`; `topcol2` and `bot col2`; and `topcol3` and `botcol3`.

In the following steps, you code the top asteroid turtles to move across the screen and include the scoring procedure, and code the bottom asteroid turtles to move along with their partners at the top:

1. First, you need to code the top asteroid turtles. Right-click (Windows) or Ctrl-click (Mac) the `topcol1` turtle and select Open Backpack from the pop-up menu.

   Note that all top asteroid turtles are already pointed in the direction they will travel and this direction never changes.

2. On the backpack Rules tab, type `fd 1 wait 0.1 checkpass` in the OnClick field and set it to Forever, as shown in Figure 11-16.

   After the top asteroid turtle is clicked on, this command sequence causes it to move forever one pixel at a time at a medium speed (`fd 1 wait 0.1`), and execute the `checkpass` procedure after each step. `checkpass` checks to see whether the asteroid turtle has an x-coordinate of 0, meaning if it is moving past the UFO; if it does, the player scores a point.

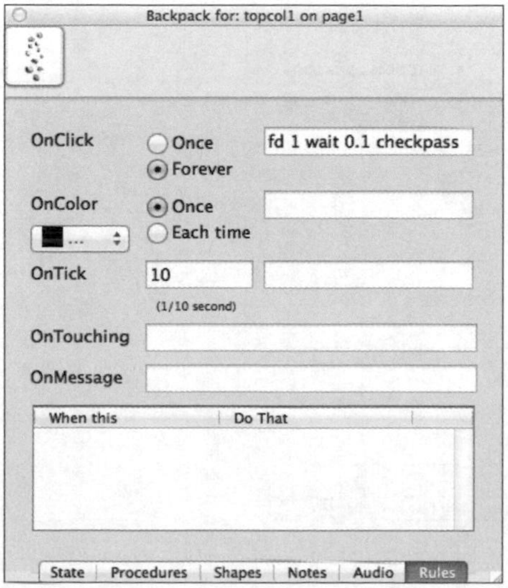

Figure 11-16

3. Repeat Steps 1–2 for the `topcol2` turtle and the `topcol3` turtle.

   Each top asteroid turtle will now move according to the same commands.

   Because each top asteroid turtle is only moving one pixel at a time, at some point it will have `xcor` = 0. If you adjust the speed of the asteroid, change only the wait time, not the forward distance. Otherwise, the asteroid may not have an `xcor` = 0 (for example, it may go from `xcor` = 1 to `xcor` = -1 or similar); if this happens, the score does not increase as it should.

4. Next, you code the bottom asteroid turtles. Right-click (Windows) or Ctrl-click (Mac) the `botcol1` turtle and select Open Backpack from the pop-up menu.

   Again, note that all bottom asteroid turtles are already pointed in the direction they will travel and this direction never changes.

5. On the backpack Rules tab, type `setx topcol1's "xcor` in the OnClick field and set it to Forever, as shown in Figure 11-17.

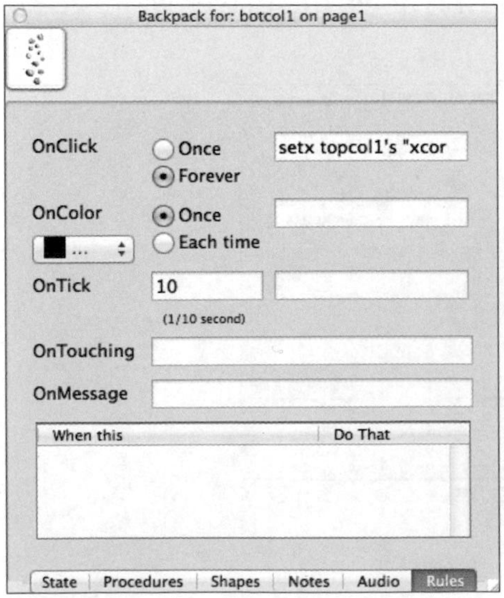

Figure 11-17

After the bottom asteroid turtle is clicked on via the `clickon` command (in the Go! button, which you will create in the next section), this command sequence causes it to forever set its x-coordinate to match the x-coordinate of its partner top asteroid. This *mirrored motion* has the effect of making the top and bottom asteroid pair move together — they stay vertically aligned.

6. Repeat Steps 4–5 for the `botcol2` turtle, matching it with the motion of `topcol2` (`setx topcol2's "xcor`). Then repeat these same steps for the `botcol3` turtle, matching it with the motion of `topcol3` (`setx topcol3's "xcor`).

Why not just make the bottom asteroids move like the top asteroids? Try coding it that way, but be sure to leave out the `checkpass` command from the OnClick fields of the bottom asteroid columns (otherwise, the score will double). You will notice a staggered effect in the motion: the top asteroid turtles move at different rates than the bottom asteroid turtles due to the additional time it takes to execute the `checkpass` command.

Create a Go! Button to Start the Game

This is it, the final step! A Go! button starts the game. Create a Go! button as follows:

1. On the toolbar, click the Create a Button button. Then click anywhere on the workspace.

2. In the Button dialog box, fill in the following information, as shown in Figure 11-18:

   • *Label:* Type `Go!` in the Label field.

   • *Instruction:* Type `everyone [clickon] ufo, fly` in the Instruction field.

Here's how the commands in the Instruction work. The
`everyone [clickon]` command clicks all turtles on. For
the asteroids, this means putting them in motion and checking to determine whether the score needs to be increased.
For the UFO, that means making it constantly fall. Then,
`ufo, fly` commands the ufo to execute the `fly` procedure — keyboard-controlled thrusters.

- *Do It:* Select the Forever radio button.

  Because Go! is set to Forever, the execution of the `clickon`
  and the `fly` commands continues over and over until a collision occurs — at which point `stopall` ends the game.

- *Visible:* Select this check box to leave the button visible.

Figure 11-18

3. Click OK to close the Button dialog box.

   The Go! button is added to the workspace.

4. Drag the button to a position near the Reset button and Score
   text box.

Freeze your UFO turtle and your asteroid turtles to prevent the
player from clicking and moving them during the game.

Save, Test, and Debug

Choose File⇨Save Project from the menu bar to save your game.
Your finished game should look similar to Figure 11-19. (*Note:*
Some of the commands in the procedures wrap onto the following
line. This is normal for long procedures. It does not indicate a line
break, so be sure to type the code as shown in the project text.)

Test your game by clicking Reset and then Go! to start the action.
Use the arrow key to pilot the UFO through the asteroid field.
Invite friends to play and see who can earn the highest score! If
you notice any bugs, go back and revise your code, and then retest
the gameplay.

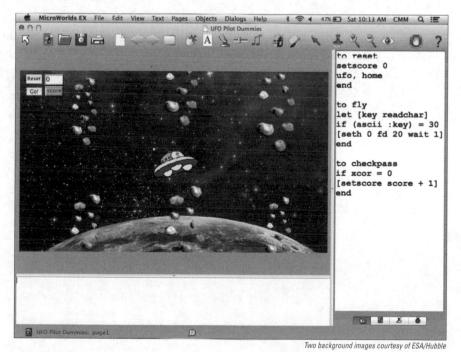

Two background images courtesy of ESA/Hubble

Figure 11-19

Enhance your game

Consider enhancing your game with new features . . .

✔ **Varied asteroid cluster sizes:** Increase or decrease the size of the asteroid clusters, and adjust their positions to impact the difficulty of game play.

✔ **More asteroid clusters:** Add another pair of asteroid clusters, but note that the more you add, the more your game slows down.

✔ **Bonus targets:** Add in an additional turtle that randomly appears and disappears. Give the turtle a special shape. If the player touches this bonus target, he earns extra points!

✔ **Variable speed (challenging):** Create a variable, `time`, that the top asteroids use as their wait time. Decrease the value of time from something like 0.1 to 0.01 after the player reaches a target score, such as 10. Add these new commands into the `checkpass` procedure using an `IF-THEN` conditional.

Squid Ink

When you're a simple, nonviolent squid, it can be hard to
defend your ocean home. But armed with ink sacs, you can swim
around safely, releasing a disorienting, black cloud whenever a
nasty shark gets too close!

In Squid Ink, you build a shooter-style game. The squid's motion is
keyboard controlled, and the shark glides constantly in a direction
towards the squid. Additionally, the squid carries hidden cargo —
his ink cloud — that matches the squid's x and y coordinates until
it is shot at the shark. The `touchedturtle` commands in IF-THEN
conditionals check whether the ink touches the shark, as well as
whether the shark touches the squid. Recorded audio plays if
either touching condition is met.

Brainstorm

Shooter games can be adapted to a wide variety of themes, including

   ✔ A shooting gallery at the fair in which the player aims a water gun at rubber ducks

   ✔ A humanitarian mission in which airplane flyovers drop food packages into refugee camps

   ✔ A *Galaga*- or *Asteriods*-style game in which the player navigates a spacecraft and shoots at incoming invaders or space debris

Start a New Project

Begin creating your Squid Ink game by starting a new project as follows:

1. Start MicroWorlds EX.

2. From the yellow MicroWorlds EX startup screen, select Free Mode.

   A new project opens.

3. From the menu bar, choose File⇨New Project Size⇨MicroWorlds Standard.

Add an Ocean-Themed Background

Follow these steps to add a background for your Squid Ink game that conveys an ocean theme:

1. On the toolbar, click the Hide/Show Painting/Clipart button.

   The Painting/Clipart palette opens.

2. Click the Backgrounds button to show the backgrounds.

3. Click on a background image you want to apply to your Squid Ink game. (Here, I selected the sea floor background.) Then click in the workspace to apply the background image.

4. Right-click (Windows) or Ctrl-click (Mac) the background image. From the pop-up menu, select Stamp Full Page.

   The image is stamped to fill the entire workspace.

 5. Switch to the Painting Tools on the Painting/Clipart palette. Use the Painting Tools to customize the background.

   The completed background is shown in Figure 12-1.

Figure 12-1

Leave the Painting/Clip Art palette open.

Create an Animated Squid Character

Create a squid character for your game as follows:

1. On the toolbar, click the Create a Turtle button. Move into the workspace and click to hatch a turtle.

2. Next, you need to name the turtle that will be your squid. Right-click (Windows) or Ctrl-click (Mac) on the turtle and select Open Backpack from the pop-up menu.

3. On the backpack State tab, click the Edit button beside the Name field. In the dialog box that appears, type squid in the Name field, as shown in Figure 12-2. Click OK to close the Name dialog box.

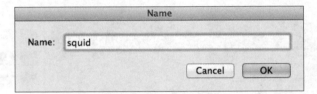

Figure 12-2

4. With the Painting/Clipart palette still open, click the Animation button.

5. Scroll down to the two pink squid shapes. Add the animated squid to the turtle as follows: Click the first squid shape. Hold down the Shift key on the keyboard and then click the second squid shape.

All the squid shapes are selected, as shown in Figure 12-3.

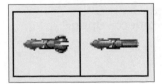

Figure 12-3

6. Move into the workspace and click on the turtle.

   The turtle now wears the animated sequence of squid, as shown in Figure 12-4.

7. Close the Painting/Clipart palette by clicking its X button.

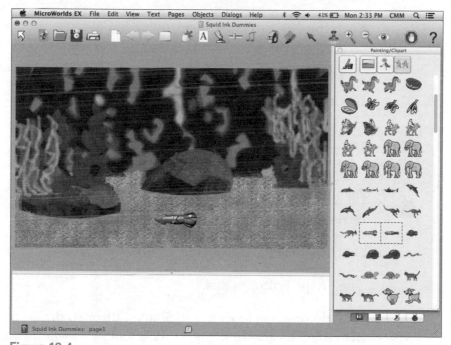

Figure 12-4

Create an Ink Cloud Character

Create an ink cloud character for your squid to shoot as follows:

1. On the toolbar, click the Create a Turtle button. Move into the workspace and click to hatch a turtle.

2. Next, name the turtle that will be your ink. Right-click (Windows) or Ctrl-click (Mac) on the turtle and select Open Backpack from the pop-up menu.

3. On the backpack State tab, click the Edit button. In the dialog box that appears, type `ink` in the Name field, as shown in Figure 12-5. Click OK to close the Name dialog box.

   Keep the `ink` turtle backpack open, but move it out of the way.

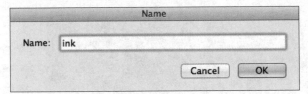

Figure 12-5

4. Click the project Shapes tab (located in the lower-right corner of the window).

5. On the project Shapes pane, double-click a shape spot.

   The Shape Editor opens.

6. Use the drawing tools in the Shape Editor to draw your own ink cloud, as shown in Figure 12-6. Click OK when you're finished.

   To increase the size of the drawing space, decrease the zoom percentage and then pull the sizing dots.

It is always good coding practice to name all elements of your program. However, in this program, it is only *necessary* to name the objects (the turtles), not the shapes they wear. Only the elements of a program that are specifically referenced by name require names.

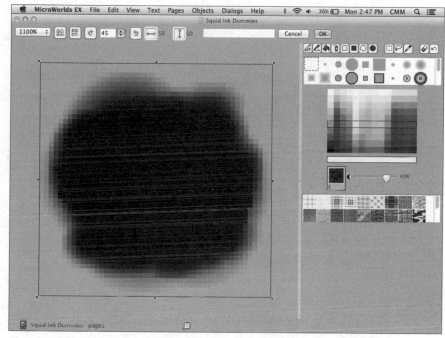

Figure 12-6

The completed ink cloud shape now appears on the project Shapes pane.

7. Click the ink shape on the project Shapes pane and then move into the workspace and click on the turtle named `ink`.

The turtle now wears the shape, as shown in Figure 12-7.

If you accidentally click somewhere other than the turtle, the ink cloud shape will appear on the background — simply right-click (Windows) or Ctrl-click (Mac) the shape and select Remove from the pop-up menu to get rid of it.

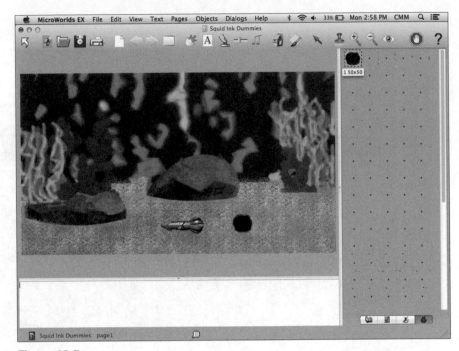

Figure 12-7

Create an Animated Shark Character

A shark character roams the ocean scene and serves as a target where the squid shoots its ink. Create an animated shark character as follows:

 1. Follow Steps 1–3 in the preceding section to create and name a turtle. In the dialog box, type shark in the Name field, as shown in Figure 12-8.

Figure 12-8

2. On the Shapes pane, double-click a shape spot.

The Shape Editor opens.

3. Use the drawing tools in the Shape Editor to draw your own shark, as shown in Figure 12-9. When you're finished, click OK.

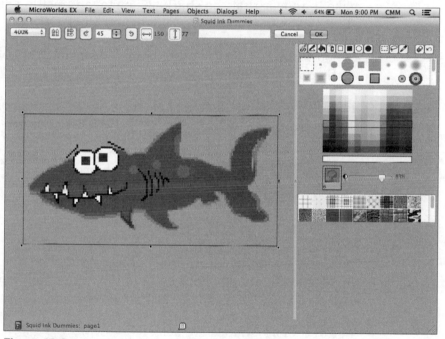

Figure 12-9

4. Right-click (Windows) or Ctrl-click (Mac) the shark shape and then select Copy from the pop-up menu.

5. Right-click (Windows) or Ctrl-click (Mac) an empty shape spot and then select Paste from the pop-up menu. Repeat so that you have three identical shark shapes.

6. Double-click a shape spot containing a copy of the shark shape.

   The Shape Editor opens.

7. Using the Paint tools in the Shape Editor, add a little light shading to adjust the dorsal fin and the tail fin. Your goal is to make it appear that the shark has changed position slightly while swimming. When you're finished, click OK.

8. Repeat Steps 6–7 on the other copy of the shark shape to add a little dark shading to the fins.

   Now, all three shark shapes appear in spots on the project Shapes pane, as shown in Figure 12-10.

Figure 12-10

9. Next, add the animated shark shapes to the shark turtle. Click the first shark shape and then hold down the Shift key on the keyboard and then click the last shark shape.

   All three shark shapes are selected.

10. Move into the workspace and click the shark turtle.

    The turtle now wears the animated sequence of sharks, as shown in Figure 12-11.

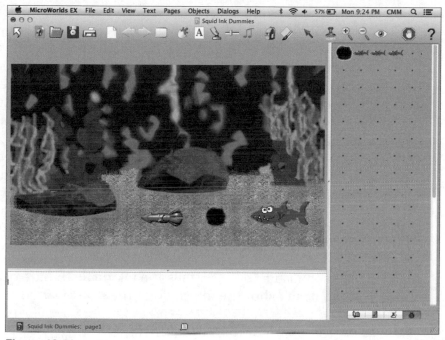

Figure 12-11

Write a Go Procedure and Make a Button

Your game will use a go procedure to start the game action. Write the go procedure and then make an associated Go button.

Write the go procedure

Follow these steps to write the go procedure:

 1. Click the project Procedures tab (located in the lower-right corner of the window).

2. Type the following go procedure:

```
to go
everyone [setx random 740 clickon]
tto [squid shark] st
ink, ht
end
```

The `go` procedure instructs `everyone` — the `squid` turtle, the `ink` turtle, and the `shark` turtle — to set its x-coordinate to a random number up to 740, which is the width of the workspace. This has the effect of placing the turtles in random positions horizontally across the screen, with the objective being to separate the squid from the shark at the start of the game. (See Project 10 for an explanation regarding how this command scatters turtle objects into random positions.) The `clickon` portion of the `everyone` command then clicks on all three turtles. You will write instructions in the OnClick fields of each turtle so that they know what commands to perform when clicked on.

The procedure then talks to (`tto`) the `squid` and `shark`, instructing them to show turtle (`st`).

The command `ink, ht` tells the ink turtle to hide because the squid hasn't shot the ink cloud at the shark — yet!

As an additional challenge, add a line of code to the `go` procedure to disperse the objects vertically as well. This helps further separate the squid and shark. Using only horizontal separation, there will be occasions when the shark and squid end up touching each other at the start of the game. Using both horizontal and vertical random positioning helps reduce the chance of an initial collision.

Create a Go button

After you have written the `go` procedure, MicroWorlds EX recognizes it as a new command that you can use. Follow these steps to create a Go button to run the procedure:

1. On the toolbar, click the Create a Button button. Then click anywhere on the workspace.

2. In the Button dialog box, fill in the following information (as shown in Figure 12-12):

   • *Label:* Type Go in the Label field to name the button.

   • *Instruction:* Type go in the Instruction field.

- *Do It:* Select the Once radio button.

- *Visible:* Select this check box to leave the button visible.

button

Name: button1
Label: Go
Instruction: go
Do It: ⦿ Once   ☑ Visible
             ○ Forever
                                 [Cancel] [OK]

Figure 12-12

3. Click OK to close the Button dialog box.

   The Go button is added to the workspace.

4. Drag the button to an out-of-the-way position in a corner of the workspace.

5. Test the Go button to make sure it functions as expected. Note that the ink turtle should disappear because it is given the hide turtle command.

Write a Swimshoot Procedure and Add It to the Squid

A swim and shoot (swimshoot) procedure lets a player move the squid around the ocean and shoot ink by using the keyboard. Follow these steps to write the procedure and add it to the squid:

1. On the project Procedures pane, write a swimshoot procedure.

   For a Windows game:

   ```
   to swimshoot
   let [key readchar]
   if (ascii :key) = 37 [seth 270 fd 10]
   ```

```
if (ascii :key) = 38 [seth 0 fd 10]
if (ascii :key) = 39 [seth 90 fd 10]
if (ascii :key) = 40 [seth 180 fd 10]
if (ascii :key) = 32 [shoot]
end
```

For a Mac game:

```
to swimshoot
let [key readchar]
if (ascii :key) = 28 [seth 270 fd 10]
if (ascii :key) = 30 [seth 0 fd 10]
if (ascii :key) = 29 [seth 90 fd 10]
if (ascii :key) = 31 [seth 180 fd 10]
if (ascii :key) = 32 [shoot]
end
```

swimshoot begins with a basic keyboard-control procedure that allows the player to use the keyboard to move the squid around the ocean in four directions. It then extends the procedure by adding the execution of a shoot procedure whenever the spacebar is pressed: if (ascii :key) = 32 [shoot]. Don't worry about the shoot procedure yet; you will write it in the next section.

2. Next, you need to tell the squid turtle to use the swimshoot procedure. Right-click (Windows) or Ctrl-click (Mac) the squid turtle and select Open Backpack from the pop-up menu.

3. On the backpack Rules tab, type swimshoot in the OnClick field and set it to Forever, as shown in Figure 12-13. Click OK to close the backpack.

After players click the Go button — a process that clicks on the squid — they can use the keyboard arrows to move the squid around the ocean, and press the spacebar to fire ink.

If you plan to distribute your game on both Windows and Mac platforms, you can put both sets of ASCII keyboard commands into the swimshoot procedure so that the game operates everywhere. Just follow the "if" line of code for Windows with the "if" line of code for Mac on the next line.

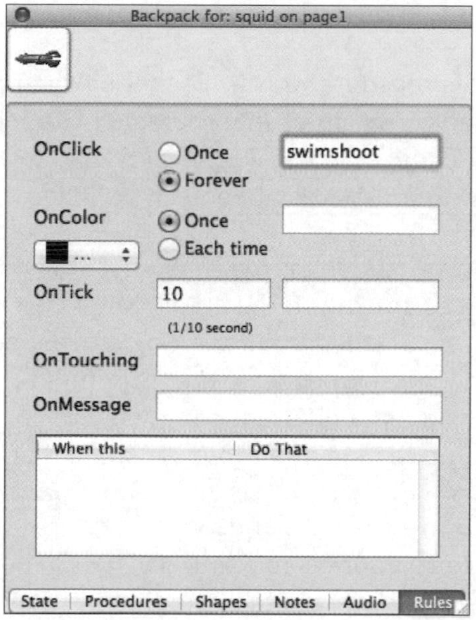

Figure 12-13

Creating keyboard control

Many games involve moving or driving a character around its environment, and keyboard control is necessary to facilitate that movement. Keyboard control is one of the most important — and fun! — coding activities you'll perform. You can assign any keys to move an object, many times using the up, down, left, and right arrows because they are logically analogous to the desired motion.

Sometimes, you'll want to move an object in one direction, as the alien does in the UFO Pilot project: Only the up-arrow key is used to make the ship fly. Other times, you'll want an object to move in two directions — for example, creating paddle control in a game such as Pong. Most often, you'll want an object to move in the four directions of a compass as when swimming the squid around the ocean.

Here's how a keyboard-control procedure works: When the player presses a key on the keyboard, the variable `key` stores that character. Every keyboard character has its own number code, called an *ASCII value,* and the values are different on Windows keyboards and Mac keyboards.

For example, on a PC (Windows), the left arrow has an ASCII value of 37. The keyboard-control procedure says if the ASCII value of a key is 37 — `if (ascii :key) = 37` — then point the object west and move it forward some distance. In the `swim` procedure, that motion command is `fd 10`. Every arrow key is assigned a different compass direction so that the turtle points in the chosen direction and moves a small distance.

You can assign a key to perform any commands you want. `swimshoot` assigns the four arrow keys to swim the squid left, up, right, and down, and it also assigns the spacebar to execute the `shoot` command.

Because ASCII values differ between PC and Mac keyboards, you should consider using both sets of commands in keyboard-control procedures so that users running Windows and also those running Mac OS can use your program. That way, everyone can play your game!

Arrow Key	Windows	Mac
Left arrow	37	28
Up arrow	38	30
Right arrow	39	29
Down arrow	40	31

Write a Shoot Procedure

A *shoot procedure* allows the squid to suddenly reveal a secret weapon — a puff of ink! When shoot executes, the ink cloud changes from hidden to showing, and moves at a target in the direction the squid is headed.

Continue working on the project Procedures pane and write a shoot procedure as follows:

```
to shoot
tto [ink]
setx squid's "xcor
sety squid's "ycor
seth squid's "heading
st
glide 200 0.4
ht
tto [squid]
end
```

When a player is driving the squid around the ocean using the swimshoot procedure, the shark approaches. The player presses the spacebar to shoot at the squid. This action executes the shoot procedure, which works as follows:

✔ The ink turtle becomes the active object using tto [ink], meaning "talk to the ink turtle."

✔ The ink turtle sets its x-coordinate (xcor), its y-coordinate (ycor), and its heading (heading) to match the squid's coordinates and heading.

✔ Then the ink becomes visible (st). This makes it appear that the squid has been secretly carrying the ink as it swims around.

✔ The ink then moves away from the squid in the direction the squid is heading using the glide command. This looks like the ink is being fired. After the ink moves 200 pixels at a speed of 0.4, it hides (`ht`). The `shoot` procedure doesn't address whether the ink hits the shark — that will occur in a different procedure.

`glide` is an alternative motion command for forward, and it is useful whenever you want to create smoother movement. To use the `glide` command, indicate both a distance and a speed, as in `glide 200 0.4`, which means move 200 pixels at a speed of 0.4. Tinker with the distance and speed to create the motion you desire.

📍 Finally, the `shoot` procedure transfers control back to the squid using `tto [squid]` so that the player can return to driving the squid. Note that while the ink approaches the shark, the squid cannot move . . . he's exhausted from firing off his ink!

Nesting procedures

The `shoot` procedure is *nested* inside the `swimshoot` procedure. *Nesting* means that a procedure is called from inside another procedure. In reality, all of the instructions of the `shoot` procedure could have been included in `swimshoot`, but it would have been really messy to write the code that way.

Here's an analogy from the kitchen to better understand why we need nesting: When making a cake, you need flour, eggs, sugar, milk, and frosting, all put together in a certain way. Frosting is made from its own set of ingredients in a process that follows the main cake recipe. It's too complicated to explain how to make frosting in the middle of explaining how to make the cake — so the "frosting" ingredient is simply nested in the cake recipe, with details about making the frosting following later.

Record "Argh, Inked Again" and "Chomp" Sounds

Although squid and sharks don't actually talk, you can guess what they might say if they did! If you have a microphone available on your computer, the audio recording feature of MicroWorlds EX allows you to record voices and sounds for inclusion in your programs. Create new recordings as follows:

1. Choose Objects⇨New Record from the menu bar.

   The Record dialog box opens.

2. Select the Show Name and Embed into Project check boxes, and leave the Visible check box unchecked, as shown in Figure 12-14.

Figure 12-14

You want to see the name of the recorded sound when you look for it on the Project tab, but you don't want the sound icon visible in the workspace. Also, embedding the sound into the project means you won't have to worry about the location of the sound if you want to share your game file — the sound will be part of the file — although it does cause your file size to increase quite a bit.

3. Click the Record button and speak into the microphone to record your sound. The first sound to record is what the shark would say when the squid inks him, something to effect of, "Argh, I'm inked!"

4. Click Stop when you're finished recording.

5. Click the Play button to play back your recording. If you're satisfied with your recorded sound, click OK to dismiss the dialog box. Otherwise, click Cancel and try again.

A Media dialog box appears, as shown in Figure 12-15.

6. Type a short name for your sound, such as *argh*, and then click OK.

(The check boxes will already be checked according to the preferences you set previously.)

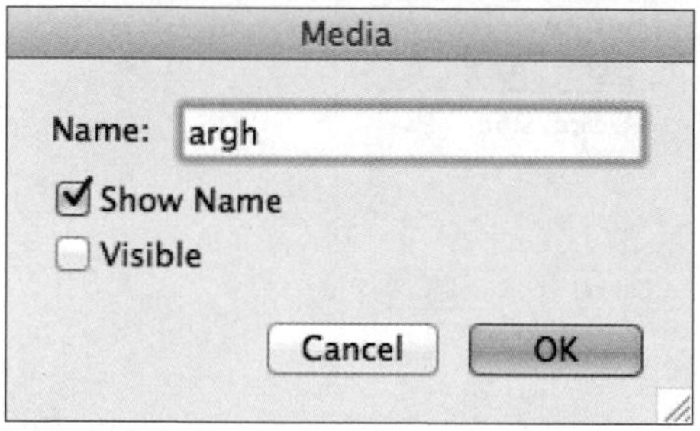

Figure 12-15

The argh sound is added to your project. The icon representing the sound does not appear in the workspace because the Visible check box was not selected.

7. Repeat Steps 1–6 to record a *chomp* sound to play when the shark eats the squid.

8. Click the Project tab (located in the lower-right corner of the window).

   The Project tab opens and shows all pages and elements in your project.

9. Click the arrow next to `page1` to see all elements on `page1` and verify that the `argh` sound and the `chomp` sound have been added to the project, as shown in Figure 12-16.

You can edit or show a project element that is hidden by right-clicking (Windows) or Ctrl-clicking (Mac) the element at the Project tab, and then selecting Edit or Show from the pop-up menu that appears.

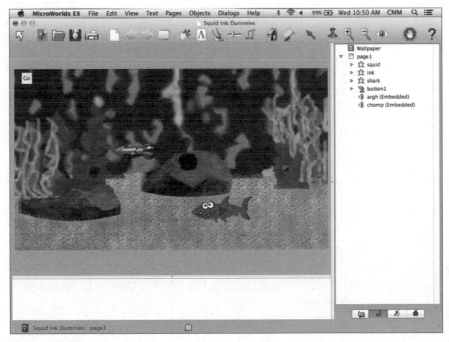

Figure 12-16

Write a Geteaten Procedure and Add It to the Squid

If the shark touches the squid, it's calamari time! A geteaten procedure is executed when the squid and shark are touching. Follow these steps to write the procedure and add it to the squid:

 1. On the Procedures pane, write a geteaten procedure as follows:

```
to geteaten
if touchedturtle = "shark [squid, ht chomp
    stopall]
end
```

Because this procedure will be placed in the squid backpack, the touchedturtle command evaluates whether the squid is touching the shark. If they do touch, the consequence of the IF-THEN statement is executed: [squid, ht chomp stopall]. The squid is instructed to hide (because he has been eaten!), and the chomp recorded sound plays. The game then halts via the stopall primitive.

2. Next, you need to tell the squid turtle to use the geteaten procedure. Right-click (Windows) or Ctrl-click (Mac) the squid turtle and select Open Backpack from the pop-up menu.

3. On the backpack Rules tab, type geteaten in the OnTouching field, as shown in Figure 12-17.

If the squid is touching the shark, the geteaten procedure is executed.

Figure 12-17

Commands used in the OnTouching field look for *coordinate convergence,* meaning two objects are in the same place at the same time. Coordinate convergence means that two objects have crashed, like a frog and a car; or one object has eaten another object, like a shark eats a squid! Coordinate convergence also occurs between the squid and its ink, but you don't want there to be a consequence of the squid-ink convergence. You must specify in the OnTouching field that the only convergence resulting in a consequence is that of the squid-shark.

In MicroWorlds EX, the `touchedturtle` command allows you to program a turtle object to respond only to specific turtles it bumps into, while ignoring others. All programming languages allow you to specify the parameters of a collision and how participants will react in a collision.

4. Close the squid backpack — it is no longer needed.

Freeze your squid and shark turtles to prevent the player from clicking and moving them during the game.

Write a Hit Procedure and Add It to the Ink

If the `ink` turtle touches the shark, he's been inked! A `hit` procedure is executed to indicate a successful hit. The `hit` procedure will be placed inside the `ink` turtle's backpack. Follow these steps to write the procedure and add it to the `ink` turtle:

 1. On the Procedures pane, write a `hit` procedure as follows:

```
to hit
if touchedturtle = "shark [ink, ht launch [argh]
    shark, bk 10]
end
```

Because this procedure will be placed in the `ink` backpack, the `touchedturtle` command evaluates whether the ink is touching the shark. If they do touch, the consequence of the IF-THEN statement is executed: `[ink, ht launch [argh] shark, bk 10]`. The ink is instructed to hide (because it hit the shark), the `argh` recorded sound is launched for play (see the nearby "Launching a parallel process in a procedure" sidebar), and then the shark backs up (`bk 10`) as if recoiling from being hit.

2. Next, you need to tell the `ink` turtle to use the `hit` procedure. The ink backpack should be open from creating the ink turtle. If you closed the ink backpack, open it by right-clicking (Windows) or Ctrl-clicking (Mac) the `ink` turtle and selecting Open Backpack from the pop-up menu.

 If you closed the backpack earlier and the `ink` turtle is hidden, access it by opening the Project pane, expanding Page 1, and double-clicking on the `ink` turtle icon.

3. On the backpack Rules tab, type `hit` in the OnTouching field, as shown in Figure 12-18.

If the `ink` touches the shark, the `hit` procedure is executed.

Launching a parallel process in a procedure

The `launch` command is useful when you want to execute a command, and then immediately execute the next command without waiting for the first command to finish executing. In Squid Ink, the `argh` recorded sound is about 3 seconds in duration (refer to Figure 12-14) and is executed by the squid. If the game waits until `argh` finishes playing prior to executing the squid's next step, the program will not read and respond to keyboard input — and thus the squid cannot move in the water. Meanwhile, the shark who will be swimming along according to his own OnClick commands, continues swimming and will likely catch up to (and eat) the squid. The `launch` command ensures that the game action proceeds at the same time that `argh` plays.

In computer programming, there are occasions when you want code commands to execute *sequentially* (or *serially*), meaning one step ends before the next step begins. There are other occasions when you want code to execute *simultaneously* (or in *parallel*), meaning at the same time. In MicroWorlds EX, a launched command in an object executes simultaneously with the command that follows. In essence, you are causing two things to happen at once. In practice, you could launch several commands in a procedure and have three, four, five, or more commands happen at once!

Parallel code execution is useful not only within a procedure but also among multiple objects. For example, one object runs its instructions at the same time another object is running *its* own instructions. This is how the shark keeps swimming towards the squid simultaneously with the squid swimming or the ink cloud moving to the shark. See Project 4 (Horse Race) for additional information on objects executing code in parallel.

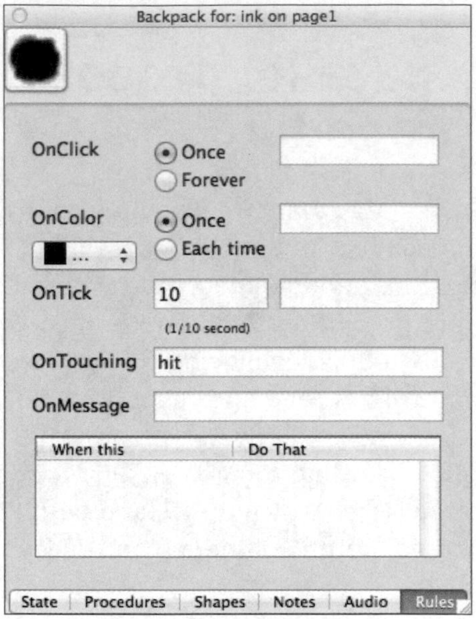

Figure 12-18

Write a Float Procedure and Add It to the Shark

Like all sharks, your game shark moves around the ocean looking for a tasty treat. A *float procedure* is executed so that the shark can move around. Float includes not only the speed at which the shark moves, but also the direction: He should always be headed towards the squid!

Follow these steps to write the `float` procedure and then place it inside the shark turtle's backpack:

1. On the Procedures tab, write a `float` procedure as follows:

```
to float
glide 3 0.01
towards "squid
end
```

`float` consists of a simple `glide` command, followed by `towards "squid`. The `towards` command sets the heading of the shark to constantly point towards the squid. Feel free to change the parameters of the `glide` command to adjust the speed of the shark.

2. Next, tell the `shark` turtle to use the `float` procedure. Right-click (Windows) or Ctrl-click (Mac) the `shark` turtle and select Open Backpack from the pop-up menu.

3. On the backpack Rules tab, type `float` in the OnClick field and set it to Forever, as shown in Figure 12-19.

Backpack for: shark on page1

OnClick	○ Once ● Forever	float
OnColor [■ ... ↕]	● Once ○ Each time	
OnTick	10 (1/10 second)	
OnTouching		
OnMessage		

When this	Do That

State | Procedures | Shapes | Notes | Audio | **Rules**

Figure 12-19

Save, Test, and Debug

Choose File⇨Save from the menu bar to save your game. Your finished game should look similar to Figure 12-20. (*Note:* I've moved the divider between the workspace and the project Procedures pane so that you can see all the procedures.)

Test your game by clicking the Go button to start the action. Use the arrow keys to swim the squid around the ocean, and press the spacebar to ink the shark. Play it repeatedly and ask friends to help test it as well. Remember to click the Stop All button if the game is glitchy and you want to stop and examine your code. This will help you work out the bugs and obtain a polished, playable game!

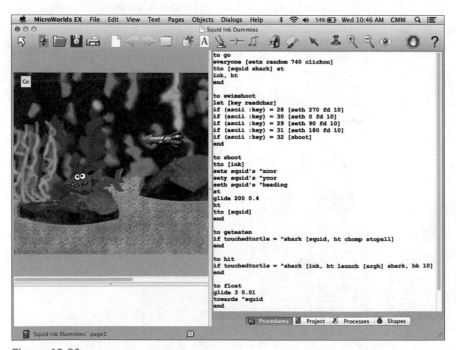

Figure 12-20

Enhance your game

Consider enhancing your game with new features:

- **Shape changes:** Create an inked shark shape and use the `setsh` primitive to change the shape of the shark when he gets inked.

- **Safe house:** Add a safe alcove or hole where the squid can hide out from the shark. In the shark's OnColor field, add code so that the shark retreats a certain distance when it touches the "safe house."

- **Levels:** Add new pages (or duplicate the page) with new challenges, such as a hungry octopus that attaches himself to the squid.

- **Silly school:** Add a little school of baby sea turtles (several turtles with `setsh "green` and `setsize 20` that swim around together). Give one turtle in the school a `glide` motion with `random` heading, and all the other turtles a `towards` the lead turtle command so that they all follow him.

Week 5

Advanced Coding

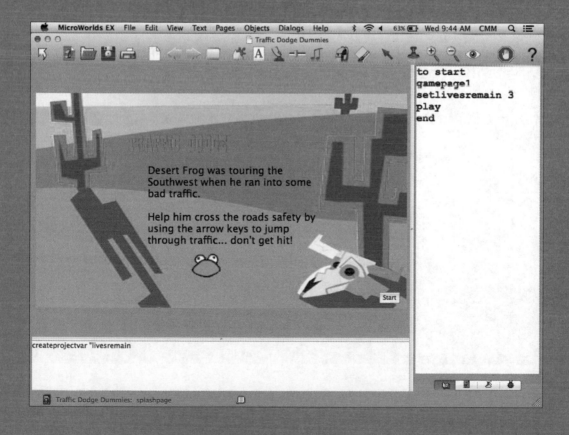

This week you'll build . . .

Rock, Paper, Scissors is a classic game, but you can play with the format just like the characters on the popular TV show, *The Big Bang Theory*. After you complete your Rock, Paper, Scissors project, try adding a lizard and Spock, as Sheldon does on the show, or add different elements of your own design. Check out the article at www.dummies.com/extras/codingforkids for tips that help you modify your game.

Rock, Paper, Scissors

Few recess games are as familiar or fast as Rock, Paper, Scissors. Using only your hands, you and an opponent randomly choose an object and reveal your choice at the same time. Based on the choices, one competitor wins, and one loses: Rock beats scissors, paper beats rock, and scissors beat paper. If both competitors choose the same object, the game is a draw (tie).

In this project, you build your own Rock, Paper, Scissors game with player versus computer. The game uses compound conditionals to determine the winner of each round. A compound conditional has an `if-then` plus conjunctions (and, or, not) in the code. This code format is used when more than one condition must be met in order for a consequence to happen. "If it is Monday and it is 8 a.m., then I ride the bus to school." If the player chooses rock and the opponent chooses scissors, rock beats scissors (player wins).

Brainstorm

You can make rock, paper, scissors into any game in which players choose three objects for comparison. The key is that each object must be able to win against another object, and also lose against the third object. What will your game feature?

- Pop stars, such as Beyoncé, Justin Timberlake, and Selena Gomez

- Pokémon characters, such as Pikachu, Squirtle, and Snowball

The rules of rock, paper, scissors are shown in Figure 13-1. Remember that if both competitors choose the same object, the game is a draw.

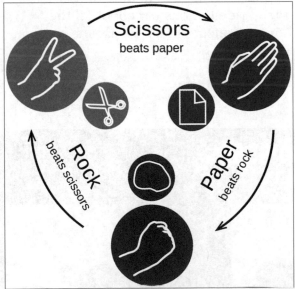

"Rock-paper-scissors" by Enzoklop - Own work. Licensed under Creative Commons Attribution-Share Alike 3.0 via Wikimedia Commons - http://commons. wikimedia.org/wiki/File:Rock-paper-scissors. svg#mediaviewwer/File:Rock-paper-scissors.svg

Figure 13-1

Start a New Project

Begin creating your Rock, Paper, Scissors game by starting a new project as follows:

1. Start MicroWorlds EX.

2. From the yellow MicroWorlds EX startup screen, select Free Mode. A new project opens.

3. From the menu bar, choose File⇨New Project Size⇨MicroWorlds Standard.

Paint the Game Page

The game page is where the player plays the game. On this page, the player will be able to select an object — rock, paper, or scissors — and then the computer will randomly show an object. Paint the game page as follows:

1. On the toolbar, click the Hide/Show Painting/Clipart button.

   The Painting/Clipart palette opens.

2. Use the Painting Tools to paint your own background in the workspace. Include two large rectangular regions (as shown in Figure 13-2):

   • One to show the player's choice of rock, paper, or scissors

   • One to show the computer's choice

3. When you're finished, close the Painting/Clipart palette by clicking its X button.

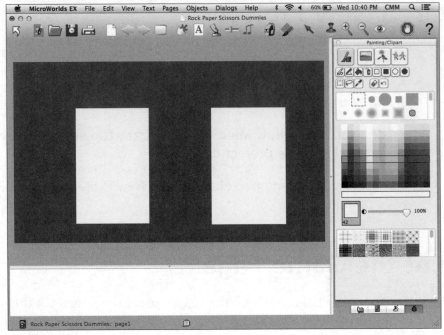

Figure 13-2

Add a Title and Text Labels to the Game Page

Add a title and text labels to the game page as follows:

1. On the toolbar, click the Create a Text Box button; move into the workspace and draw a long rectangle for the text box; type the name of your game — Rock, Paper, Scissors — in the white area of the text box.

2. Select the text inside the text box. From the menu bar, select the Text menu options and format the text.

   See Project 1 for details on formatting text.

3. Right-click (Windows) or Ctrl-click (Mac) inside the text box and select Transparent from the pop-up menu.

4. Drag the text box title to the top of the workspace.

5. Repeat Steps 1–3 to create a text box named CHOOSE! Drag this label into a position where the player buttons will be located.

6. Repeat Steps 1–3 to create two text boxes: PLAYER and COMPUTER. Drag the PLAYER label into the left rectangle where the player's choice will be located and drag the COMPUTER label into the right rectangle where the player's choice will be located, as shown in Figure 13-3.

To make sure that players don't accidentally move your text labels, right-click (Windows) or Ctrl-click (Mac) any label and select Freeze from the pop-up menu to freeze it in place.

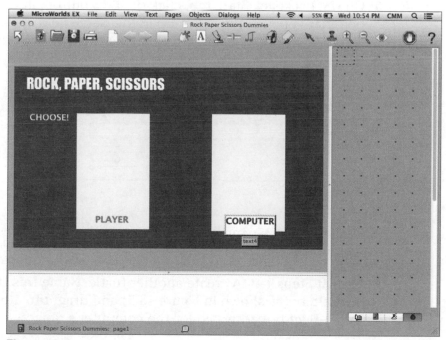

Figure 13-3

Create Rock, Paper, and Scissors Characters

You'll need two turtle objects for the game: one player turtle and one computer turtle. Each turtle can appear as a rock, a piece of paper, or a pair of scissors. Create two turtle objects and the rock, paper, and scissors character shapes as follows:

1. On the toolbar, click the Create a Turtle button. Move into the workspace and click to hatch a turtle.

2. Next, name the turtle that will be your player's object. Right-click (Windows) or Ctrl-click (Mac) the turtle and select Open Backpack from the pop-up menu.

3. On the backpack State tab, click the Edit button. In the dialog box that appears, type `player` in the Name field, as shown in Figure 13-4. Then click OK to close the Name dialog box. Close the backpack by clicking its X button.

Name		
Name: `player`		
	Cancel	OK

Figure 13-4

4. Drag the `player` turtle to a position in the left box reserved for the player's object.

5. Repeat Steps 1–3 to create another turtle. Name this turtle `computer` (as shown in Figure 13-5) and drag it to a position in the right box reserved for the computer's object.

Figure 13-5

Your game now looks something like Figure 13-6.

Figure 13-6

 6. Next, paint some shapes for the rock, paper, and scissors characters. Click the project Shapes tab (located in the lower-right corner of the window).

7. On the project Shapes pane, double-click a shape spot.

The Shape Editor opens.

8. Because you need to draw large shapes, it is helpful to resize the drawing area in the Shape Editor so that you have more room to draw. Click the Zoom tab and select 600%. Then drag the sizing dots of the drawing area until the Shape Dimension Indicators (width and height) each read 100 (see Figure 13-7).

Figure 13-7

9. Use the drawing tools in the Shape Editor to draw a rock shape, as shown in Figure 13-8.

10. Name the shape rock (in the empty white field at the top of the Shape Editor) and then click OK.

   The Shape Editor closes, and the rock shape appears in a spot on the project Shapes pane.

11. Repeat Steps 7–10 to create a paper shape and also a scissors shape.

   Now, all three shapes appear in spots on the project Shapes pane, as shown in Figure 13-9.

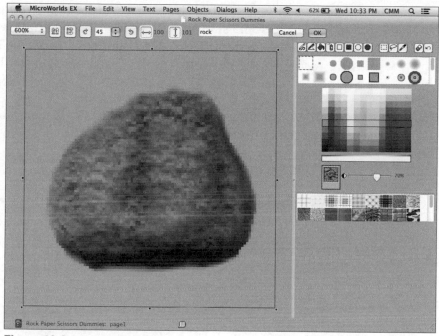

Figure 13-8

Figure 13-9

12. Click any shape on the project Shapes pane and then move into the workspace and click the `player` turtle.

The turtle now wears the shape.

13. Repeat Step 12 to place a shape on the `computer` turtle.

If you accidentally click somewhere other than the turtle, the shape will appear on the background — simply right-click (Windows) or Ctrl-click (Mac) the shape and select Remove from the pop-up menu to get rid of it.

14. Even though you painted the shapes fairly large, you may still need to make some size adjustments once the shapes are applied to the turtles. Right-click (Windows) or Ctrl-click (Mac) the `player` turtle and select Open Backpack. On the backpack State tab, type in a number for the Size. Close the backpack.

Remember, the default size of a turtle is 40. The smallest size is 5, and the largest is 160.

15. Repeat Step 14 for the `computer` turtle.

In Figure 13-10, the backpack shows a `computer` turtle size of 60.

	Backpack for: computer on page1	
Name:	computer	Edit...
Xcor:	191	**Ycor:** -23
Heading:	0	**Size:** 60
Shape:	scissors	
Animate:	● Setshape	○ Setrotate
Pen:	● Up (pu)	☑ Visible?
	○ Down (pd)	
	○ Erase (pe)	
	I have	Value
	State Procedures Shapes Notes Audio Rules	

Figure 13-10

Make Rock, Paper, and Scissors Buttons

The player needs a way to make a choice of rock, paper, or scissors. You can do that by creating a button for each choice. The button will change the shape of the player's turtle to show the choice. Then, the button will execute a procedure that makes the computer randomly select its own shape.

Follow these steps to make the rock, paper, and scissors buttons:

1. On the toolbar, click the Create a Button button. Then click anywhere in the workspace.

2. In the Button dialog box, fill in the following information, as shown in Figure 13-11:

   • *Label:* Type `Rock` in the Label field to name the button.

   • *Instruction:* Type `player, setshape "rock wait 5 compchoose` in the Instruction field.

     The instruction tells the `player` turtle to set its shape to rock, then `wait 5` (about half a second) to help pace the game so that an element of excitement is added regarding what the computer will choose and who will win the match! It then executes the nested `compchoose` procedure, which causes the computer to randomly make a choice. (See the next section, "Write a Compchoose Procedure.")

   • *Do It:* Select the Once radio button.

   • *Visible:* Select this check box to leave the button visible.

Figure 13-11

3. Click OK to close the Button dialog box.

   The Rock button is added to the workspace of the game.

4. Drag the Rock button to a position just below the CHOOSE! Label.

5. Repeat Steps 1–4 to create a button for the player to choose Paper and then have the computer randomly make a choice. In the Instruction field, enter `player, setshape "paper wait 5 compchoose`, as shown in Figure 13-12.

button		
Name:	button2	
Label:	Paper	
Instruction:	player, setshape "paper wait 5 compchoose	
Do It:	● Once ○ Forever	☑ Visible
	Cancel	OK

Figure 13-12

6. Repeat Steps 1–4 to create a button for the player to choose Scissors and then have the computer randomly make a choice. In the Instruction field, enter `player, setshape "scissors wait 5 compchoose`, as shown in Figure 13-13.

button		
Name:	button3	
Label:	Scissors	
Instruction:	player, setshape "scissors wait 5 compchoose	
Do It:	● Once ○ Forever	☑ Visible
	Cancel	OK

Figure 13-13

The game now looks like Figure 13-14.

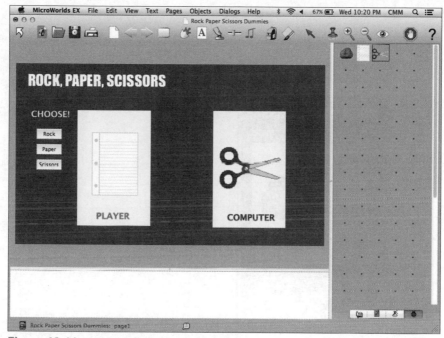

Figure 13-14

Write a Compchoose Procedure

 A compchoose procedure causes the computer to randomly make its choice of rock, paper, or scissors. Switch to the project Procedures pane, and write the compchoose procedure as follows:

```
to compchoose
repeat 10 [computer, wait 1 setshape pick [rock
    paper scissors]]
checkwin
end
```

 When writing procedures that have long lines of code, it is helpful to extend the width of the Procedures pane. Just grab the divider between the pane and the workspace and open up the pane as much as you need, as shown in Figure 13-15. Another way to see your code more clearly is to break up long commands over several lines by inserting your own lines breaks between parts of the command.

Divider

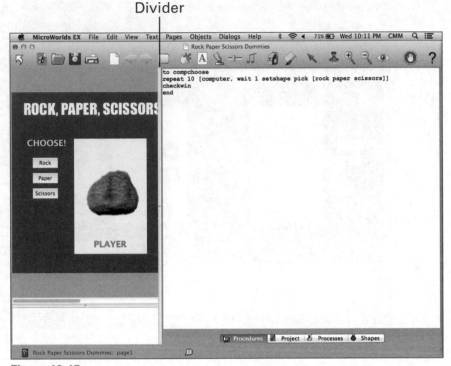

Figure 13-15

The `compchoose` procedure works like this:

✔ It repeats `10` times a process of telling the `computer` turtle to set its shape to one picked from three possibilities: `rock`, `paper`, and `scissors`. From the player's view, the computer is "deciding" what object to reveal by picking a shape and then picking another shape over and over until it settles on a final choice. Here again, the coding is used merely to heighten the player experience. (See the nearby sidebar, "Picking — selecting with replacement," for more on the `pick` command.)

✔ The `wait 1` command simply slows down the process.

✔ The `checkwin` procedure (which you write in the next section) determines who wins the match.

Picking — selecting with replacement

The `pick` command operates similarly to the `random` command. While `random` selects a random number from a range, `pick` is used to pick an item from a list, or a single character out of a word. There is equal probability of picking any item from a list: In a list of three items, each item has a 1/3 probability of being selected. Also, each item can be picked at any time — after an item is picked, it can be picked again — it is not removed from the list. This is called *selecting with replacement*.

Write a Checkwin Procedure

A checkwin procedure determines who wins the two-way match by comparing the player shape with the computer shape.

The checkwin procedure checks for all possible outcomes of a rock, paper, scissors game. What are those?

✔ The player and the computer choose the same object — this is a draw.

✔ The player chooses rock, and the computer picks paper or scissors.

✔ The player chooses paper, and the computer picks rock or scissors.

✔ The player chooses scissors, and the computer picks rock or paper.

On the Procedures pane, type the checkwin procedure (see Figure 13-16):

```
to checkwin
; check for draw
if (player's "shape) = (computer's "shape) [say [DRAW]]
```

```
; player chooses rock
if and (player's "shape) = "rock (computer's "shape) = "paper [say
         [PAPER COVERS ROCK] ]
if and (player's "shape) = "rock (computer's "shape) = "scissors [say
         [ROCK CRUSHES SCISSORS] ]
; player chooses paper
if and (player's "shape) = "paper (computer's "shape) = "rock [say
         [PAPER COVERS ROCK] ]
if and (player's "shape) = "paper (computer's "shape) = "scissors
         [say [SCISSORS CUT PAPER] ]
; player chooses scissors
if and (player's "shape) = "scissors (computer's "shape) = "rock [say
         [ROCK CRUSHES SCISSORS] ]
if and (player's "shape) = "scissors (computer's "shape) = "paper
         [say [SCISSORS CUT PAPER] ]
end
```

Note that each comparison begins with a comment line that is introduced by a semicolon symbol (;).

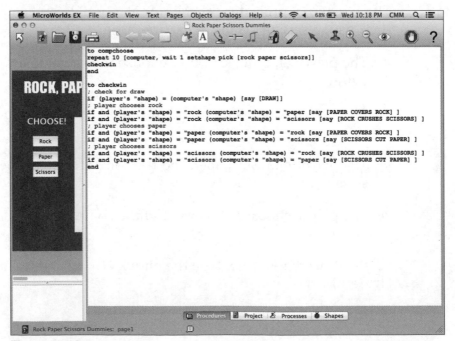

Figure 13-16

When using parentheses in writing MicroWorlds EX code, you can leave them off of single words such as `"rock`. Parentheses are needed only to eliminate confusion with double words such as contractions, for example, `(player's "shape)`.

As you write longer and more complicated procedures, it's a good idea to include *comment lines* in your code. Comment lines are notes about what each procedure or program section does. Comments help you remember the purpose of your code and are especially helpful to others who may read your code, or collaborators who may be coding with you on a team project. They are also ideal for keeping your program visually and structurally organized, and may be written to serve as a plan before creating any actual code. A semicolon symbol (;) usually starts a comment line. Comment lines are not executed. In Figure 13-16, the words in red are comments. Note that longer comments can wrap to additional lines, but you should not use a line break to split them as this will generate an error.

Following each comment is a *compound conditional* to compare the objects and say an outcome. Here is an example:

- *Plain words:* If the player's shape is a rock, and the computer's shape is paper, then say PAPER COVERS ROCK.

- *MWEX code:* `if and (player's "shape) = "rock (computer's "shape) = "paper [say [PAPER COVERS ROCK] ]`

In the compound "and" conditional, both conditions must be true for the consequence to be executed.

The `checkwin` procedure compares all possible combinations of player and computer choices and gives a consequence for each pair. `checkwin` uses the `say` command to inform the player of the outcome of each match. The `say` command uses your computer's artificial voice to say the words in the square brackets.

One branch of mathematics where compound conditionals of all sorts appear is logic. From formal logic that forms the basis of argumentation and proofs (you'll do these in geometry!) to puzzle logic — including classics such as Wolf, Sheep, and Cabbage (see `www.plastelina.net`) — you'll find conditionals.

Exploring conditional statement formats

The format of a conditional statement is very different depending on the programming language used:

✔ *Plain words:* If a first condition is satisfied or a second condition is satisfied, `then` give the consequence.

✔ *MWEX:* If or condition1 condition2 [consequence]

✔ *Python:* If condition1 or condition2: consequence

Here is an example you can probably relate to:

✔ *Plain words:* If I'm tired or I'm hungry, then I can't concentrate

✔ *MWEX:* If or (I'm tired) (I'm hungry) [I can't concentrate]

✔ *Python:* If I'm tired or I'm hungry: I can't concentrate

Save, Test, Debug, and Enhance

Chose File➪Save Project from the menu bar to save your game. Test your game by playing it several times. Test out each button and make sure that each combination says the correct result. This will help you work out the bugs.

Where's Wallace Walrus?

Where's Wallace Walrus? is a classic search-and-find game. Wallace is an ordinary walrus lounging on the ice among a rather large population of walrus friends. Some are wearing earmuffs; others are wearing scarves, hats, or goggles. But Wallace is the only walrus on the floe not sporting accessories — and it's the player's job to find him! The game features a common coding command called a do loop to create the population of walruses. Random shape assignment and positioning make every game unique. Your players will find themselves asking, "Where's Wallace Walrus?"

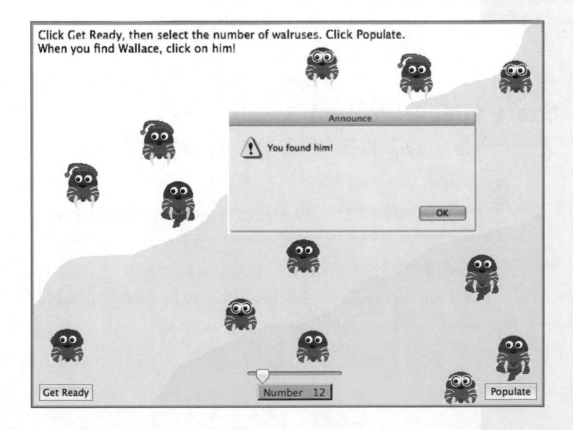

Brainstorm

Search-and-find or hidden-object games come in a variety of formats. Create any type of character population and setting, such as

- City scenes with a population of colorful characters in the tradition of Where's Waldo?

- Aliens varying in number of eyes, all living on a distant planet

- Amoebas in a petri dish

- Letters in a bowl of alphabet soup

- Books on a bookshelf or beads and jewelry in a drawer

- Gears or robot parts on a factory floor

- Cars on a track in a NASCAR race, with slightly different colors and decals

Start a New Project

Start a new project for your game as follows:

1. Start MicroWorlds EX.

2. From the yellow MicroWorlds EX startup screen, select Free Mode.

   A new project opens.

3. From the menu bar, choose File⇨New Project Size⇨Full Screen 640 x 480.

Name the Search-and-Find Page

Follow these steps to name the page:

1. From the menu bar, choose Pages⇨Name Page.

2. Type searchpage in the Name dialog box, as shown in Figure 14-1. Then click OK.

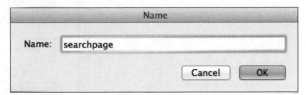

Figure 14-1

Paint the Background of the Search Page

Paint a simple background in the workspace of your searchpage as follows:

1. From the toolbar, click the Hide/Show Painting/Clipart button.

   The Painting/Clipart palette opens.

2. Open the Painting Tools.

3. Select any shade of light blue and then use the pencil tool with a wide tool tip to paint a simple band of icy water across the background (see Figure 14-2). The band can be any size.

4. If you want to, fill a white section of the background with a light gray shade using the Paint Bucket tool.

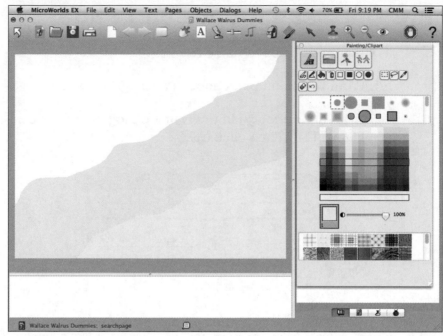

Figure 14-2

Create a Main Character

The main character is the object that players search for on your `searchpage`. Here's how to create your main character — in this game, Wallace Walrus:

1. From the toolbar, click the Create a Turtle button. Move into the workspace and click to hatch a turtle.

2. Next, you need to name the turtle that will be your player's object. Right-click (Windows) or Ctrl-click (Mac) the turtle and select Open Backpack.

3. On the backpack State tab, click the Edit button beside the Name field. In the dialog box that appears (see Figure 14-3), type `walrus` in the Name field. Click OK to close the Name dialog box.

Leave the backpack open — you will use it again soon.

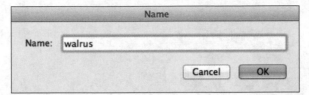

Figure 14-3

4. Now paint a shape for this walrus turtle. Click the project Shapes tab (located in the lower-right corner of the window).

5. On the project Shapes tab, double-click a shape spot.

The Shape Editor opens.

6. You may want to draw a slightly larger shape than the default size of 40 x 40 pixels. To do so, resize the drawing area in the Shape Editor so that you have more room to draw. Click the Zoom tab and select 1100% or 1200%. Drag the sizing dots of the drawing area until the Shape Dimension Indicators each read approximately 50 x 50.

7. Use the drawing tools in the Shape Editor to draw a walrus head, as shown in Figure 14-4.

8. Name the shape wallace in the empty white field at the top of the Shape Editor, as shown in Figure 14-4. Click OK.

The Shape Editor closes, and the wallace shape appears in a spot on the project Shapes pane.

9. Click the wallace shape on the project Shapes pane and then move into the workspace and click on the walrus turtle.

The turtle now wears the shape.

Figure 14-4

Create Distracter Character Shapes

A search-and-find game hides the main character among many distracter characters. This makes it challenging for the player to find the main character — and fun when he finally does! In the following steps, you will make copies of the main character shape and then create distracter shapes from the copies:

 1. On the project Shapes pane, right-click (Windows) or Ctrl-click (Mac) the `wallace` shape and then select Copy from the pop-up menu to copy the shape.

2. Right-click (Windows) or Ctrl-click (Mac) an empty shape spot and then select Paste from the pop-up menu. Repeat to create a total of four copies of `wallace`.

3. Double-click a shape spot containing a copy of `wallace`.

The Shape Editor opens.

4. Using the Paint tools in the Shape Editor, add an additional feature to the shape, such as earmuffs as shown in Figure 14-5.

You may need to pull the sizing dots to slightly increase the size of the workspace if the additional feature takes up a lot of space.

Figure 14-5

5. Name the shape `earmuffs` in the empty white field at the top of the Shape Editor, as shown in Figure 14-6. Click OK.

The Shape Editor closes, and the `earmuffs` shape appears in a spot on the project Shapes pane.

6. Repeat Steps 3–5 to create a `scarf` shape, a `hat` shape, and a `goggles` shape.

Now, Wallace and all four distracter shapes appear in spots on the project Shapes pane, as shown in Figure 14-6.

Figure 14-6

To undo the last step when painting in the workspace or the Shape Editor, choose Edit⇨Undo at the Menu bar, or press Ctrl-Z (Windows) or Command-Z (Mac).

Make a Slider to Vary the Number of Distracters

Players will want to adjust the difficulty of your search-and-find game. New or younger players may only want to have five or six walruses to look at. But experienced players may want to challenge themselves with a hundred walruses! Follow these steps to create a slider so that players can adjust the number of walruses in the game:

 1. From the toolbar, click the Create a Slider button. Then click anywhere on the workspace.

Or, from the menu bar, choose Objects⇨New Slider.

2. In the Slider dialog box, fill in the following information (as shown in Figure 14-7):

- *Name:* Type Number, which represents the number of walrus distracters in the game.

- *Minimum and Maximum:* Type a minimum and maximum value for the number of walrus distracters in the project.

- *Value:* Type a starting value for the number of walrus distracters. This is the number that shows on the slider before the player changes it.

- *Show Name:* Select this check box.

- *Visible:* Select this check box.

- *Vertical:* If you want to make the slider vertical (up and down), select the Vertical check box.

slider	
Name:	Number
Minimum:	2
Maximum:	100
Value:	2

☑ Show Name
☑ Visible
☐ Vertical

Cancel   OK

Figure 14-7

3. Click OK to close the Slider dialog box.

The Number slider appears in the workspace.

4. Drag the slider to where you want it to appear in the workspace.

Write a Populate Procedure and Make a Button

To create a population of distracter walruses around Wallace the walrus, you need to write a `populate` procedure and make a button to execute that procedure.

Write a populate procedure

On the project Procedures pane, type the following `populate` procedure:

```
to populate
newturtle "t1
st
repeat Number [clone "t1 setsh pick [earmuffs scarf
    hat goggles]]
```

```
remove "t1
everyone [setx random 640 sety random 480]
end
```

The `populate` procedure works as follows:

✔ A `newturtle` is added to the `searchpage` and named `t1`. It then makes `t1` visible with the command `st` (show turtle). `t1` is wearing a special shape — it just appears as the default turtle shape.

✔ `repeat` executes `Number` times the commands inside the square brackets. The value of `Number` is set by the slider and represents the number of distracter turtles who hang out with Wallace. On each repetition, the `t1` turtle is cloned so that a new numbered turtle is added (`t2`, `t3`, `t4`, and so on). As each new turtle is added, a shape is picked randomly from the distracter shapes: `earmuffs`, `scarf`, `hat`, or `goggles` and applied to the turtle. *Note:* Don't forget that Wallace the `walrus` turtle is still sitting there nicely in the workspace — he is the only turtle with a special name.

✔ Following completion of the `repeat`, the `t1` turtle is removed using the command `remove "t1`. The `t1` turtle serves only as a *seed* for cloning the distracter turtles.

✔ Finally, the command `everyone [setx random 640 sety random 480]` gives `everyone` in the workspace a random coordinate position. Wallace and each of the distracters set their x-coordinate to `random 640`, the width of the workspace. Wallace and all distracters also set their y-coordinate to `random 480`, the height of the workspace.

Many games and simulations require objects to be scattered into random positions. Examples include distributing cows in a field, people in a mall, or battleships in the ocean. You will likely find yourself writing code to generate a random x-coordinate and a random y-coordinate for each object so that the entire group appears scattered. See Project 10 for details on randomly scattering objects.

Coding languages typically feature primitives for executing loops. MicroWorlds EX uses `repeat` in a similar way that many languages use a `for` command. Other languages employ a `do` command, which is also used for looping and usually provides a way to exit the loop when a certain condition is met (`do until`). MicroWorlds EX features a related command, called `dotimes`. Choose Help⇨Vocabulary from the menu bar for additional information on using this command in your code.

Create a Populate button

Next, follow these steps to create a Populate button to execute the `populate` procedure:

1. From the toolbar, click the Create a Button button. Then click anywhere on the workspace.

2. In the Button dialog box (see Figure 14-8), fill in the following information:

   • *Label:* Type `Populate` in the Label field to name the button.

   • *Instruction:* Type `populate` in the Instruction field.

   • *Do It:* Select the Once radio button.

   • *Visible:* Select this check box.

Figure 14-8

3. Click OK to close the Button dialog box.

   The Populate button is added to the workspace.

4. Drag the button to reposition it to where you want it located.

5. Click the Populate button to check that it functions as expected.

Write a Get Ready Procedure and Make a Button

When testing the Populate button, did you notice that the population of walruses just keeps growing, and growing, and growing? That's because you haven't created a way to remove walruses and return the workspace to containing only Wallace. A getready procedure and button will solve that problem.

Write a getready procedure

 On the project Procedures pane, type the following getready procedure:

```
to getready
everyone [ifelse who = "walrus [home][remove who]]
end
```

The getready procedure has a single line of code that speaks to everyone — all turtles in the workspace, including Wallace the walrus and his distracters. who is the currently active turtle and determines which turtle is receiving the command at the moment, although everyone will eventually get a turn at being who. who executes the ifelse command within one of the sets of square brackets, and then a different turtle becomes who, and so on.

Here's how the ifelse command works. Speaking to the turtle population in the workspace, it says:

If who = Wallace the walrus, then move to the home position

else, remove the currently selected turtle (who)

The getready procedure eventually removes all turtles from the workspace except Wallace the walrus.

An IF (or IF-THEN) conditional differs from an IF-ELSE (or IF-THEN-ELSE) conditional. In an IF conditional, if the condition is true, then the consequence in square brackets is executed; if the condition is false, then the consequence is ignored, and the next line of code is executed. In an IF ELSE conditional, if the condition is true, then the consequence in the first set of square brackets is executed; if the condition is false, then the consequence in the second set of square brackets is executed.

Create a Get Ready button

Next you need to create a Get Ready button to execute the getready procedure. Follow these steps:

1. From the toolbar, click the Create a Button button. Then click anywhere on the workspace.

2. In the Button dialog box, fill in the following information (see Figure 14-9):

   - *Label:* Type Get Ready in the Label field to name the button.

   - *Instruction:* Type getready in the Instruction field.

   - *Do It:* Select Once.

   - *Visible:* Leave the Visible check box selected.

button		
Name:	button2	
Label:	Get Ready	
Instruction:	getready	
Do It:	● Once	☑ Visible
	○ Forever	
		Cancel OK

Figure 14-9

3. Click OK to close the Button dialog box.

The Get Ready button is added to the workspace.

4. Drag the button to reposition it to where you want it located.

5. Click the Get Ready button to check that it functions as expected.

It should clear all the walrus turtles from the workspace, leaving behind only Wallace the `walrus`.

Add Page Directions to the Search Page

Add directions to the search page as follows:

1. From the toolbar, click the Create a Text Box button; click on the page and drag to create a long rectangle for the text box.

2. Type directions — *Click Get Ready, then select the number of walruses. Click Populate. When you find Wallace, click on him!* — in the white area of the text box.

3. Select the text inside the text box. From the menu bar, select the Text menu options and format the text.

See Project 1 for details on formatting text.

4. Right-click (Windows) or Ctrl-click (Mac) inside the text box and select Transparent from the pop-up menu.

To make sure that players don't accidentally move your directions or buttons, simply right-click (Windows) or Ctrl-click (Mac) any opaque text box or button and select Freeze from the pop-up menu to freeze it in place.

Write a Found Him Procedure and Add It to the Main Character

When a player locates Wallace the walrus, the player clicks him. walrus needs an instruction that indicates to the player that he's been successfully found. A foundhim procedure accomplishes this. Follow these steps to create the procedure and add it to the main character:

 1. On the project Procedures pane, type the following foundhim procedure:

```
to foundhim
announce [You found him!]
end
```

2. To cause the foundhim procedure to execute when walrus is clicked, you need to add foundhim to the OnClick field of the turtle backpack. Move to the open backpack of the turtle named walrus.

3. On the backpack Rules tab, type foundhim in the OnClick field, as shown in Figure 14-10.

Because only walrus carries foundhim in the OnClick of his backpack, he is the only turtle in the game to react to being clicked.

4. Close the backpack.

5. Test the buttons and slider on the game page to ensure they work as expected. Click on Wallace to ensure that he responds when found.

Backpack for: walrus on searchpage

OnClick	⦿ Once ○ Forever	foundhim
OnColor ■ ... ⇳	⦿ Once ○ Each time	
OnTick	10 (1/10 second)	
OnTouching		
OnMessage		

When this	Do That

State | Procedures | Shapes | Notes | Audio | Rules

Figure 14-10

Create and Name the Splash Page

A splash page helps introduce a search-and-find game. It also shows the players what the main character and the distracter characters look like! Follow these steps to create and name this page:

1. From the toolbar, click the New Page button. Alternatively, you can create a new page from the menu bar by choosing Pages⇨New Page.

2. From the menu bar, choose Pages⇨Name Page and type splashpage in the Name dialog box, as shown in Figure 14-11. Then click OK.

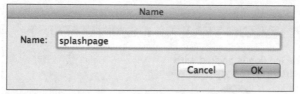

Figure 14-11

Paint a Background on the Splash Page

Paint a simple background in the workspace of your splash page as follows:

1. From the toolbar, click the Hide/Show Painting/Clipart button.

   The Painting/Clipart palette opens.

2. Open the Painting Tools. Paint any background you want, but keep the design simple because you will be adding other elements to the splashpage.

3. Add the wallace shape to the background by clicking wallace on the Shapes pane, and then moving into the workspace and clicking the splashpage.

4. Adjust the sizing dots to resize the wallace shape to whatever size you choose.

   Hold down the Shift key while you resize to maintain the shape proportions.

5. Right-click (Windows) or Ctrl-click (Mac) the shape and select Stamp from the pop-up menu.

6. Repeat Steps 3–5 for each distracter shape, adding the shapes for earmuffs, scarf, hat, and goggles to the splash page, as shown in Figure 14-12.

Figure 14-12

Add a Title and Backstory to the Splash Page

Use text boxes to create a title and backstory on the splash page as follows:

1. From the toolbar, click the Create a Text Box button; click on the page and drag to create a long rectangle for the text box.

2. Type a title — Where's Wallace Walrus? — in the white area of the text box.

3. Select the text inside the text box. From the menu bar, select the Text menu options and format the text.

   See Project 1 for details on formatting text.

4. Right-click (Windows) or Ctrl-click (Mac) inside the text box and select Transparent from the pop-up menu.

5. Repeat Steps 1–4 to create additional text boxes to label Wallace the Walrus as well as the distracter characters. Also include a text box with directions — *Click on Wallace when you find him!*

   Your splash page should look similar to Figure 14-12 (in the preceding section).

Add a Let's Play to the Splash Page

After viewing the splash page of your game, a player needs a way to move to the search page. Add a Let's Play! button to do so:

1. From the toolbar, click the Create a Button button. Then click the workspace anywhere.

2. In the Button dialog box, fill in the following information (see Figure 14-13):

   • *Label:* Type Let's Play! in the Label field to name the button.

   • *Instruction:* Type searchpage in the Instruction field.

   • *Do It:* Select the Once radio button.

   • *Visible:* Select this check box to leave the button visible.

button		
Name:	button1	
Label:	Let's Play!	
Instruction:	searchpage	
Do It:	⦿ Once	☑ Visible
	◯ Forever	
	Cancel	OK

Figure 14-13

3. Click OK to close the Button dialog box.

   The Let's Play! button is added to the workspace.

4. Drag the button to reposition it to where you want it located.

Adding a transition between pages is a nice finishing touch to your game. See Project 15 for instructions on adding page transitions.

Remove Turtle Tooltip Naming

By default, each turtle is identified by a tooltip. When you point to a turtle, the arrow pointer tells you the name of that turtle. However, this would ruin the fun of trying to find Wallace because the player could just point to each turtle and the arrow pointer would reveal the turtle name.

You should eliminate the display of the turtle name when the arrow points at the turtle on the game page. Do so by typing `settooltip "` in the Command Center, as shown in Figure 14-14.

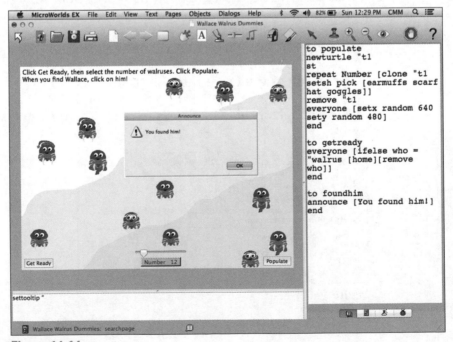

Figure 14-14

Save, Test, and Debug

 Click the Save Project button on the toolbar to save your search-and-find game. Test all the buttons and run the game several times to ensure the game runs the way you want. Troubleshoot and fix bugs until the game functions just the way you want.

Enhance your game

Consider enhancing your search-and-find game with new features:

✔ Add distracting features to the background.

✔ Add additional shapes for the distracter characters.

✔ Add a timer to measure how long it takes the player to locate Wallace (be sure to reset the time on each new game).

Traffic Dodge

What's a desert frog to do when faced with racing cars, speeding motorcycles, and oh-so-slow camels? That's what your player must contend with while crossing busy highways in Traffic Dodge!

In this project, you build your own Frogger-style game that includes levels. You build *game pages* — both Level 1 and Level 2. These are the pages where the player plays the game. Then you create a *splash page* — a page that introduces your game and gives a backstory.

The player controls the frog by using keyboard controls. If the jumping frog and a vehicle collide, the hit is announced, and the frog shape changes to appear squished. Also, the game has a variable that indicates lives remaining — each hit subtracts one life, and when the player runs out of lives, the game is over. Get jumping!

 In the classic version of Frogger, game play is more complicated: You must first dodge traffic, and then jump onto lily pads to avoid drowning in the raging river. Here, you need only worry about programming a game in which the frog must avoid getting squished by vehicles and other moving objects.

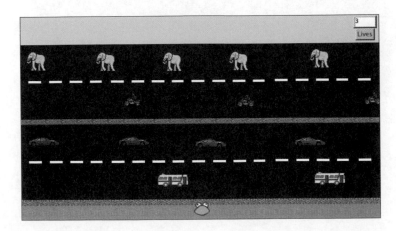

Brainstorm

Don't feel limited to jumping a frog through obstacles. You can choose any "mark" to move through any obstacle:

- An iPod-wearing vocalist being bombarded with music notes as he attempts to reach his recording session unscathed

- A germ-evading, white-blood-cell trooper as it moves through the body (like in the movie *Osmosis Jones*)

- A student moving through busy hallways during passing period on her way to class

- A hover-taxi navigating high-speed air traffic to pick up and deliver a passenger (like from the movie *The Fifth Element*)

Start a New Project

Begin creating your Traffic Dodge game by starting a new project as follows:

1. Start MicroWorlds EX.

2. From the yellow MicroWorlds EX startup screen, select Free Mode.

   A new project opens.

3. From the menu bar, choose File⇨New Project Size⇨ MicroWorlds Standard.

Paint and Name the Level 1 Game Page

The level 1 *game page* is where the player starts playing the game. Paint the level 1 game page and name it as follows:

1. On the toolbar, click the Hide/Show Painting/Clipart button.

   The Painting/Clipart palette opens.

2. Use the Painting Tools to paint your own traffic scene (gray roads, terrain, and sidewalks) in the workspace.

Painting the background gray — not black — makes it easier to see the turtle objects (which are black) when you add them to the workspace.

3. At the top of the workspace, paint a blue sky as the goal area for the frog.

Figure 15-1 shows what the traffic scene and sky look like in the example.

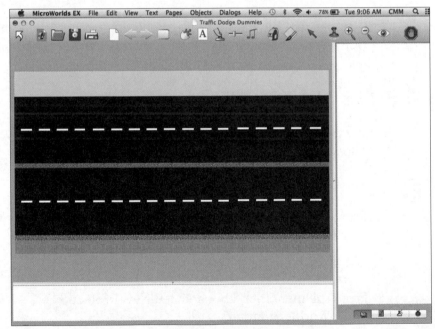

Figure 15-1

4. Close the Painting/Clipart palette by clicking its X button.

5. From the menu bar, choose Pages⇨Name Page.

6. In the dialog box that appears, type gamepage1 in the Name field, as shown in Figure 15-2.

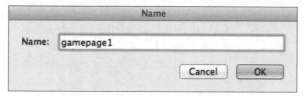

Figure 15-2

7. Click OK to close the Name dialog box.

The name of the page now shows in the lower-left corner of the window (refer to Figure 15-1).

Create a Frog Character

The frog is the character that the player moves through the game. The frog character is a turtle object that wears one of two shapes: `greenie` or `squished`. Follow these steps to create the frog character:

1. On the toolbar, click the Create a Turtle button. Move into the workspace and click to hatch a turtle.

2. Open the turtle backpack: Right-click (Windows) or Ctrl-click (Mac) on the turtle and select Open Backpack. On the backpack State tab, click the Edit button.

3. In the Name dialog box that appears, type `frog` in the Name field. Click OK to close the dialog box.

4. Drag the frog turtle to a starting position near the bottom center edge of the workspace.

Now is a good time to find the coordinates of the `frog` turtle position . . . you'll need them later! To find the coordinates, on the backpack State tab, note the Xcor and the Ycor — the (x,y) coordinates — of this position. Write them down. Click the X button to close the backpack of `frog`.

If the frog turtle is centered horizontally, its x-coordinate is 0, and it lies on the y-axis.

5. Now you're ready to paint some shapes! Click the project Shapes tab (located in the lower-right corner of the window).

6. On the project Shapes pane, double-click a shape spot.

   The Shape Editor opens.

7. Use the drawing tools in the Shape Editor to draw your own frog shape.

   The frog shape for the example is shown in Figure 15-3.

Figure 15-3

8. Name the frog shape `greenie` (in the empty white field at the top of the Shape Editor; see Figure 15-3) and then click OK.

   The Shape Editor closes, and the `greenie` frog shape appears in a spot on the project Shapes pane. This is the shape the frog turtle usually wears.

9. Repeat Steps 6–8 to create a shape for the frog when it is hit. Name this frog shape `squished`.

The completed `greenie` and `squished` shapes now appear on the project Shapes tab, as shown in Figure 15-4.

Figure 15-4

10. Click the `greenie` shape on the project Shapes tab and then move into the workspace and click the turtle.

The turtle now wears the shape.

If you accidentally click somewhere other than the turtle, the frog shape will appear on the background — simply right-click (Windows) or Ctrl-click (Mac) the shape and select Remove from the pop-up menu to get rid of it.

Blast from the past

Ask your parents to list their favorite video games from their teen years — I'll bet Frogger is one of them! In Frogger, the player jumps a frog through speeding cars and pond water perils to safely reach his lily pad.

A variation that was also wildly popular — Freeway — asked players to answer the question, "Why did the giant yellow chicken cross the road? To get to the other side!"

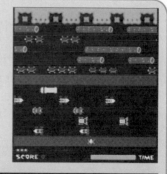

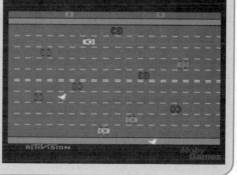

Create Traffic Characters

Traffic characters are turtles wearing a variety of shapes and speeding along the roads. Follow these steps to create the traffic characters:

 1. On the toolbar, click the Create a Turtle button. Move into the workspace and click to hatch a turtle. Drag this traffic turtle into a lane.

 2. On the toolbar, click the Hide/Show Painting/Clipart button.

   The Painting/Clipart palette opens.

 3. Look at the clip art in the Painting/Clipart palette by clicking the Singles button or the Animation button. Click on a vehicle shape (a car, a bus, or even an elephant!) and then move into the workspace and click on the traffic turtle.

   The turtle now wears the vehicle shape.

4. Close the Painting/Clipart palette by clicking its X button.

5. Next, set the turtle heading so that the vehicle matches the direction in which the shape is pointing. Right-click (Windows) or Ctrl-click (Mac) on the traffic turtle and select Open Backpack from the pop-up menu.

6. On the backpack State tab, type in a number for the Heading.

   For east, the heading is 90. For west, the heading is 270. For the example, set the heading to 90, as shown in Figure 15-5.

 Remember, a circle has 360 degrees. In MicroWorlds EX, north is 0 degrees, and measurement around the circle is in the clockwise direction.

7. With the backpack still open, set the size of the vehicle. In the Size field, type in a number less than 40 to shrink the vehicle. Type in a number greater than 40 to grow the vehicle.

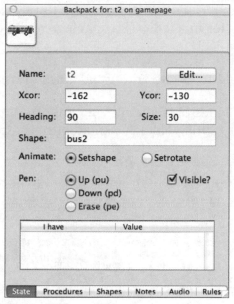

Figure 15-5

The default size of a turtle is 40. For the example, enter 30 for the size, as shown in Figure 15-5.

Click the vehicle shape thumbnail in the upper-left corner of the turtle backpack to apply a change and see the effect of the change.

8. Close the backpack.

9. Make a few copies of your traffic turtle as follows. Right-click (Windows) or Ctrl-click (Mac) the traffic turtle and select Copy from the pop-up menu. Click on the background and select Paste from the pop-up menu.

    A copy of your traffic turtle appears.

10. Click Paste again to drop another traffic turtle on the background. Repeat three or four times to add several copies of traffic turtles to the lane.

11. Click and drag the traffic turtles, one at a time, into positions that mimic vehicles in a lane. The spacing can be even or uneven, your choice!

12. Repeat Steps 1–11 to create additional lanes of traffic.

Be sure to form lanes of traffic moving in both directions, and set the headings of the vehicles to match their directions of movement.

In Figure 15-6, you can see four lanes of traffic in Level 1 made up of elephants, motorcycles, race cars, and buses.

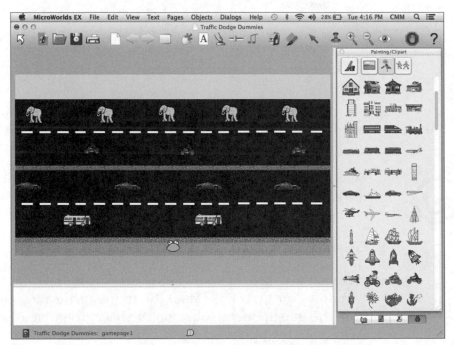

Figure 15-6

Freeze your frog turtle and your traffic turtles to prevent the player from clicking them and moving them during the game. Right-click (Windows) or Ctrl-click (Mac) each turtle and then select Freeze from the pop-up menu.

Make Traffic Move

Traffic moves through the lanes and gets in the way of the frog crossing safely. Turtle objects in a single lane should all move at the same rate of speed, but different lanes can move at different speeds. Make traffic move as follows:

1. Open the backpack of one of the traffic turtles. On the backpack Rules tab, enter a speed value in the OnClick field and select the Forever radio button.

   For example, set the speed value in the OnClick field to fd 10 wait 1.

2. In the workspace, click the traffic turtle to *click it on* and see it move. Click the turtle again to *click it off* and stop its motion.

Try increasing or decreasing the value of fd or wait to see how it affects the speed of the turtle. Each has a different effect: fd controls the distance covered during each command execution, and wait controls the pause time during each execution.

The more objects there are moving in your game, the slower they move — just like real traffic!

An easy way to stop a moving turtle — and the action of the entire workspace — is to click the Stop All button on the toolbar.

3. Close the traffic turtle backpack by clicking its X button.

4. Repeat Steps 1–3 for each traffic turtle, setting different speeds for each lane of traffic.

A quick way to get a turtle moving is to right-click (Windows) or Ctrl-click (Mac) the turtle and select Animate from the pop-up menu. This automatically inserts the commands fd 5 wait 1 into the turtle's OnClick field and sets it to execute Forever.

A shortcut for setting speeds for each traffic turtle is to set the speed of one turtle, and then copy and paste the turtle several times in the workspace or execute a `clone` command in the Command Center.

Create a Project Variable for Lives

Your game needs a way to show how many lives are left. Traffic Dodge begins with three lives, and each time the player's frog is hit by a traffic turtle, it loses a life. When the player has lost all three lives, the game is over.

In projects with a single page, you can just create a text box variable for lives. But the value of a text box variable exists on the page where it's located. This means that you can't carry over the value of a lives variable from a Level 1 page to a Level 2 page.

A *project variable* is a variable that exists everywhere in your game and whose value carries over from one page to another. To create a project variable that will be used to keep track of frog lives, enter the following command in the Command Center:

```
createprojectvar "livesremain
```

This command creates a new project variable with the name `livesremain`. The new project variable is visible on the Project pane, as shown in Figure 15-7.

Figure 15-7

Show Lives Remaining

The `livesremain` project variable tracks how many lives the frog has left. To show this value to the player, create a text box and then show the `livesremain` value in the text box. Follow these steps:

1. On the toolbar, click the Create a Text Box button and then click in the workspace to create a new text box.

   This text box will be used to show how many lives remain.

2. Right-click (Windows) or Ctrl-click (Mac) inside the text box and select Edit from the pop-up menu.

3. In the Name field, enter `lives` to name the text box.

   Don't set the text box to transparent — text boxes that show information that changes, such as variable values, must remain opaque.

4. When you're finished, click OK.

5. Reposition the text box in the upper-right corner of the screen.

The code for showing the value of the `livesremain` variable in the `lives` text box will be added later in the "Write a Play Procedure" section.

Create the Splash Page

A *splash page* is the first page players see when they open a game. It shows the title of the game and a colorful graphic with the main characters. The splash page usually explains the goal of the game and how to play. It may also show a short backstory that explains how the characters found themselves in the middle of the action.

Follow these steps to create the splash page:

1. From the menu bar, choose Pages⇨New Page.

   A new page appears.

2. On the toolbar, click the Hide/Show Painting/Clipart button.

   The Painting/Clipart palette opens.

3. Click the Backgrounds button to show the available background images.

4. Click on a background image you want to apply to your splash page. Then click in the workspace to drop the image on the page.

5. Right-click (Windows) or Ctrl-click (Mac) the background image. From the pop-up menu, select Stamp Full Page.

   The selected image is stamped to fill the entire background area.

6. Close the Painting/Clipart palette by clicking its X button.

7. From the menu bar, choose Pages⇨Name Page.

8. In the dialog box that appears, type `splashpage` in the Name field.

9. Click OK to close the page Name dialog box.

   The name of the page — `splashpage` — now shows in the lower-left corner of the window.

10. Use text boxes to add the game title, instructions, and a back-story to the splash page. (See Project 14 for details on adding text to the splash page.)

The title, instructions, and backstory for the example are shown in Figure 15-8.

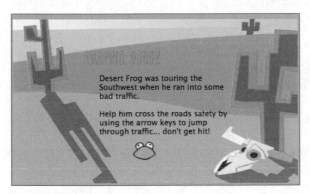

Figure 15-8

Write a Start Procedure

Your game will use a `start` procedure to move to the Level 1 game page, set the lives remaining project variable to a starting value, and then begin the game action.

 On the project Procedures pane, write this `start` procedure:

```
to start
gamepage1
setlivesremain 3
play
end
```

When the `start` procedure is executed, it moves to `gamepage1`. It then sets the value of the `livesremain` project variable to 3. Next, it runs the `play` procedure (which you will write later) to begin the game action.

Make a Start Button

After you've written the `start` procedure, MicroWorlds EX now recognizes it as a new command that you can use. Follow these steps to create a button on the `splashpage` to run the procedure:

1. On the toolbar, click the Create a Button button. Then click anywhere in the workspace.

2. In the Button dialog box, fill in the following fields:

   - *Label:* Type `Start` in the Label field to name the button.

   - *Instruction:* Type `start`, which is the procedure that will be executed when this button is clicked.

   - *Do It:* Select the Once radio button.

   - *Visible:* Select this check box to leave this button visible.

   The dialog box for the example is shown in Figure 15-9.

button	
Name:	button1
Label:	Start
Instruction:	start
Do It:	⦿ Once ☑ Visible
	◯ Forever Cancel OK

   Figure 15-9

3. Click OK to close the Button dialog box.

   The Start button is added to the workspace of the `splashpage`.

4. Drag the button to an out-of-the-way position in a corner of the workspace.

Figure 15-10 shows the completed splash page, `start` procedure, and Start button.

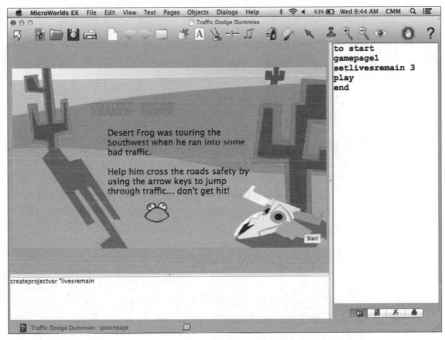

Figure 15-10

Move Between Pages and Add a Page Transition

One function of the Start button is moving from the `splashpage` to `gamepage1`. You can add a page transition to make the change from one page to another more eye-catching. Add a page transition as follows:

1. On the toolbar, use the Previous Page and Next Page arrow buttons to move to the page where you want to add the transition.

Add the transition to the page you are going to.

2. From the menu bar, choose Pages⇨Transitions.

The Transitions dialog box appears, as shown in Figure 15-11.

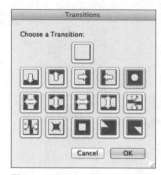

Figure 15-11

3. Click a transition and then click OK.

The transition is applied to the page. Test the transition by using the arrow keys to turn away from the page, and then turn back to the page.

Write a Play Procedure

A `play` procedure begins the game action by placing the correct shapes on all characters, positioning characters in their starting positions, and then setting all the characters in motion. Turn to `gamepage1`.

 On the project Procedures pane, write the following `play` procedure (see Figure 15-12):

```
to play
lives, ct pr livesremain
frog, setshape "greenie
```

```
frog, setpos [0 -190]
everyone [clickon]
end
```

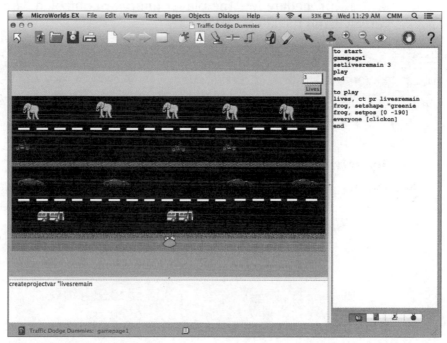

Figure 15-12

Replace [0 -190] with whatever Xcor and Ycor values you discovered in the earlier section "Create a Frog Character."

When the play procedure is executed, it tells the lives text box to clear its text and then print the value of the livesremain project variable in the box. Next, the play procedure tells the frog turtle to set its shape (setshape) to "greenie. It then positions the frog turtle at its starting coordinates — the Xcor and Ycor you found earlier. Finally, it clicks on all the turtles on the current page, activating the motion commands in their OnClick fields (everyone [clickon]), setting the game in motion.

Write a Jump Procedure and Add It to the Frog

A `jump` procedure lets the player jump, or control, a game character by using the keyboard.

Other programming software, including Game Salad, uses built-in keyboard control commands. However, MicroWorlds EX enables you to learn and control the underlying details of keyboard control, a skill that will prove useful in more complex coding endeavors.

Writing the jump procedure

 On the project Procedures tab, write a `jump` procedure as follows:

For a Windows game:

```
to jump
let [key readchar]
if (ascii :key) = 37 [seth 270 fd 40]
if (ascii :key) = 38 [seth 0 fd 40]
if (ascii :key) = 39 [seth 90 fd 40]
if (ascii :key) = 40 [seth 180 fd 40]
end
```

For a Mac game:

```
to jump
let [key readchar]
if (ascii :key) = 28 [seth 270 fd 40]
if (ascii :key) = 30 [seth 0 fd 40]
if (ascii :key) = 29 [seth 90 fd 40]
if (ascii :key) = 31 [seth 180 fd 40]
end
```

The `jump` procedure reads the arrow key pressed on the keyboard by the player. It then points and moves the `frog` in the associated direction. Every arrow key is assigned a different compass direction so that the turtle points in the chosen direction and moves a small distance. (See Project 12 for details on writing a procedure for keyboard control of a character.)

Adding the jump procedure to the frog

Tell the `frog` turtle to use the `jump` procedure as follows:

1. Right-click (Windows) or Ctrl-click (Mac) the `frog` turtle and select Open Backpack from the pop-up menu.

2. On the backpack Rules tab, type `jump` in the OnClick field and select the Forever radio button.

   After the `play` procedure player "clicks on" the `frog`, the player can use the keyboard arrows to jump it through the traffic.

   Leave the `frog`'s backpack open.

Write a Hit Procedure and Add It to the Frog

A `hit` procedure lets the `frog` turtle know it has collided with a traffic turtle.

Writing the hit procedure

 On the project Procedures pane, type the following `hit` procedure:

```
to hit
frog, setshape "squished
wait 10
announce [SPLAT]
setlivesremain livesremain - 1
if livesremain = 0 [endgame]
play
end
```

When it's executed, the hit procedure checks for a collision between the frog and any other turtle. If a collision occurs, it sets the alternate shape of the frog (setshape "squished), waits briefly (wait 10), and then announces the collision (announce [SPLAT]). It then removes one life (setlivesremain livesremain - 1).

Next, the procedure checks to see if the player has lost all lives remaining (if livesremain = 0). If so, it runs the endgame procedure (which you'll write later in this project); otherwise, it runs the play procedure to continue the gameplay.

Adding the hit procedure to the frog

Tell the frog turtle to use the hit procedure. On the backpack Rules tab, type hit in the OnTouching field. Now whenever the frog collides with a traffic turtle during the game, the hit procedure is executed.

A collision takes place when there is *coordinate convergence* between two turtles. This means that some part of a shape on one turtle touches some part of a shape on another turtle. When coordinate convergence occurs, it means the objects have collided.

Collisions are detected different ways in different programming languages. In MicroWorlds EX, collision detection is precise — actual touching of shapes takes place. GameMaker has precise collision detection and also non-precise collision detection (see Figure 15-13), in which only the bounding boxes of the shapes touch. In GameMaker, precise collision detection requires a lot more processing power than non-precise, and if you have a lot of objects moving around, this can really slow down the game. However, precise collision detection creates a more realistic gameplay experience for players because it more accurately depicts real-world physics.

Figure 15-13

Write an End Game Procedure

An endgame procedure ends the game action when the frog has failed to cross the roadways in three attempts. In the Procedures pane, type the following endgame procedure:

```
to endgame
everyone [clickoff]
announce [GAME OVER]
splashpage
end
```

The endgame procedure is executed when the livesremain variable equals zero. The value of this variable is checked in the hit procedure, which you created in the earlier section, "Writing the hit procedure."

endgame stops the motion of all characters (everyone [clickoff]) and then announces that the game is over (announce [GAME OVER]). Finally, it returns the player to the splash page (splashpage).

Write a Succeed Level 1 Procedure and Add It to the Frog

A succeed1 procedure lets the player know that the frog turtle made it safely through the traffic of gamepage1 to the target zone.

Write the succeed1 procedure

 On the project Procedures pane, write a succeed1 procedure as follows:

```
to succeed1
everyone [clickoff]
wait 10
gamepage2
play
end
```

When it's executed, the succeed1 procedure clicks off all objects on the page to halt the flow of traffic on Level 1. It then pauses briefly before moving to Level 2, gamepage2 (which you will make in "Lay Out and Code the Level 2 Game Page"). succeed1 then executes the play procedure to continue the game action.

Add the succeed1 procedure to the frog

Follow these steps to add the succeed1 procedure to the frog on Level 1:

1. With the backpack of the frog turtle open on gamepage1, switch to the backpack Rules tab.

2. Click the OnColor drop-down list and scroll to the color of the target zone in your game. (In this example, the sky color is cyan blue.)

3. Type succeed1 in the OnColor field and set it to Once, as shown in Figure 15-14.

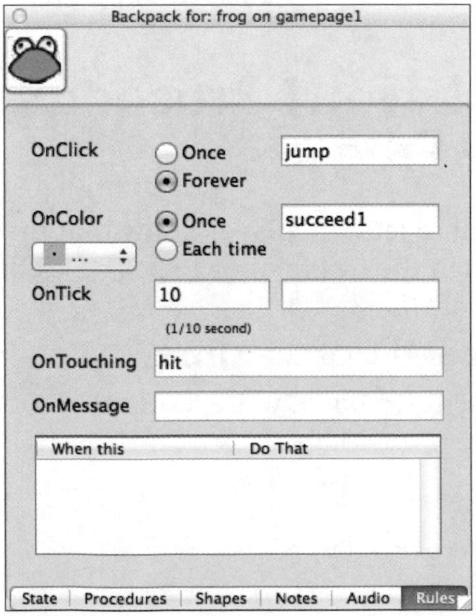

Figure 15-14

When the player moves the `frog` turtle into the Level 1 target zone during the game, the color that the `frog` touches matches its backpack OnColor. When this occurs, the OnColor command is activated. Here, the `succeed1` procedure is executed, advancing the player to Level 2.

4. Close the Level 1 `frog`'s backpack on `gamepage1` by clicking its X button.

Lay Out and Code the Level 2 Game Page

Adding additional levels to Traffic Dodge is a snap! In this example you will add a Level 2, but note that you can add as many new levels as you want. The key tasks in adding a new level are duplicating the existing game page, creating a new succeed procedure, and adding the new procedure to the frog turtle's backpack.

Create the level 2 game page

Follow these steps to create `gamepage2`:

1. Move to `gamepage1`. Then from the menu bar, choose Pages⇨Duplicate Page.

   The duplicate page appears in the workspace and is named page1.

2. Rename the page. From the menu bar, choose Pages⇨Name Page and type `gamepage2` in the dialog box.

   This page is your Level 2 page.

3. Edit traffic on Level 2. You may want to add additional obstacles, edit shapes, and edit speeds in order to add variety to this new level.

4. Add a page transition that the player will see when moving from Level 1 to Level 2. (See the earlier section "Move Between Pages and Add a Page Transition.")

Write the succeed2 procedure

 When a player successfully completes Level 2, the game is won! Write a `succeed2` procedure on the project Procedures pane as follows:

```
to succeed2
everyone [clickoff]
announce [YOU WIN!]
splashpage
end
```

When it's executed, the `succeed2` procedure halts traffic by clicking everyone off. It then announces that the player has won the game (`announce [YOU WIN!]`) and returns the player to the `splashpage`.

Add the succeed2 procedure to the frog

Follow these steps to add the `succeed2` procedure to the frog on Level 2:

1. Open the backpack of the `frog` turtle open on `gamepage2`, and switch to the backpack Rules tab.

2. The OnColor drop-down list is already set to the target zone in your game. (In this example, the sky color is cyan blue.)

3. Type `succeed2` in the OnColor field and set it to Once.

   When the player moves the `frog` turtle into the Level 2 target zone during the game, the color that the `frog` touches matches its backpack OnColor. When this occurs, the OnColor command is activated. Here, the `succeed2` procedure is executed, informing the player that the game is won.

4. Close the Level 1 `frog`'s backpack on `gamepage1` by clicking its X button.

Save, Test, and Debug

Choose File⇨Save Project from the menu bar to save your game.

The completed Traffic Dodge game with all procedures is shown in Figure 15-15. The figure shows Level 2 (gamepage2) in the workspace. Also note that the createprojectvar command in the Command Center is now deleted.

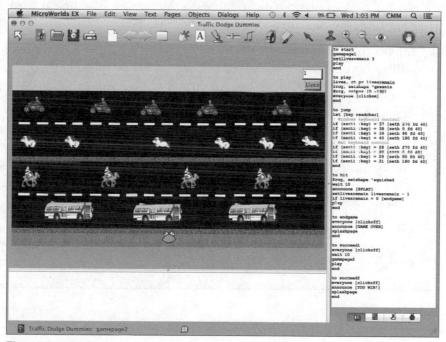

Figure 15-15

Test your game by playing it repeatedly. After you have worked out all the bugs, you can challenge friends to determine the Traffic Dodge champion!

Enhance your game

Consider enhancing your game with new features:

- **Levels:** Add new pages (or duplicate the game page) with new challenges.

- **Characters:** Add animated characters to traffic. Create additional shapes for the frog to orient his body in the direction he is jumping, and set each shape in the `jump` procedure.

- **Music and sound effects:** VG Music (`www.vgmusic.com`) offers a huge collection of video game sound effects and music you can add to your game. All the classics are available, including Frogger!

- **Prevent cheats:** Some players figure out that by jumping backwards, you can reach the goal and avoid the traffic. You can prevent cheats by eliminating the ability to jump backwards — just remove the down-arrow control. Or, you can add a color band at the bottom of the screen through which the frog can't move — a lava pit, or an abyss — and that announces his doom. Get creative!

- **Win Page:** Add a win page that appears when a player wins the game. The `succeed2` procedure moves the player to the `winpage` as opposed to the `splashpage`.

Index

Y

X

About the Author

With childhood activities that included tinkering with her Apple II+ computer and conducting science fair research, Camille McCue, Ph.D. developed an early love of STEM (science, technology, engineering, and mathematics). She earned her math degree at the University of Texas at Austin and worked in IBM PC marketing for two years prior to becoming a physics teacher to rural youth via BUD (big ugly dish) satellite. For the next 12 years, Camille produced and anchored live television programming for NASA and PBS, connecting kids with experts on topics as varied as orbiting astronauts and Antarctic penguin researchers.

Since 2005, she has taught video game programming, math enrichment, tech mashup, and future cities engineering at the Alexander Dawson School in Las Vegas, Nevada. Additionally, she teaches at the University of Nevada, Las Vegas (UNLV), as well as speaks frequently at professional conferences.

She has served on the editorial board of the *Mathematics Teaching in the Middle School* journal (published by the National Council of Teachers of Mathematics) and written lessons for the NCTM *Illuminations* website. In 2012, she was selected by the Gaming2Learn initiative to pilot-teach *Survival Master,* engineering gaming software developed through a multimillion-dollar National Science Foundation grant.

She earned her advanced degrees in curriculum and instruction with her doctoral research at UNLV focused on tween coding. Camille currently serves as Director of Dawson College Bound, a program mentoring citywide youth towards academic success in high school and university. Camille and her fantastic husband Michael are the proud parents of two incredible sons, Ian and Carson. *Coding For Kids For Dummies* is Camille's sixth technology book for Wiley.

Dedication

To Carson.

Author's Acknowledgments

Thanks to the indefatigable team at Wiley for their work in helping craft this first installment of the *For Kids For Dummies* series! Steve Hayes, although your professional title has changed and become increasingly more impressive over the years — now Executive Editor — you have always been a boots-on-the-ground kind of guy who magically turns ideas into products. Thank you so much for your guidance, collaboration, and friendship over many years of creating books. Senior Project Editor Kim Darosett: I am in your debt for your deep expertise in communicating technology, your flexibility in managing this bag of snakes, and your patience in listening to my opinions (also known as soapbox rants) about adapting the writing for a kid audience. I was elated when you caught errata — because you were actually working through *every* step of *every* project! I am honored and humbled by your incredibly detailed work.

I'd also like to thank marketing manager Raichelle Weller and copyeditor Linda Morris for their efforts in polishing and packaging this book just so. Many thanks also to the brilliant Susan Einhorn, president of Logo Computer Systems Inc. (LCSI), who served as technical editor for this project. Your exceptional knowledge of programming pedagogy "kicked it up a notch" (as they say in *Futurama*) and ensured that the projects are not only technically accurate, but also instructionally sound. Thank you also to Michael Quinn of LCSI's Board of Directors for providing day-in and day-out support for my use of MicroWorlds EX at the Alexander Dawson School over the past decade, and for supporting the marriage between the highly-organized *For Dummies* approach and the exploratory playground approach of all things Logo.

Many thanks to the Alexander Dawson Foundation Board of Trustees and our school leadership for affording me the opportunity to bring innovative approaches to curriculum and instruction to our school, including the creation of courses featuring coding, and to the many students whom I have had the privilege of teaching — and learning from — over the years. Additionally, I'd like to acknowledge the tireless support of my colleagues and mentors at UNLV who helped shape my research activities addressing middle-school math and coding. Thank you also to Dawson students Sophie Gray and Stella Gray and to UNLV professor Dr. David James, who provided review and commentary of project concepts; to my Dawson fifth graders who critiqued the book cover design; and to my Dawson College Bound coordinator Cathi Muckle for her always-steadfast assistance.

Most of all, an enormous, heartfelt thank you to my husband Michael, my children, and my mother Beverly Dempsey-Moody who have championed my efforts to "lean in" professionally (as Sheryl Sandberg would say). I am especially grateful to my boys, Ian McCue and Carson McCue, for serving as in-house testers of MicroWorlds EX projects all these years (and to Carson for his Monster Mashup character designs in this book). Finally, thank you to the legendary Dr. Seymour Papert, the man who envisioned children using computers as tools for expressing creativity through his Logo programming environment. You changed the world and fostered a love of coding among millions. I hope this book celebrates and continues your work by encouraging a new generation of kids to embrace and appreciate the power of programming.

Publisher's Acknowledgments

Executive Editor: Steven Hayes

Senior Project Editor: Kim Darosett

Copy Editor: Linda Morris

Technical Editors: Susan Einhorn and Michael Quinn

Editorial Assistant: Claire Johnson

Sr. Editorial Assistant: Cherie Case

Project Coordinator: Erin Zeltner

Cover Image: ©iStock.com / Portugal2004